Bhagavad Gītā

Home Study Course

(Text in Sanskrit with transliteration, word-to-word and verse
meaning, along with an elaborate commentary in English
based on Śaṅkara-bhāṣyam)

Volume 3

Chapter 3
Summary of Chapters 1-3

Swami Dayananda Saraswati
Arsha Vidya

Arsha Vidya
Research and Publication Trust
Chennai

Published by :

Arsha Vidya Research and Publication Trust
4 'Srinidhi' Apts 3rd Floor
Sir Desika Road Mylapore
Chennai 600 004 INDIA
Tel   : 044 2499 7023
Telefax : 2499 7131
Email   : avrandpt@gmail.com
Website: www.avrpt.com

ISBN : 978-93-80049-32-8

ISBN : 978-93-80049-39-7 (Set of 9 Volumes)

New Edition & Format : July   2011   Copies : 1200
1st Reprint   : July   2012   Copies : 1000

Design & Layout :
Graaphic Design

Printed at :
Sudarsan Graphics
27, Neelakanta Mehta Street
T. Nagar, Chennai 600 017
Email : info@sudarsan.com

Preface

I am very happy that the 'Bhagavad Gītā Home Study Course' will now be available in nine compact volumes so that one can carry a given volume while travelling. As I said in my foreword for the last edition, I want the readers to be aware that these books do not constitute another set of books on the *Bhagavadgītā*. They are different in that they are edited transcript-pages of classroom discussions; they are presented to the reader as a program for self-study. If this is borne in mind, while reading, one can enjoy the same attitude of a student in the classroom, making oneself available to the whole process of unfoldment of the content of the words of Bhagavān. The study will then prove to be as rewarding as directly listening to the teacher. This attitude would prove to be *ātma-kṛpā*. Once this *kṛpā* is there, the other two, *śāstra-kṛpā* and *īśvara-kṛpā* would follow.

The enormous job of patient editing of the pages, thousands of them, and presenting them, retaining the original words and content without any compromise, was done by Dr. Martha Doherty. These books have created a number of committed students of the *Bhagavadgītā*, thanks to Martha's invaluable contribution to the teaching tradition of Vedanta. I also congratulate the staff of our Publication division ably led by Ms. K. Chandra, a dedicated student of Vedanta.

Swami Dayananda Saraswati
Arsha Vidya
June 19 2011

KEY TO TRANSLITERATION AND PRONUNCIATION OF SANSKRIT LETTERS

Sanskrit is a highly phonetic language and hence accuracy in articulation of the letters is important. For those unfamiliar with the *Devanāgari* script, the international transliteration is a guide to the proper pronunciation of Sanskrit letters.

अ	*a*	(b*u*t)		ट	*ṭa*	(*t*rue)*3
आ	*ā*	(f*a*ther)		ठ	*ṭha*	(an*th*ill)*3
इ	*i*	(*i*t)		ड	*ḍa*	(*d*rum)*3
ई	*ī*	(b*ea*t)		ढ	*ḍha*	(go*dh*ead)*3
उ	*u*	(f*u*ll)		ण	*ṇa*	(u*n*der)*3
ऊ	*ū*	(p*oo*l)		त	*ta*	(pa*th*)*4
ऋ	*ṛ*	(*rh*ythm)		थ	*tha*	(*th*under)*4
ॠ	*ṝ*	(ma*ri*ne)		द	*da*	(*th*at)*4
ऌ	*ḷ*	(reve*lry*)		ध	*dha*	(*breathe*)*4
ए	*e*	(pl*ay*)		न	*na*	(*n*ut)*4
ऐ	*ai*	(*ai*sle)		प	*pa*	(*p*ut) 5
ओ	*o*	(g*o*)		फ	*pha*	(loo*ph*ole)*5
औ	*au*	(l*ou*d)		ब	*ba*	(*b*in) 5
क	*ka*	(see*k*) 1		भ	*bha*	(a*bh*or)*5
ख	*kha*	(bloc*kh*ead)*1		म	*ma*	(*m*uch) 5
ग	*ga*	(*g*et) 1		य	*ya*	(lo*y*al)
घ	*gha*	(lo*g h*ut)*1		र	*ra*	(*r*ed)
ङ	*ṅa*	(si*ng*) 1		ल	*la*	(*l*uck)
च	*ca*	(*ch*unk) 2		व	*va*	(*v*ase)
छ	*cha*	(cat*ch h*im)*2		श	*śa*	(*s*ure)
ज	*ja*	(*j*ump) 2		ष	*ṣa*	(*sh*un)
झ	*jha*	(he*dg*ehog)*2		स	*sa*	(*s*o)
ञ	*ña*	(bu*nch*) 2		ह	*ha*	(*h*um)

•	*ṁ*	*anusvāra*	(nasalisation of preceding vowel)
:	*ḥ*	*visarga*	(aspiration of preceding vowel)
*			No exact English equivalents for these letters

1.	Guttural	–	Pronounced from throat
2.	Palatal	–	Pronounced from palate
3.	Lingual	–	Pronounced from cerebrum
4.	Dental	–	Pronounced from teeth
5.	Labial	–	Pronounced from lips

The 5th letter of each of the above class – called nasals – are also pronounced nasally.

Contents

Chapter 3

कर्म-योगः

Karma-yogaḥ
Topic of *Karma*

In the previous chapter, beginning at verse 55, Lord Kṛṣṇa pointed out that a wise person, a *sthitaprajña*, is one who gives up all desires, being happy with oneself in oneself. This is the ultimate human end and is what is meant by *mokṣa*, liberation or freedom.

Giving up desires implies giving up all activities also. An activity is pursued because there is a desire to accomplish a given end. If there is no desire to accomplish a given end, there is no pursuit.

Arjuna wanted *śreyas*, liberation, and understood that in order to gain it, knowledge alone was required and *karma* was of no use. Kṛṣṇa explained all this when Arjuna asked him to describe a *sthitaprajña*. Before that, Kṛṣṇa talked about the nature of *ātmā* being free from any limitation. Then he asked Arjuna to listen to what he had to say about *karma-yoga*; he said, *yoge tu imām śṛṇu (Gītā 2.39)*.

Arjuna's confusion about knowledge and karma

During this discussion, Kṛṣṇa asked Arjuna to perform action, remaining rooted in *karma-yoga* – *yogasthaḥ kuru karmāṇi (Gītā 2.48)*. This mandate confused Arjuna. He wondered, 'should I continue to do *karma* or should I pursue knowledge? If I pursue knowledge, I will definitely gain *mokṣa*, whereas if

I perform *karma* I will be bound by *karma-phala*. Even *karma-yoga* is not adequate for *mokṣa*. How then am I to gain *mokṣa* if I perform action?'

Arjuna had made it very clear to Kṛṣṇa, early in the second chapter, that he wanted *mokṣa*. He told Kṛṣṇa in so many words, 'I am your student. Please teach me so that I will gain *śreyas*, *mokṣa*.' Arjuna naturally expected Kṛṣṇa to tell him exactly what would give him *mokṣa*. Kṛṣṇa pointed out that knowledge would give him *mokṣa*, thereby implying that all *karma* was to be renounced in order to pursue knowledge. Why, then, was Kṛṣṇa advising him to do *karma*? Having said that knowledge would give Arjuna *mokṣa*, Kṛṣṇa had then said, 'Get up and fight!' What did this mean?

Did Kṛṣṇa think that Arjuna was unfit for *mokṣa* or did he think that *karma-yoga* would also result in *mokṣa*? Arjuna wanted to know what Kṛṣṇa's contention really was. The situation was like a man going to a doctor, being told that he had diabetes, and being advised to start and end each day with sweet-rolls and pastries! Such a prescription would result only in a quick death and is not at all befitting the man's condition.

Here, Arjuna wanted *mokṣa*, absolute freedom, and *karma* was prescribed for him. He knew that the *karma*s enjoined by the Veda were strictly for achieving results within *saṁsāra*, a life of limitation, and that they would not deliver him from *saṁsāra*. Kṛṣṇa himself had said to Arjuna, 'May you not get involved with any *karma* unfolded in the Veda.' Arjuna was therefore confused by all these conflicting statements. Since *mokṣa* was said to be purely in the form of knowledge, he concluded that he should go for knowledge. And if he was to pursue knowledge, why do *karma*? This was why Arjuna wanted to become a renunciate, a monk, and renounce all activities so that he could dedicate his life to the pursuit of knowledge.

'Giving up everything, may you go after this knowledge, *sannyasya-śravaṇaṁ kuryāt*' was a popular statement. Arjuna had seen the *sannyāsīs* giving up everything to pursue knowledge. He therefore thought that if he was interested in *mokṣa*, he should do the same. This is the case for anything one wants in life. If money is what you are interested in, you must give up a lot of things and go after money. Or, if you want power, you should go after it to the exclusion of everything else, spending whatever money is necessary to get it. You cannot expect to retain your money and, at the same time, gain power. No election was ever won that way. However, after gaining power, whether you are able to regain the money is a different issue!

Arjuna therefore thought, 'if I want knowledge, it is only reasonable that I should give up *karma*, action.' For a person who is dedicated to pursue knowledge, giving up everything is not an unreasonable requirement. This is why a life of renunciation, *sannyāsa*, loomed so large in Arjuna's mind and it was all he wanted. In his eyes, *sannyāsa* seemed to be the only destination and was the right thing to do. But Kṛṣṇa had said, 'Having decided to fight, please get up and fight, *tasmāt uttiṣṭha kaunteya yuddhāya kṛta-niścayaḥ*' (*Gītā* 2.37).

Arjuna's confusion was based on his incorrect understanding of renunciation. Kṛṣṇa seems to have dismissed the pursuit of *karma* for good by not allowing it to be considered in the pursuit of *mokṣa*. Therefore, *sannyāsa* had to be the answer. At the same time, however, Kṛṣṇa had praised *karma*. This apparent contradiction caused Arjuna to ask, 'What exactly should I do?' He did not think of pursuing both *karma* and *mokṣa* because nowhere in the second chapter did Kṛṣṇa mention combining them.

Knowledge, *jñāna*, is adequate for *mokṣa*. *Mokṣa* does not depend on any *karma* because it is not something that is created. Being the very nature of the *ātmā*, *mokṣa* is already accomplished. The self is already liberated, already free, and needs only to be recognised as such. Therefore, knowledge alone is adequate for *mokṣa*. And after knowledge, *karma* is also not required because the person is happy with himself or herself as he or she is. What *karma* is to be done then? And for what purpose?

Doing *karma* for the pleasure of it is not what is being discussed here. To do *karma* merely for the pleasure of it means that one may or may not do it. Some people will do *karma* and enjoy themselves, while others may not do any *karma* at all and still enjoy themselves. If one does something for the enjoyment of it, there is no question of doing it as a bounden duty. Therefore, one need not do it or one may do it. But for *mokṣa*, why should one do *karma*, when all that is required is knowledge? If knowledge is adequate, then one must only pursue that knowledge.

So, from what Lord Kṛṣṇa had said so far, it looked to Arjuna as though knowledge was the prime pursuit. But it was also very clear to Arjuna that he had been commanded to perform action. Therefore, the first dose of teaching, contained in the second chapter, was confusing to Arjuna, who was already confused when the teaching began. In an attempt to resolve his confusion he asked Kṛṣṇa to describe a *sthitaprajña*, a wise person. This was an indirect question in that, by knowing exactly what a *sthitaprajña* was, Arjuna thought he would know whether it was knowledge or *karma* that would make him wise and therefore free.

In response, Lord Kṛṣṇa did not mention *karma* at all. He talked only about self-mastery and knowledge. He never said that one who does *karma* becomes a *sthitaprajña*. All of Kṛṣṇa's descriptions of a wise person implied knowledge alone. He had said that what is night for the ignorant is day for the wise and what is night for the wise is day for the ignorant. In this way, he talked about two visions – that of the wise and that of the ignorant, the vision of one who is ignorant being different from the vision of one who is wise.

From all that Kṛṣṇa had told him, Arjuna received confirmation that knowledge was adequate for *mokṣa*. There was no question of *mokṣa* requiring a little bit of knowledge and a little bit of *karma*. *Mokṣa* is not like an English trifle or granola! Only knowledge is necessary and all other little bits are useless. Thus, Arjuna concluded, 'If knowledge alone is going to liberate me, then the pursuit of knowledge is enough.' If knowledge is adequate *karma* never comes into the picture, neither before knowledge nor after knowledge. Because this was Arjuna's thinking, he had a doubt to raise. Thus, when Kṛṣṇa finished talking, Arjuna asked his question.

There are two types of question. One is a question that is asking for an explanation, called *praśna*, in Sanskrit. 'What is a wise person?' is such a question. Another type of question involves doubt, *saṃśaya*, which comes in the form of, 'Does the *sthitaprajña* walk, talk, sit, etc., or not?' Only when there are two or more opinions about a topic is there a possibility of a doubt.

Throughout the *Gītā*, Arjuna raised doubts and also asked questions involving definitions or descriptions. When Arjuna wanted to know what a wise person was, he was not expressing a doubt, although he may have had one. He only wanted to know. 'What is *sannyāsa*?' for example, is not a doubt; it is purely a question asking for a definition. But when Arjuna asked which was better, *sannyāsa* or *karma-yoga*, he was expressing a doubt.

Verses 1&2

Arjuna expresses his doubts

अर्जुन उवाच ।
ज्यायसी चेत्कर्मणस्ते मता बुद्धिर्जनार्दन ।
तत्किं कर्मणि घोरे मां नियोजयसि केशव ॥ १ ॥

arjuna uvāca
jyāyasī cetkarmaṇaste matā buddhirjanārdana
tatkiṁ karmaṇi ghore māṁ niyojayasi keśava (1)

arjunaḥ – Arjuna; *uvāca* – said (asked)

janārdana – O Janārdana (Kṛṣṇa)!; *karmaṇaḥ* – than action; *buddhiḥ* – knowledge; *jyāyasī* – better; *te matā cet* – if it is your contention; *tat* – then; *ghore karmaṇi* – in the gruesome action; *mām* – me; *kiṁ niyojayasi-* – why do you impel; *keśava* – O Keśava (Kṛṣṇa)!

Arjuna said:

Janārdana (Kṛṣṇa)! If in your contention knowledge is better than action, why then do you impel me into this gruesome action, Keśava (Kṛṣṇa)?

Arjuna addressed Lord Kṛṣṇa here as Janārdana, a name for the Lord, which means one who upholds the law of *karma* by giving the fruits of wrong action to the performer of the action. Wrong *karma* results in pain, *duḥkha*, either immediately or later.

Kṛṣṇa's contention, as Arjuna saw it, was that knowledge and the pursuit of knowledge are better than or superior to action, *karma*. The action being referred to here was no ordinary action such as performing a ritual or cooking. It was a terrible, gruesome action involving bloodshed and the destruction of many people. Therefore, Arjuna asked Kṛṣṇa, 'Why do you engage me in this terrible action? If, with reference to *mokṣa* knowledge is superior, if knowledge alone is going to give me *mokṣa*, why are you asking me to do *karma*?

In Arjuna's understanding, Kṛṣṇa was asking him to act, but at the same time he was praising knowledge and its pursuit. Kṛṣṇa seemed to be saying that knowledge liberates, but at the same time, he was asking Arjuna to do *karma*, and terrible *karma* at that! Arjuna wanted to be a *sannyāsī* and Kṛṣṇa seemed to be pushing him into the ring to fight. He had not even signed a contract with him! He had asked only that Kṛṣṇa be his driver, not his agent who would arrange fighting matches for him.

Arjuna's question, 'Why are you asking me to perform this terrible action?' extends into the next verse as well.

व्यामिश्रेणेव वाक्येन बुद्धिं मोहयसीव मे ।
तदेकं वद निश्चित्य येन श्रेयोऽहमाप्नुयाम् ॥ २ ॥

vyāmiśreṇeva vākyena buddhiṁ mohayasīva me
tadekaṁ vada niścitya yena śreyo'hamāpnuyām (2)

vyāmiśreṇa – self-contradictory; *vākyena* – with words; *iva* – seemingly; *me* – my; *buddhim* – mind; *mohayasi iva* – you seem to confuse; *yena* – by which; *aham* – I; *śreyaḥ* – liberation, *mokṣa*; *āpnuyām* – shall gain; *tat* – that; *ekam* – one; *niścitya* – deciding for good; *vada* – tell

> With words that are seemingly contradictory, you seem to confuse my mind. Deciding for good, which is better; tell me the one thing by which I shall gain liberation.

Arjuna did not say that Kṛṣṇa's words were self-contradictory, but that they were seemingly contradictory. In Arjuna's understanding, there was contradiction. Even then, he did not say to Kṛṣṇa, 'You confuse me with self-contradictory words,' which would have been an accusation.

Here, we are given an indication of how one should talk in such situations. When Arjuna said, 'By words which are seemingly contradictory, you seem to be confusing me,' he meant that, in fact, Kṛṣṇa's intention was not to confuse him.

We know that there is often accusation involved in a dialogue between two people. If your perception is that a person did something to you, you may say, 'You did this to me.' The person becomes defensive and will not accept your statement. You then feel that your feelings are invalidated, and you are not understood. The other person also feels that he or she is accused and not understood at all! In other words, there is not only no communication but also miscommunication! Here, Arjuna's use of the word *iva*, as though, reveals an important principle in communication – never evoke the defensive person in the one with whom you are communicating.

Arjuna was not accusing Kṛṣṇa of confusing him. Nor did he say that his words were contradictory. Instead, he said that Kṛṣṇa's words seemed to be contradicting themselves and, therefore, Kṛṣṇa seemed to confuse him. But Arjuna did not think that Kṛṣṇa was confusing him, only that this was how he perceived it. He says, 'My perception is that I have not understood what you have taught because you seem to praise knowledge.'

Mokṣa is not produced by *karma*.

For a wise person, all the *karma*s and their results that are mentioned in the Veda are like a well that has been completely flooded over by water. Of what use is the well water when there is water everywhere? You need not search for the well. When the river is dry, the well water is useful, but when the river is overflowing, and the well is underneath it, you are not going to look for the well because it is not going to be of any use to you. Similarly, for the one who knows oneself to be full, free from limitation, of what use is an object of security and happiness except for its empirical value? This was how Kṛṣṇa had praised the wise person.

By praising the wise, wisdom is praised. Kṛṣṇa had praised wisdom in this way and had made it very clear that knowledge was adequate for *mokṣa*. So Arjuna told Kṛṣṇa that the basis for his confusion was because he was asked to perform action, *karma*, and at the same time knowledge was praised as a means for *śreyas*.

Karma is something that can be produced, something that is born out of one's will, whereas *mokṣa* cannot be produced. Four types of results can be produced by *karma* – something can be created by you, something that has already been created can be modified or destroyed by you, something can be cleansed or purified by you, and a place that is already there and can be reached by you. Whether actions are worldly or religious, they can only produce one of these four types of results.

Here, we are talking about *mokṣa*, which cannot be produced. If it could be produced, it would also be lost. If, for example, *mokṣa* could be achieved by purifying the *ātmā*, it would take no time at all for the *ātmā* to become impure again. You would have to scrub it everyday!

Nor can the *ātmā* be reached because *ātmā* is myself. It is not something I have to reach because it is not away from myself. Therefore, reaching it is impossible. Modification of the *ātmā* is also not *mokṣa*. What can be modified is subject to time.

So, *mokṣa* gained will be lost. Also, in order for the *ātmā* to be subject to modification, it would have to be an object objectifiable by me. But, because *ātmā* is myself, it cannot be an object in my hands. Therefore, it is not something that I can modify. The self is already accomplished and *mokṣa* is identical with it.

But Kṛṣṇa was asking Arjuna to do *karma*. Therefore, Arjuna asked him to settle on one or the other – either knowledge or *karma*. If it was to be *karma*, he wanted to know why.

The nature of knowledge:

Knowledge is not something that is produced and is therefore different from *karma*. Knowledge is knowing things as they are. To know that an unclean object is unclean or that a clean object is clean is knowledge, *jñāna*. To know untruth as untruth or truth as truth is also *jñāna*. To know the real, *satya*, as *satya*, is *jñāna* and to know the unreal, *mithyā*, as *mithyā*, is also *jñāna*.

Because knowledge is as true as the object, it is not dependent upon your will. I cannot decide that this is how knowledge should be. I can only see the object as it is. Nor can knowledge be modified by my will. The will can set me up to pursue knowledge, but it cannot interfere in the perception of an object. This being the case, *jñāna* and *karma* are two entirely different things.

Arjuna wanted Kṛṣṇa to tell him whether knowledge or *karma* would liberate him, 'Tell me whether I will gain *śreyas* by *karma* or by knowledge. Tell me which one will do it.

Do not tell me that knowledge is all right and *karma* is also all right and that I can go this way or that way.'

Suppose you go to a teacher who tells you that you should perform *karma*. Then you decide to go to another teacher for a second opinion, just as you might if a doctor you have consulted recommends a surgery. The second teacher may say, 'What *karma*! You should do *yoga*.' Yet another teacher might say you must pursue knowledge. It is to be expected that if you go to three different teachers, each one may give you a different set of instructions. You then have to find out for yourself, which of the three is proper. Which teacher is right? There may be a fourth person who is right.

It is also understandable that the same teacher may give different advice to different students. One student may ask, 'Should I marry or not,' and be told that he or she should marry. Another student may be told not to marry because he or she does not know how to take care of himself or herself. The person is already a *duḥkhī* and risks making another person a *duḥkhī* by marrying prematurely. So, a teacher may advise his or her students differently.

In the *Gītā* there are only two people involved – Kṛṣṇa, the teacher, and Arjuna, the student. It seemed to Arjuna that Kṛṣṇa was saying, 'Knowledge liberates; therefore, do *karma*!' Only one student was involved here, Arjuna. It looked as if he was being told, 'Knowledge is okay and *karma-yoga* is okay.' Arjuna was, therefore, understandably confused by Kṛṣṇa's seemingly contradictory words. There was a similar situation in the epic, *Rāmāyaṇa*, between Prahasta and Rāvaṇa.

Rāvaṇa had kidnapped Rāma's wife, Sītā. This was probably the first kidnapping ever reported and was definitely a federal case! Rāma, who was a king, took the case into his own hands. When negotiations for Sītā's return were unsuccessful, Rāma declared war on Rāvaṇa. Rāvaṇa had a minister, Prahasta. Summoning him, Rāvaṇa asked, 'Prahasta, what do you think? Should I give Sītā back to Rāma? I think we are inviting trouble by keeping her here.' To which Prahasta replied, 'Yes, Maharaj you should give her back because we are definitely inviting danger by doing otherwise. We will all be destroyed.'

Hearing this, Rāvaṇa became very angry, and said, 'Are you saying that we will be destroyed by this Rāma, a mere mortal, an ordinary human being? Are you telling me, Rāvaṇa, who has ten heads and great powers, that this puny little Rāma is going to destroy me?'

'Never, Maharaj, never!' Prahasta replied. 'Rāma is a nobody. He has only two hands and two legs. With his bow and arrows what can he possibly do to you?' Then Rāvaṇa, said, 'But I am told that this Rāma is not an ordinary mortal.' Prahasta's reply came promptly; he said, 'Maharaj do you know what I have heard about this Rāma? They say he is an *avatāra*, an incarnation of the Lord himself, and not an ordinary mortal.'

Getting angrier, Rāvaṇa asked, 'Do you think that Rāma and Lakṣmaṇa with these monkeys can beat us? We can beat anybody. When I am the Lord of the three worlds, are you saying that these two are going to destroy me?' 'Never, Maharaj,' Prahasta replied.

'How can these two fellows with their monkeys do anything to you?' Rāvaṇa then said, 'But I am told that the monkey, Hanumān, is a very powerful fellow!'

'Maharaj, there is not only one Hanumān,' Prahasta responded, 'there are thousands of monkeys; some of them are as great as Hanumān. There are so many of them that if they all come here, we are done for.' Then Rāvaṇa asked, 'Are we afraid of monkeys?' 'What, Maharaj,' exclaimed Prahasta. 'Of course, we are not afraid of monkeys. Varuṇa, the god of water comes and waters our gardens. Vāyu, the god of air, comes and sweeps our floors. Why should we be afraid of these monkeys?'

It would seem that Prahasta had read a book equivalent to 'How to Win Friends and Influence People.' The advantage of being a Prahasta is that, in every cabinet reshuffle, his name always appears on the top of the list because he says 'yes' to everything.

Such pleasantries may be acceptable to those who are anxious to maintain a position, but, in Arjuna's case, the relationship was one of teacher and student. 'I am your student,' Arjuna had told Kṛṣṇa. A teacher should not be afraid to tell a student what is true and what is not true. If a teacher does not tell you what is true, who else is going to do it? Arjuna wanted Kṛṣṇa to tell him what was true and not true. Therefore, he was not looking for pleasantries. He wanted to be told what was the one thing that would give him *mokṣa*, and did not want to hear about anything in between. He did not want to be told that *karma* is good and knowledge is also good. He did not see it that way, even though it looked as though this was what Kṛṣṇa was saying.

Arjuna was as though saying to Kṛṣṇa, 'From your own words, I understand that knowledge liberates and *karma* binds. Why, then, do you want me to be bound to this *karma*? Every *karma* I perform only makes the knot more complicated. If I am to resolve this knot, this tie to *saṁsāra*, a life of limitation, for which I need and want *mokṣa*, then I need to pursue knowledge. But you are asking me to act. Therefore, you must have something in mind. Please tell me what it is because I do not understand.'

This, then, was the thinking behind Arjuna's question, which was really a doubt.

Verse 3

Kṛṣṇa's answer – two-fold committed lifestyles

श्रीभगवानुवाच ।
लोकेऽस्मिन्द्विविधा निष्ठा पुरा प्रोक्ता मयानघ ।
ज्ञानयोगेन साङ्ख्यानां कर्मयोगेन योगिनाम् ॥ ३ ॥

Śrībhagavān uvāca
loke'smin dvividhā niṣṭhā purā proktā mayānagha
jñānayogena sāṅkhyānāṁ karmayogena yoginām (3).

śrī-bhagavān – the Lord; *uvāca* – said;
anagha – O sinless one (Arjuna)!; *asmin* – in this; *loke* – world;
dvividhā – two-fold; *niṣṭhā* – committed lifestyles; *purā* – in the beginning; *mayā* – by me; *proktā* – was told; *jñāna-yogena* – in

the form of the pursuit of knowledge; *saṅkhyānām* – for the renunciates; *karmayogena* – in the form of the pursuit of *karma-yoga*; *yoginām* – for those who pursue activity

Śrī Bhagavān said:

The sinless one (Arjuna)! The two-fold committed lifestyles in this world, was told by Me in the beginning[1]– the pursuit of knowledge for the renunciates and the pursuit of *karma-yoga* for those who pursue activity.

Kṛṣṇa was not talking here as Mr. Kṛṣṇa, who was born on a given day at a given time, but as Īśvara, the Lord. Throughout the *Gītā*, Kṛṣṇa talked as the Lord, except in one or two places where he said to Arjuna, 'You are my friend.' In fact, anyone who understands the nature of Īśvara can talk as an *avatāra*, as Īśvara incarnate, just as Vyāsa had Kṛṣṇa do in the *Mahābhārata*. In the fourth chapter of the *Gītā*, Kṛṣṇa himself talked about what an *avatāra* is, as we shall see.

Here, in this verse, Kṛṣṇa said that in the Veda, the two-fold *niṣṭhā* was expounded by him. *Niṣṭhā* means a committed lifestyle. For example, a person who is committed to the practice of *japa*, chanting the Lord's name, is called *japa-niṣṭhā*, and when performing austerities, *tapas*, as the emphasis in one's life, the person is called *taponiṣṭhā*. One for whom the pursuit of Brahman is the *niṣṭhā* is a *brahma-niṣṭhā* and *jñāna-niṣṭhā* is one whose commitment is to knowledge.

---

[1] In the Vedas

In this verse, Kṛṣṇa said that one of the *niṣṭhās* he revealed to the world in the beginning is for the *sāṅkhyas*, the *sannyāsīs*, and is in the form of *jñāna-yoga*, meaning that knowledge is the means. Knowledge is the means for the *jñāna-yogī* who is a *sannyāsī* because he has no *karma* to do, other than the pursuit of knowledge in order to gain *mokṣa*. The other *niṣṭhā*, *karma-yoga*, he revealed to the world in the beginning is for everyone else – *karma-yogīs*.

Kṛṣṇa then revealed the two-fold *niṣṭhā* to Arjuna. The word *sāṅkhya* means knowledge and is also used in the *Gītā* by Lord Kṛṣṇa to mean *sannyāsa*, the life of renunciation. Those who are committed to knowledge are called *sāṅkhyas*[2] and the knowledge that is unfolded so clearly by all the *Upaniṣads*, the subject matter referred to as Vedanta is called *sāṅkhya*. The only topic that Vedanta deals with is, 'ātmā is Brahman.' Therefore, *sāṅkhya* means Brahman and what is unfolded by the Vedas, by the Vedanta, is *sāṅkhyaṁ brahma*. Because the knowledge of Brahman is called *sāṅkhya*, and those who pursue that knowledge are also called *sāṅkhyas*, we find in the *Gītā* that the word is also used as a synonym for *sannyāsa*, the lifestyle of renunciation in which knowledge alone is pursued.

Because Arjuna wanted *śreyas*, *mokṣa*, Kṛṣṇa told him about this two-fold *niṣṭhā*. *Mokṣa* is clearly the end in view and the *niṣṭhā* is a means to this end. The *niṣṭhā* is two-fold because

---

[2] सम्यक् ख्यायते सा वैदिकी सम्यग्बुद्धिः सङ्ख्या । तया प्रकाश्यत्वेन सम्बन्धि तत्त्वं साङ्ख्यम् । (आनन्द गिरि)

तद्विषया बुद्धिः सांख्य बुद्धिः । सा सांख्य बुद्धिः येषां ज्ञानिनाम् उचिता भवति ते साङ्ख्याः । (शङ्कर भाष्यम् २.११- उपक्रम भाष्यम्)

there are two different groups of people. One group is called *karma-yogīs* or just *yogīs* and includes everyone who does not live a life of renunciation. For these people there is *karma-yoga*, whereas for the *sannyāsī* there is *jñāna-yoga*. These two styles are in accordance with the four stages of life found in the Vedic culture.

The first stage is called *brahmacarya-āśrama*, wherein the person lives a studious life with learning as the main focus. The *brahmacarya-āśrama* prepares one for the next *āśrama*, the *gṛhastha-āśrama*, marriage. In the *Chāndogyopaniṣad* we read that, Śvetaketu spent twelve years in the *gurukula*, which he joined when he was twelve years old. So the first twenty four years of one's life is the first stage of the *brahmacarya-āśrama*.

The second stage of life, *gṛhastha-āśrama*, where being a householder and raising a family is the primary focus, prepares one for the third stage, called *vānaprastha-āśrama*. In this stage, a person remains married, but husband and wife live as friends, rather than as a married couple. The person continues to perform the various rituals enjoined by the Veda for householders, but withdraws from worldly activities and lives a contented life. The *vānaprastha-āśrama* prepares one for the fourth and final stage, *sannyāsa*, a life of renunciation. *Sannyāsa* is the best retirement plan because one does not require money for it. One simply renounces whatever one has.

Renunciation is possible at any stage. Arjuna, who was in the *gṛhastha-āśrama* wanted to renounce. He did not want to go through the intermediary stage as a *vānaprastha*. Nor was it necessary to do so, for the day a person wants to get out of any of the first three *āśrama*s, it can be done. When one discovers the readiness, the dispassion in oneself, on that very day, one can take *sannyāsa*. There is a Vedic sanction for it.

The *sannyāsa-āśrama* is a stage in life where one is absolved from performing *karma*s. One is freed from the duties in order to pursue knowledge. This pursuit is all that is to be done. Therefore, the person must already be a *jñānī* or want nothing but knowledge.

Types of sannyāsa

There are two main types of *sannyāsa*. For a person who is already a *jñānī*, there is *vidvat-sannyāsa*, a *sannyāsa* taken because of knowledge. The person has knowledge, and there is nothing more for him or her to do in the world – no obligations whatsoever. If the knowledge has been gained in any of the other three *āśramas* – *brahmacarya-āśrama, gṛhastha-āśrama,* or *vānaprastha-āśrama* – the person can take to the *sannyāsa-āśrama* directly, taking *vidvat-sannyāsa*, so that he or she is no longer subject to obligations. Otherwise, for the person with knowledge, there will still be obligations because each of the first three *āśramas* implies certain duties on one's part, which cannot be left undone as long as one is in that *āśrama*. Thus, the person takes *sannyāsa* to be free of these obligations—to make it perfect, in other words.

The other main type of *sannyāsa* is *vividiṣā-sannyāsa* and is meant for knowing.[3] This *sannyāsa* is for those who desire to know the self, *ātmā*, as Brahman. The person knows exactly what is to be done. He or she has heard that this *ātmā* is Brahman

---

[3] वेदितुम् इच्छा – विविदिषा – desire to know

and wants to know it. Such a person is not interested in anything else and has certain *viveka*, discrimination, with reference to the real and the unreal. He or she also has *vairāgya*, dispassion, *mumukṣutvam*, the desire for liberation, and other qualifications in various degrees. And with these qualifications, the person takes to the life of *sannyāsa*, called *vividiṣā-sannyāsa*.

The third type of *sannyāsa* is *āpat-sannyāsa*. When a person thinks he or she is going to die and does not want to die a *gṛhastha* or a *vānaprastha*, but rather as a *sannyāsī*, he takes *āpat-sannyāsa*. *Āpat* means danger. Because *sannyāsa-āśrama* is always praised in the *śāstra*, it is natural for a person to want the results of this *āśrama*. It is as though the person has had a blank cheque all along and now wants to encash it. For one who has already lived a *gṛhastha* life and has been told that death is near, there seems to be no use in continuing in the *gṛhastha-āśrama*.

A man who is not about to die will usually want to remain a *gṛhastha* because he is fond of his wife and children. But if he knows he is going to die fairly soon, he may go for *āpat-sannyāsa*. At such a time, one does not require a *guru* but can simply declare oneself to be a *sannyāsī*. With the sun, the elements, and all the gods as witness, one can make vows, for which there is a particular *mantra*. And if one happens to survive, the vows taken can always be ratified later. This is how Śaṅkara became a *sannyāsī*.

How Śaṅkara became a sannyāsī

Śaṅkara wanted to become a *sādhu* at a very young age, but his mother was not at all agreeable. As the story of his life goes, he had the help of a crocodile that had caught hold of his leg while he was bathing in the river. Śaṅkara's mother was waiting for him on the bank and he called out to tell her what was happening. It may have been a ploy or perhaps the crocodile was symbolic of *saṁsāra*. We do not know. In any case, when his mother began crying, Śaṅkara told her that if he took the vows of *sannyāsa*, the crocodile would let go of him. Because there was danger to his life involved, this was *āpat-sannyāsa*. Śaṅkara then took the vows and, lo! behold! The crocodile released him!

When he walked out of the river, his mother said, 'Come on, let's go home.' 'What!' Śaṅkara replied, 'I am a *sannyāsī* now.' When his mother told him the vows were only for the crocodile's sake, he said, 'Not at all! I have made the vows and I am going.' In this way, Śaṅkara became a *sannyāsī*. Later, he went to the *guru*, Govinda-bhagavat-pāda, who lived on the banks of *Narmadā* in the middle of India, and became his disciple. It was Govindapāda who ratified Śaṅkara's vows of *sannyāsa*. Ratification is always possible whenever one has taken *āpat-sannyāsa* and survives.

Expecting some good end from the *sannyāsa-āśrama*, people have value for it. This expectation is based on the belief that a *sannyāsī* does not take another birth. And if there is a birth, the hope is that one will at least get a better chance in the next life. This is a belief and one has faith, *śraddhā*, in it. A person may be born into a family where he or she can start life as a *sādhu*, so that directly from the *bramacarya* stage he or she will become a *sannyāsī* and not a *gṛhastha*. Thus, those who have become *sannyāsīs* this way may have been *āpat-sannyāsīs* in their previous life.

The last ritual of a sannyāsī

Arjuna's heart was not in *āpat-sannyāsa*. He was not dying, but he did want to know. Therefore, he wanted to take *vividiṣā-sannyāsa*. In *sannyāsa* one gives up all *karmas*, for which there is a special ritual, the last fire ritual that a *sannyāsī* performs. You may see a *sannyāsī* doing a *pūja*. But you will never see a *sannyāsī* sitting around a fire performing a Vedic ritual. Such a person has been freed of all obligatory fire rituals, of all *karmas*, in fact. A *sannyāsī's* last fire ritual is one in which all are given up.

In this ritual, the *sannyāsī* bids goodbye to all the ancestors, to whom there has been an obligation – father, mother, grandfather, grandmother, great grandfather, great grandmother, then *ṛṣi*s and *deva*s. The person taking *sannyāsa* says that self-knowledge will be pursued to the exclusion of all else, asks for the blessings of the paternal and maternal ancestors, and takes a vow of *abhaya*, a vow not to harm any living being, including trees and plants. The *sannyāsī* also vows to be a non-competitor in this world and all others, thereby becoming a person who does not compete for the sake of status politically, economically, or socially. Knowledge is the only interest for the *sannyāsī*.

Having taken these vows, the *sannyāsī* takes a few symbolic steps towards the north, the direction that stands for *mokṣa*. South stands for death. Thus, Lord Death, Lord Yama, is a southerner. This symbolism may be based on the polar attraction in the north. Death never attracts you, whereas freedom from death does. Moving towards the north in search of *mokṣa*, having discarded all clothing, the *sannyāsī* is called back by the *guru*, given a set of simple clothing, and asked to serve and continue studying with the *guru*. This, then, is the ritual of *sannyāsa*, be it either *vidvat-sannyāsa* or *vividiṣā-sannyāsa*. Both are mentioned by Śaṅkara in his commentary.

In *vidvat-sannyāsa*, one may or may not take *sannyāsa* formally. The main aim is that, by knowledge, one gives up all *karma*s. The knowledge is that 'I am a non-doer. I perform no action.' This is *naiṣkarmya*, the state of actionlessness. I perform no action at any time because *ātmā*, which is 'I,' does not perform any action. Nor does *ātmā* cause anyone to perform action. I am not a doer in spite of all the actions I do. This knowledge is real *sannyāsa* described as *jñāna-karma-sannyāsa*.

For the sake of this *jñāna-karma-sannyāsa*, one takes to the lifestyle of *sannyāsa*, pursuing self-knowledge. The other *niṣṭhā*, *karma-yoga*, is for those seekers in the other *āśramas*.

The purpose of karma-yoga

There is no doubt that *karma* binds, with its limited results. But, if you do *karma* for *antaḥ-karaṇa-śuddhi*, for neutralising your *rāga-dveṣas*, for gaining the grace of Īśvara, if you perform your prayers, rituals, and duties for the sake of these alone, the *karma* you perform becomes a means, *yoga*, for *mokṣa*.

Sannyāsa is only possible if one has lived a life of *karma-yoga*. Otherwise, one becomes a *sannyāsī* who has *rāga-dveṣas* and one will be miserable. A *karma-yogī* has the means, a world, a field, where his or her *rāga-dveṣas* can be neutralised. Such a field is not there for a *sannyāsī*. *Sannyāsa* means a life of study from morning to night. No other activity is available. A *sannyāsī* cannot even sing much because the pursuit of music, along with everything else, has already been given up.

A *sannyāsī* is one who has to pursue knowledge for which certain capacity to contemplate is required. If the pressure from *rāga-dveṣas* is there, one cannot sit in contemplation. One will find, instead, all kinds of agitation or one will fall asleep. After a few days, the lifestyle of a *sannyāsī*, traditionally indicated by the wearing of orange robes, will become a source of irritation. Naturally, then, *sannyāsa* is meant only for those who, to an extent at least, have taken care of their *rāgas* and *dveṣas*.

The two-fold *niṣṭhā* is meant only for *śreyas*. Arjuna wanted Kṛṣṇa to tell him which one was better and Kṛṣṇa replied that one can be a *sannyāsī* or a *karma-yogī*. Both are meant for the same end – *mokṣa, śreyas*. One can live a life of *karma-yoga* and gain *mokṣa* and one can live a life of *sannyāsa* and gain *mokṣa*. The only difference is that for a *sannyāsī* there is only knowledge, whereas for a *karma-yogī* there is knowledge and *karma*. This difference must be understood well because this is where there is a lot of confusion.

Arjuna was a *karma-yogī*, not a *sannyāsī*. By listening to Kṛṣṇa, he was pursuing knowledge. Although *gṛhasthas* pursue other activities, they are qualified for knowledge. This pursuit of knowledge plus the performance of *karma* made Arjuna a *karma-yogī*. If the pursuit of knowledge had not been there, if he had no discrimination, and if *mokṣa* had not been the end for him, he would not have been a *karma-yogī*. He would have been a simple doer, a *karmī*, a *karmaṭha*. When *mokṣa* is the end in view, then *karma* becomes *yoga* because it is done with a particular attitude in order to gain *antaḥ-karaṇa-śuddhi*, purification of the mind.

In this way, *karma-yoga* is important in gaining knowledge. One can take *sannyāsa* and gain *sarva-karma-sannyāsa* or one can live a life of *karma-yoga* and gain the same thing. *Sarva-karma-sannyāsa* is an end in itself for which the means is either of the two lifestyles – *sannyāsa* or *karma-yoga* revealed by the Lord in the beginning itself, in the *Upaniṣad*s.

Among the ten *Upaniṣad*s commonly studied, the first one is *Īśāvasyopaniṣad*. The first *mantra* of this *Upaniṣad* is meant for the *sannyāsī*, the *jñāna-yogī*. It says, 'In this moving world, everything should be looked upon by you as Parameśvara, the Lord – *īśāvāsyamidaṁ sarvam*. The Lord being everything, what is there that is yours? Or, not yours? Live a life of renunciation and pursue self-knowledge alone,' this *mantra* advises. Pursuit of this knowledge, giving up every other pursuit, is the life of *sannyāsa* or *jñāna-yoga*, said Śaṅkara in his commentary.

The second *mantra* of the same *Upaniṣad* says, 'Even if you want to live one hundred years, live doing *karma* with the proper attitude.[4] This is the best way for you. If *karma* is done in the proper way, it will not affect you at all.' This is *karma-yoga*.

---

4 कुर्वन्नेवेह कर्माणि जिजीविषेच्छतं समाः ।
एवं त्वयि नान्यथेतोऽस्ति न कर्म लिप्यते नरे ॥ (ईशावास्योपनिषद् १.२)
kurvanneha karmāṇi jijīviṣecchataṁ samāḥ
evaṁ tvayi nānyatheto 'sti na karma lipyate nare (Īśāvāsyopaniṣad 1.2)

Thus, we see here the two-fold *niṣṭhā* being unfolded, *sannyāsa*, wherein the pursuit of knowledge alone is allowed, and *karma-yoga*, the pursuit of knowledge along with whatever *karma* is to be done. Throughout the *śāstra*, these two *niṣṭhās* are always discussed in the same way.

Choice of lifestyle

In the Vedic vision, *śreyas* is *mokṣa*. *Mokṣa* is the end, the human destiny to be gained in this life. Here, itself, *saṁsāra* is crossed. To have taken a human birth means that you have already made it. Because you have an intellect, *buddhi*, *viveka* is possible. It is true that experience teaches, but you do not need to get knocked around for seventy five years to develop discrimination. Twenty-five years are good enough! Once you develop *viveka*, *śreyas* alone looms large before you; it becomes the only real end for you.

You become either a *karma-yogī* or a *sannyāsī*. The *niṣṭhā* was told in a two-fold way because there are two kinds of people. But there is only one means for *mokṣa*, knowledge. Depending on the kind of person you are, you can be either a *sannyāsī* and pursue knowledge to the exclusion of everything else or a *karma-yogī* and pursue knowledge along with *karma*. In both lifestyles, the pursuit of knowledge is common. Knowledge is *mokṣa*. Therefore, the choice is not between *jñāna* and *karma*. It is between *sannyāsa* and *karma-yoga*.

When the choice is between *karma-yoga* and *sannyāsa*, it is natural to look to *sannyāsa*. Given a choice, why do *karma* at all? *Sannyāsa* seems to be the better choice since performing *karma* implies so much effort, problems, and even bloodshed.

Karma can be such a nuisance. When two lifestyles are available, why should I put up with a life of *karma*?

The choice is like asking which is the better way to catch hold of my nose in order to do breathing exercises. Shall I take my hand directly to my nose or shall I reach around from behind my head? It can be done either way, but when the first way is obviously so easy where is the question of choosing? *Sannyāsa* seems to be easier – just give up all the *karma*s and pursue knowledge. Why do both? For instance, a *karma-yogī*, living in an agricultural society, has to milk the cow, graze it, wash it, and take care of the children, among other things. One child is crying, the other is on his lap, and the third one is tugging at him from behind. The mosquitoes are biting and his wife is shouting. In between, he has to perform the fire ritual called *agnihotra-karma*, with all its problems. The firewood is wet, everything is smoking, and his eyes become filled with all kinds of tears – tears born out of the smoke, tears born out of the nagging children, tears born out of his helplessness, and so on. When will such a person have time to pursue knowledge? Whenever he picks up the *Gītā* book, all that comes is sleep!

Is it therefore not better to go for *sannyāsa*? Arjuna definitely thought so. However, *sannyāsa* is not as easy as it appears. It looks as though you need only to sit and study. But try, and you will find that it does not always work that way. Instead, you may vegetate the whole day because you are not able to study so intensively. This is not the way. Kṛṣṇa continued to tell Arjuna exactly what *sannyāsa* and *karma-yoga* are. Even though a choice is there, *karma-yoga* will pave the way for *sannyāsa*.

It will even pave the way for the desire for knowledge and, therefore, for *vividiṣā-sannyāsa*. Kṛṣṇa told Arjuna that *sannyāsa* is not at all easy in spite of how pleasant and simple it appears to be. After all, *sannyāsa* is giving up everything.

Arjuna thought that giving up everything would not present any great problem, especially since he had lived in the forest for twelve years. But during those twelve years, he had been thinking about Duryodhana and the kingdom, and the injustice of it all. Twelve years of meditation upon Duryodhana did not make Arjuna a *sannyāsī*. Arjuna had been nursing a big hurt for a long time. Therefore, *sannyāsa* was not going to come so easily to him. One does not become a *sannyāsī* by decision alone – all of which Kṛṣṇa would tell him later in the *Gītā*.

Verse 4

Actionlessness with reference to gaining mokṣa

न कर्मणामनारम्भान्नैष्कर्म्यं पुरुषोऽश्नुते ।
न च संन्यसनादेव सिद्धिं समधिगच्छति ॥ ४ ॥

na karmaṇām anārambhānnaiṣkarmyaṁ puruṣo'śnute
na ca sannyasanādeva siddhiṁ samadhigacchati (4)

puruṣaḥ – a person; *karmāṇām* – of actions; *anārambhāt* – by non-performance; *naiṣkarmyam* – the state of actionlessness; *na aśnute* – does not gain; *ca* – and; *sannyasanāt- eva* – merely by renunciation; *siddhim* – success (liberation); *na samadhigacchati* – does not attain

A person does not gain the state of actionlessness by non-performance of actions. Nor does the person attain success (liberation) out of mere renunciation, *sannyāsa*.

We have seen that there are two lifestyles, *niṣṭhās*, *jñāna-yoga-niṣṭhā* and *karma-yoga-niṣṭhā*. These two *niṣṭhās* are for two types of people, the *sannyāsīs* and the *karma-yogīs*, respectively. All those seeking liberation, who are other than *sannyāsīs*, are *karma-yogīs*. Here, Kṛṣṇa explains why this is so.

There is a connection between *karma-yoga* and *sannyāsa*, *jñāna-yoga*. For a *jñāna-yogī*, the pursuit of knowledge alone is *yoga*, for which he or she must have freedom from the hold of *rāga-dveṣas*. The Gītā itself decribes *rāga-dveṣas* as the source of all our problems. Therefore, *rāga-dveṣas* must be taken care of before one becomes a *sannyāsī*.

If one becomes a *sannyāsī* without *karma-yoga*, how is one going to neutralise one's *rāga-dveṣas*? There are *rāgas*, desires, for certain things and, for a *sannyāsī*, it is impossible to fulfil them. *Dveṣas*, those situations that one wants to avoid, will also be there with no possibility of being neutralised. As a *karma-yogī*, however, one has a field in which one's *rāga-dveṣas* can be neutralised. Thus, *karma-yoga* becomes the means for *jñāna-yoga* and *jñāna-yoga* becomes the means for *mokṣa*.

We have seen how the word *sannyāsa* can have two meanings, one being a lifestyle implying the renunciation of all relationships and activities in order to pursue knowledge alone. The other meaning is that by knowledge, one gives up all action, *jñānena karma sannyāsaḥ*. Śaṅkara often took it this way, *sannyāsa* as an end in itself, knowledge being *sannyāsa*. This is because *sarva-karma-sannyāsa*, the giving up of all action, takes place in knowledge. Through knowledge, the doership of the *ātmā* is nullified. Because there is no doership in the *ātmā*, even as one performs action, it is not really being done by the *ātmā*. Only when this is clearly understood, is there the giving up of all activities through knowledge, *jñānena karma sannyāsaḥ*. This is what is meant by *sarva-karma-sannyāsa*, which is equivalent to *mokṣa*.

Nyāsa means renunciation and *sannyāsa* means perfect or complete renunciation. *Sarva-karma-sannyāsa* means perfect renunciation of all action, the renunciation being in the form of knowledge itself. This knowledge is not possible without a certain mind. Such a mind is accomplished by *karma-yoga*, performing action with the proper attitude, as we saw in the previous chapter, and will see again in this chapter. *Karma-yoga* enables one to give up all *karma*s in the sense that it becomes a means for *sarva-karma-sannyāsa*.

The necessity of karma-yoga

With a desire for *mokṣa*, one can take to a life of renunciation called *vividiṣā-sannyāsa*. In this type of *sannyāsa*, *sarva-karma-sannyāsa* has not yet taken place, but certain duties are given up so that knowledge can be pursued. However, if the person has not taken care of his or her *rāga-dveṣa*s before taking *sannyāsa*, he or she will not be able to pursue knowledge to the exclusion of everything else.

Taking *sannyāsa* is always possible because it is open to choice. If you are a *mumukṣu* and there is a choice between a life of renunciation of activity and a life of action, why should you perform activity? Since you are only interested in *mokṣa*, which can be gained by the pursuit of knowledge alone, why would you not take *sannyāsa* and pursue knowledge alone? Because, if you have not taken care of your *rāga-dveṣas*, it is not possible to do so.

Even if you do commit yourself to the pursuit of this knowledge, other interests will be there based on your *rāga-dveṣas*. For most people who take to this knowledge, it is not the predominant factor in their lives. They have a lot of other interests as well. Therefore, they are not *sannyāsīs* at all. One does not become a *sannyāsī* just by pursuing knowledge. *Sannyāsa* implies a certain mind that is only possible by *karma-yoga*.

To conclude that performing action is of no use to you when what you want is *mokṣa*, is not correct. Doing *karma* is useful because without a prepared mind, your pursuit of knowledge will be useless. Without *karma-yoga* there is no chance of neutralising your *rāga-dveṣas* and, if this neutralisation does not take place to a significant degree, there is no chance to gain the knowledge through which all action is given up. So, to take to a life of *sannyāsa* without having dealt with your *rāga-dveṣas*, is meaningless.

Knowledge alone negates doership

In this verse, Kṛṣṇa said that by not performing action a person does not gain the end called *naiṣkarmya*, the state of actionlessness, which is *sarva-karma-sannyāsa*. The renunciation of all activities is in the form of knowledge alone because there is no such thing as giving up all activities without giving up doership. Why not just give up the doership then? But how are you going to give up the doership when you are the very doer? If you think you can give it up by just deciding to do so, who is the one that makes the decision? How are you going to give up the doer who is deciding? Therefore, you are not going to give up doership this way.

Doership does go away in the wake of knowledge that 'I am *ātmā*, Brahman, which is not the doer.' This knowledge alone negates the doership in the *ātmā*. Nothing else will do it. To think that surrendering is another way to reach God is certainly not correct, for how will you surrender the one who surrenders? You are still left with having to give up the doership.

Here is a relevant verse from the *Mahābhārata*:

त्यज धर्ममधर्मं च उभे सत्यानृते त्यज ।
उभे सत्यानृते त्यक्त्वा येन त्यजसि तत्त्यज ॥

tyaja dharmamadharmaṁ ca ubhe satyānṛte tyaja
ubhe satyānṛte tyaktvā yena tyajasi tattyaja

(Mahābhārata-śānti-parva 12.329.40)

Give up *dharma* and *adharma*; give up the concept of real and unreal. Having given up the concept of real and unreal, give up that by which you give up.

Give up *dharma* and *adharma*, right and wrong, good and bad. Go beyond them. Do not just give up the right and do the wrong! To give up the wrong and do the right is only the first stage. Give up the right also. The very concepts of right and wrong must be given up. All *karma* is to be given up, both *puṇya-karma* and *pāpa-karma* have to be given up. And that giving up is what we call *sannyāsa*. A *sannyāsī* does not perform actions that will create *pāpa*; nor does he or she do actions for the sake of *puṇya*. Giving up both *puṇya* and *pāpa karmas*, the person becomes a monk, a renunciate. Having done this, all that is then done is in the form of enquiry, *vicāra*, with reference to the person's concept of what is real and what is unreal. Eventually, these concepts also are given up.

Suppose someone says that he or she has given up all concepts of reality, both empirical reality and subjective reality, meaning that the person no longer cares for the empirical world or for the false values he or she once had. The person no longer thinks that money or anything else is going to liberate him or her. In other words, one has become dispassionate towards everything that exists within the empirical reality, which we call the world. Having discovered this inner dispassion, the person now has the notion, 'I am a *sannyāsī*. I am dispassionate.' In other words, the person is still there in the form of the ego, *ahaṅkāra*, which says, 'I have given up everything.' This *ahaṅkāra* also has to be given up and this can only be done through knowledge.

In fact, you do not give up the *ahaṅkāra*. How can you, when you are the *ahaṅkāra*? Only in the wake of knowledge that you are not the *ahaṅkāra*, does it go away because it is not true. And along with the *ahaṅkāra* goes the doership and all actions too.

By absence of doership and therefore all actions, it should not be construed that the one who has knowledge of the self will be like a stone, not performing any action. In spite of all actions, the *jñānī* does not take the self to be a doer. For the *jñānī*, the doer is the self, but the self is not the doer. In this sense, *sarva-karma-sannyāsa* is the state of actionlessness, *naiṣkarmya*, in the form of knowledge.

Thus, self-knowledge and *naiṣkarmya* are identical. The word *naiṣkarmya* is used because, as long as *karma* is there, you are bound to whatever body you have at any given time and place. Even in dream, you have some kind of physical body of your own, albeit set up by your own thought. All bodies, ethereal, celestial, or corporeal, are all because of *karma* alone.

Karma makes you identify with a particular body in order to go through the experiences that are the result of *puṇya* and *pāpa*, and themselves the result of previous actions performed by you. As long as *karma* is there, *saṁsāra*, life as we know it, is there and as long as *saṁsāra* is there, *karma* is there. *Karma* will remain as long as ignorance of oneself remains.

Actionlessness is not giving up action

The word *naiṣkarmya* is important because the state of actionlessness, freedom from action, is identical with what is called *mokṣa*, which is self-knowledge, *ātmā-jñāna*. It looks so simple – by doing nothing, you will gain the state of actionlessness and, therefore, *mokṣa*. But Kṛṣṇa clearly stated here that the state of actionlessness is not accomplished by not doing *karma*. Thus, it is not as simple as one might think.

We know that the state of action means to be active. So it is natural for us to think that all we have to do now is to be inactive in order to gain the state of actionlessness called *mokṣa*. Thus the question arises, why perform all these actions? Arjuna asked Kṛṣṇa the same question, Why should he perform action, let alone such a terrible action? He, too, thought that by giving up all his actions, he would gain the state of actionlessness that is *mokṣa*.

Here, the question can be asked, how long should you be actionless in order to gain *mokṣa* – half a second, one second, two seconds, one minute, how long? If actionlessness is *mokṣa*, should you be actionless for a long time? What is the determining factor? Since, between two thoughts there is no action at all, should you not gain *mokṣa* before the second thought comes? Should you not, therefore, have gained *mokṣa* long ago? In fact, in between thoughts, you must be gaining *mokṣa* all the time! If this kind of actionlessness amounts to *mokṣa*, you would have gained it long ago.

Another factor to consider is that it is not possible for you to be actionless. In fact, Kṛṣṇa points this out in the next verse. Remaining actionless for a long time is itself an action. Since sitting is an action, someone may say, 'I will not sit; I will lie down. Then I will be actionless.' But lying down is also an action. 'What are you doing now?' 'I am lying down.' Thus, there is no way of gaining the state of actionlessness by not doing action.

Someone may think that by not initiating an activity, he or she will gain the state of actionlessness since the very act of beginning anything is to become active. The state of actionlessness is lost simply by starting an action. If an action is not started, perhaps the state of equilibrium between not acting and acting is actionlessness. If that state is not disturbed, *mokṣa* will not be disturbed, but if you begin any action, *mokṣa* will be disturbed! To correct this thinking, Kṛṣṇa made it very clear here that by not starting any activity, you do not gain actionlessness, *naiṣkarmya*.

Simply taking to sannyāsa does not guarantee mokṣa

It may also be said that *sannyāsa* can be taken, not because the person is afraid of performing actions, but simply as a vow that absolves the *sannyāsī* from all of the commitments and obligations enjoined by the Veda. The Veda itself says that *sannyāsa* can be taken, all activities can be given up, in order to pursue knowledge. Kṛṣṇa addressed this notion also, saying that by simply taking to *sannyāsa* alone, one will not gain *mokṣa*. Just because a person has become a *sannyāsī* does not mean that he or she has *naiṣkarmya* because, for this, self-knowledge is required. Śaṅkara made the same point in his commentary on this verse.

Jñāna-niṣṭhā, otherwise called *mokṣa*, is not achieved by merely becoming a *sannyāsī* because *karma-yoga* is also a means. In fact, without *karma-yoga-niṣṭhā*, *sannyāsa-niṣṭhā* is not possible. Only by *karma-yoga* can you become a real *sannyāsī*. Only then is there a choice between *karma-yoga* and *sannyāsa*.

If you have gained certain contemplativeness by a life of *karma-yoga*, if your life is more or less adequate and you are satisfied with yourself, then you can sit with yourself. Only then can *sannyāsa* be a means for you. Without *karma-yoga*, this *sannyāsa* is not possible, to say nothing of *naiṣkarmya*. Therefore, mere taking of *sannyāsa* does not amount to gaining *mokṣa*.

Not performing action is also not *naiṣkarmya*. If, not being a *sannyāsī*, you do not do the *karma* that is to be done by you, it amounts to a dereliction of duty. It is not *naiṣkarmya*. If, however, you give up *karma* by taking *sannyāsa*, you may think that the vows you have taken are enough to free you from all actions. But they are not; you still have to gain knowledge.

Verse 5

Actionlessness is not to be taken literally

न हि कश्चित्क्षणमपि जातु तिष्ठत्यकर्मकृत् ।
कार्यते ह्यवशः कर्म सर्वः प्रकृतिजैर्गुणैः ॥ ५ ॥

na hi kaścit kṣaṇamapi jātu tiṣṭhatyakarmakṛt
kāryate hyavaśaḥ karma sarvaḥ prakṛtijairguṇaiḥ (5)

jātu – ever; *kṣaṇam* – for a second; *api* – even; *kaścit* – some one; *akarmakṛt* – without performing action; *na* – not; *hi* – indeed; *tiṣṭhati* – remains; *hi* – because; *prakṛtijaiḥ guṇaiḥ* – by the three *guṇas* born of *prakṛti*; *sarvaḥ* – everyone; *avaśaḥ* – being helpless; *karma* – action; *kāryate* – is made to do

Indeed, no one ever remains for even a second without performing action because everyone is forced to perform action by the (three) *guṇas* (*sattva*, *rajas* and *tamas*) born of *prakṛti*.

There is no person who can exist even for a second, now or later, without performing any action whatsoever. It cannot be said that someone who is young and active, either meaningfully or idly, performs action and someone who is old and inactive does not. Young or old, no one exists without performing one action or the other at any time, even for the shortest period of time.

Even Kṛṣṇa performed action. He was talking; he was teaching. And if he had not been teaching, he would have been doing something else. If there were no one to teach, he would simply pick up his flute and play. He would not remain quiet for very long – and even if he did, sitting quietly would also be an action.

In India, there is an expression, 'keeping quiet,' which means the person is doing nothing. But 'keeping quiet' is definitely an activity. No one keeps quiet; one is quiet. 'Keeping quiet' is an action because 'keeping' is an action.

Karma defined

So there is no time whatsoever when you are free from activity. We can see that there are many varieties of activities with many definitions. For instance, whatever you do voluntarily is *karma*. Closing your eyelids involuntarily is also *karma*. A general definition of *karma* is that which is in the form of motion, *calanātmakaṁ karma*.

If action is motion, then non-action, *akarma*, must be motionlessness and therefore *naiṣkarmya*. But is it? How long can you be motionless? When a man who considers himself motionless is asked, 'Do you do any *karma*?' He may not answer because talking is a *karma*. Instead, he shakes his head in the negative, which is an action. Similarly, if he nods his head in agreement to the question, 'Are you doing *akarma*?' He is also performing an action.

The entire body is always in a state of activity. Breathing is motion, thinking is motion from one thought to another. Eating is an activity, even when performed by one who has given up all activities. There may be a special name for it –*bhikṣā*, but, even so, it is an action. Just see what a *bhikṣu* will do if, instead of giving him food, we simply write the word *bhikṣā* on a piece of paper and hand it to him!

Similarly, cooking, walking, and bathing are all *karma*s. Sitting in a chair, cross legged on the floor, or in any other manner is *karma*. All these *karma*s are in the form of motion. If this is so, when are you going to be motionless? Only when you know, I am motionlessness. 'In knowledge alone, there is *akarma*. There is no other *akarma*, otherwise.

Thus, at no time is there any living being who is not performing some activity or the other. We have no way of knowing whether there is activity after death, except that the *śruti* says that one takes another birth, thereby implying even more action. Therefore, when is a person not performing action? Even in deep sleep, there is activity since breathing and other vital physiological functions continue to operate. Otherwise, there would be no need to break one's fast; there would be no breakfast for the person!

Causes of action – the three *guṇa*s born of *prakṛti*

If motion is action, then, there is no time when the person in a given physical body is free from activity. Even if action is taken as something that is will based, one is always doing one thing or the other, helplessly impelled by an unseen cause, as Kṛṣṇa said in the second line of the verse when he introduced the word *prakṛti.*

Prakṛti is that out of which any product, any creation, is ultimately born and is the word given to the material cause of the world. Your mind is also born out of *prakṛti,* which has three qualities, *guṇas* – *sattva, rajas* and *tamas.* Being qualities of the cause, *prakṛti,* these three qualities will also be in the effect or the product. For example, gold is the cause for a given bangle. Gold has certain qualities, certain weight, and that weight will be there in the bangle. It also has a certain colour, which will also be in the bangle. Because gold is rustproof, the bangle will also be rustproof. The bangle will contain the malleability, strength, and so on, of the gold because it is born of gold, *prakṛti,* the cause. Its cause being gold, the bangle will necessarily have the same qualities as gold.

Similarly, the *antaḥ-karaṇa,* mind, is born of *prakṛti* and has the same qualities – *sattva, rajas,* and *tamas.* Each produces certain types of desire, the expressions of which can be classified according to these three *guṇas,* as we shall see in more detail later in the *Gītā.* For instance, there are three types of giving– giving as an investment in expectation of a return is born of *tamas;* giving for the sake of pride is born of *rajas;* giving because it must be done, and once done it is forgotten, is born of *sattva.* Thus, there is a clean division among the three.

Because *sattva, rajas* and *tamas* are present in everyone, there are three types of expression with reference to desires.

Prompted by these desires, one performs action. In this way, all living beings are made to do action. There is no escaping it. A bug keeps moving because if it stays in one place it risks getting squashed. Even while moving, it has no guarantee for its life. For a worm to go from one side of a room to another is like making a pilgrimage on foot to Benares from the South of India!

Something inside every living creature impels it to perform action. This is how the creation is. No one remains without performing action. Therefore, literally speaking, one is not going to accomplish *naiṣkarmya*, actionlessness. *Naiṣkarmya* is simply knowing oneself to be free from doership. This is the only *naiṣkarmya* available and this is *mokṣa*.

The verse under discussion here relates to the previous one. By not beginning an activity, one is not going to accomplish *naiṣkarmya*. Nor is one going to do so by giving up action, even if one adheres to the Vedic rules for *sannyāsa*. Also, by becoming a *sannyāsī*, one cannot give up activities because it is physically impossible. One will always be doing one thing or the other. One will go for food, which is an action; one will eat the food, which is another action. Thus, even a *sannyāsī* is active in some form or the other.

Therefore, if one takes *sannyāsa*, it does not mean that one has gained *sarva-karma-sannyāsa*; one has merely been absolved from certain duties. Giving up all action is a matter of knowing. When choosing between the two lifestyles, do not think that *sannyāsa* is easy. There is activity in *sannyāsa* also, just as there is in *karma-yoga*. Which one is more appropriate for you depends upon your disposition.

If one has *rāga-dveṣas*, it is better to be a *karma-yogī*. If, however, one finds oneself to be contemplative and not interested in anything other than pursuing self-knowledge, then *sannyāsa* is suitable for the person. It means that one's life has been lived meaningfully and one is now ready for *sannyāsa*. Only then should one become a *sannyāsī*. Even so, *naiṣkarmya* is equal only to knowledge.

Verse 6

A saṁsārī is one who does not know the ātmā

कर्मेन्द्रियाणि संयम्य य आस्ते मनसा स्मरन् ।
इन्द्रियार्थान्विमूढात्मा मिथ्याचारः स उच्यते ॥ ६ ॥

karmendriyāṇi saṁyamya ya āste manasā smaran
indriyārthān vimūḍhātmā mithyācāraḥ sa ucyate (6)

yaḥ – one who; *karmendriyāṇi* – organs of action; *saṁyamya* – controlling; *indriyārthān* – sense objects; *manasā* – with the mind; *smaran* – remembering; *āste* – sits; *saḥ* – that one; *vimūḍhātmā* – deluded; *mithyācāraḥ* – a person of false conduct; *ucyate* – is called

The one who, controlling the organs of action, sits with the mind remembering those sense objects is deluded and is called a person of false conduct.

One who does not know that the nature of *ātmā* is *naiṣkarmya*, actionlessness, takes himself or herself to be a doer. When, as a doer, one gives up actions by will, his or her life is false. *Mithyā* means 'false' and *ācāra* means conduct and therefore, '*mithyācāra*' literally means 'false living.'

A person who does not know the *ātmā* is a *saṁsārī* with all the problems, inadequacies, and so on, that a life of *saṁsāra* implies. Giving up all activities, such a person cannot but dwell upon the sense objects towards which he or she no longer goes. Controlling all the organs of action, the person thinks that he or she performs no action. Not speaking or doing anything, the person just sits. What happens then? Because he or she does not see the self as fullness, *ānanda*, the person cannot but think of the sense objects. Not knowing the *ātmā*, but thinking that he or she is going to be actionlessness, one who gives up all activities will necessarily dwell on the objects towards which he or she no longer goes. This is why Kṛṣṇa refers to such a person as *vimūḍhātmā*, one who is deluded and confounded. His or her conduct itself is false. It is not actionlessness at all because the person is always thinking about the sense objects.

Suppose this person does not think about the objects. He or she cannot but think about them because the person has no other object to think about unless he or she knows the *ātmā*. If the *ātmā* is known, there is no problem. The person is already actionlessness, which is why knowledge of the *ātmā* is called *mokṣa*. Without this knowledge, a person who thinks he or she is going to gain *naiṣkarmya* by not doing action is living in delusion. Instead of enjoying the knowledge of *ātmā*, the person will contemplate upon various objects already experienced or possible experiences yet to come. Kṛṣṇa told Arjuna that this type of living is false and Śaṅkara went so far as to call it sinful, *pāpācāra*.

Kṛṣṇa now describes the person who does not live in this way.

Verse 7

An asaktaḥ is one who takes to yoga of action

यस्त्विन्द्रियाणि मनसा नियम्यारभतेऽर्जुन ।
कर्मेन्द्रियैः कर्मयोगमसक्तः स विशिष्यते ॥ ७ ॥

yastvindriyāṇi manasā niyamyārabhate'rjuna
karmendriyaiḥ karmayogam asaktaḥ sa viśiṣyate (7)

arjuna – O Arjuna!; *yaḥ* – one who; *tu* – whereas; *indriyāṇi* – sense organs; *manasā* – with the mind; *niyamya* – controlling; *asaktaḥ* – unattached; *karmendriyaiḥ* – with the organs of action; *karmayogam* – the *yoga* of action; *ārabhate* – takes to; *saḥ* – that one; *viśiṣyate* – is far superior

Whereas, Arjuna! the one who, controlling the sense organs with the mind, remaining unattached, takes to the *yoga* of action (i.e., action performed with *yoga-buddhi*) with the organs of action, is far superior.

A person who can control his or her sense pursuits has discrimination, *viveka*. The control is through the mind only. The word *manasā*, through the mind, implies *viveka*, *manas* being another word for *buddhi*, intellect. To control one's organs of action and sense pursuits – in other words, having a mastery over them – is to direct them at will. Such a person, not attached to *karma-phala*, the results of action, begins, *ārabhate*, takes to a life of *karma-yoga*, meaning that the person performs *karma* as a *yoga*, as a *sādhana*, a means. One cannot do *karma-yoga*. One can only have it because *karma-yoga* is strictly an attitude with reference to action and its result. The person described by Kṛṣṇa in this verse is one who begins doing *karma* with the organs of action, speaking, walking, and whatever is to be done, with the proper attitude.

Actions to be done may be *vaidika-karma*s, scripturally enjoined rituals, or *laukika-karma*s consisting of all other activities. When one does *vaidika-karma* or *laukika-karma* with the *karma-yoga* attitude, one does not do it to fulfil one's *rāga-dveṣa*s but to neutralise them – in other words, to purify the mind for gaining the knowledge that is *mokṣa*.

Generally, people do *vaidika-karma*, rituals, prayers, and so on, in order to gain securities and pleasures. This is nothing but fulfilling their *rāga*s and *dveṣa*s. First you pray and then you present the Lord with your petition. There is nothing wrong with this, but you need to know that it is only for fulfilling *rāga-dveṣa*s.

Praying to the Lord for the cure of a disease or the solution to a problem is definitely appropriate. If you have done everything you can do and it is not enough, why not invoke the Lord also? What should be understood here is that all prayers, even those enjoined by the Veda, can be for your securities and pleasures, either here or in the hereafter. Or they can be *yoga*, a means for self-purification and self-knowledge, which is *mokṣa*.

*Karma*s even if performed according to *dharma*, is for the fulfillment of one's *rāga-dveṣa*s alone, that is for the sake of achievements in the form of securities and pleasures. Such *karmas* are called *kāmya-karmas* and the person who does the *karma* is called a *karmī* or a *karmaṭha,* one who is attached to the results of action.

The person who is unattached is one who, rather than doing *kāmya-karma,* is doing *karma* for the sake of preparing the mind for knowledge. For such a person, prayer or any other type of *vaidika-karma* is for the very joy of praying and also for purification of the mind, *antaḥ-karaṇa śuddhi.* Being for certain desired ends, that is, *antaḥ-karaṇa śuddhi* and *mokṣa,* these *karmas* also come under the category of *kāmya-karma,* but since the purpose of performing them is *antaḥ-karaṇa śuddhi,* they are not considered to be impelled by *rāga-dveṣa*s. This needs to be understood.

However, *karma* done for any other reason is a *bhoga-sādhana,* a means for enjoying security and pleasure, even if it is a prayer or ritual enjoined by the Veda. A man may perform an elaborate ritual for the sake of wealth, progeny, or for heaven, in which he spends a lot of money. But all these are for enjoyment alone even though the person does not know who is enjoying what.

When you say you enjoy an object, you do seem to be enjoying it. In time, however, you find that the object has enjoyed you because you have grown older. The objects of enjoyment have taken away your liver, kidneys, everything! You find yourself the loser because you do not know who is the enjoyer and who is the enjoyed. During the early years of your life, your body was growing. You became taller and stronger. You grew by eating. But as an adult, the emphasis shifted.

Previously, you were eating and you were growing. But now, in spite of eating, you are declining. Therefore, who is eating now? You are no longer eating the food; the food is eating you. The food itself has become the eater because, in spite of eating, you are declining! In this way, the eater can become the eaten. Therefore, you do not know which is the enjoyer and which is the enjoyed.

Action as prayer

If, when performing *vaidika-karmas*, one thinks of oneself as an enjoyer, one is referred to as a *phalāsakta*, one who is attached to the results of action. It is the same for *laukika-karma*, as well. In fact, for a *karma-yogī* there is no such thing as a *laukika-karma*. The word is merely a verbal expression for an action that is not a Vedic ritual because, for a *yogī* every action is nothing but prayer to Īśvara, the Lord, as our analysis reveals. The order that is here in the creation is nothing but Īśvara. Once one recognises this fact, any action one performs, which is in keeping with Īśvara, becomes a prayer. Therefore, there is nothing that is *laukika* or *vaidika*, the words being used only to distinguish non-ritualistic actions from ritualistic actions.

Since any action that is in keeping with *dharma*, Īśvara, becomes a form of prayer, action performed by one who is not attached to the results of action is not considered to be impelled by one's *rāga-dveṣas*. The expression, 'being unattached to the results of one's actions,' is the source of much confusion because no one performs action without expecting results. The word *asakta*, one who is unattached, has to be understood as a technical word which means one whose actions, whether *vaidika* or *laukika*, are not based purely on *rāga-dveṣas*. *Rāga* is always in terms of something desirable that is away from you and *dveṣa* is in terms of something you want to avoid or get rid of. Actions not based on *rāga-dveṣas* are considered to be in keeping with *dharma* and are meant for *antaḥ-karaṇa śuddhi*.

Thus, in the verse, *asakta* refers to a person who enjoys a certain control. Otherwise, one's *rāga-dveṣas* alone will decide what one should do. Whatever fancies happen along, the person will simply join them and do whatever comes to mind. Convenience, instead of what is right, becomes the rule here, though the action may be against *dharma*. The *karma-yogī*, on the other hand, has a certain control over his or her organs of action and sense organs. We use the word 'certain' here because, even though the person is a *karma-yogī*, he or she is still an *ajña*, one who is ignorant with reference to the self. Thus, even though this person may have some omissions and commissions, there is always a degree of control.

Being not impelled by *karma-phala* alone, interested only in *antaḥ-karaṇa śuddhi* and *mokṣa*, the *karma-yogī* does what has to be done. The idea conveyed here is that, technically, purification of the mind is a result of one's actions. But, because purification of the mind is not born out of *rāga-dveṣa* based action, it is not referred to as a *karma-phala* in the usual sense.

When you say you want to gain *mokṣa*, you mean that you want to know *ātmā*, which means you want to know Īśvara. *Antaḥ-karaṇa śuddhi* is for understanding Īśvara.

Knowledge of Īśvara is knowledge of oneself

Whether we use the word 'knowing,' 'gaining,' 'reaching,' or whatever, what is meant is knowledge of Īśvara, which is not separate from knowledge of the self. Between *jīva*, the individual, and Īśvara, the Lord, there is identity, which is expressed as an equation, 'You are that, *tat-tvam-asi*.'

'That, *tat*,' refers to Īśvara who is the cause of the world. 'That,' Īśvara, you are, *tvam asi*. This equation naturally implies self-knowledge and also Īśvara-knowledge. In this context, *karma* is performed for *antaḥ-karaṇa śuddhi* so that knowledge of Īśvara can be gained, and not for getting something out of Īśvara. Getting something out of Īśvara implies *rāga-dveṣas*, whereas here we want to know what he is. We want to have the vision of Īśvara, which is something entirely different. Therefore, *karma* becomes *yoga*. Kṛṣṇa described one who begins this *yoga* as far superior. To whom? In his commentary, Śaṅkara refers back to the person mentioned in the previous verse, the one who outwardly performs no action but dwells inwardly upon all the sense objects that have been given up. Such a person can also be called lazy.

Laziness and idleness are not the same thing. A lazy person is one who does nothing outwardly, but does everything mentally. He or she even writes letters mentally and then becomes annoyed when there is no reply! Whereas an idle person is one who is always busy, without ever accomplishing anything. He or she makes a mess of everything and then clears them up. Such a person has no time for anything and accomplishes nothing.

In a planetarium in Hawaii, there is a coin-operated machine designed to be as busy as an idle person. Every form of mechanism can be seen in this machine – moving pistons, revolving wheels, hammering devices, and so on. Everything that is mechanically possible is going on there, but nothing is ever produc=ed. Aside from being a waste of energy and genius, this machine is an excellent satire on how people are busy accomplishing nothing!

The word *'viśiṣyate'* in this verse does not mean simply superior. To say that the *karma-yogī* is far better does not mean that the *mithyācāra* mentioned in the previous verse, is good. The two are completely different. One person is sitting, dwelling on things, being lazy, and the other person is active and has a *karma-yoga* attitude. Because the *karma-yogī* accomplishes everything, he or she is far superior to the other person who is simply a hypocrite, not merely superior; there is no comparison at all. The *karma-yogī* accomplishes the ultimate *puruṣārtha*, *mokṣa* but the hypocrite achieves nothing even in a relative sense.

Verse 8

Doing what is to be done is superior to inaction

नियतं कुरु कर्म त्वं कर्म ज्यायो ह्यकर्मणः ।
शरीरयात्रापि च ते न प्रसिद्ध्येदकर्मणः ॥ ८ ॥

niyataṁ kuru karma tvaṁ karma jyāyo hyakarmaṇaḥ
śarīrayātrāpi ca te na prasiddhyed akarmaṇaḥ (8)

tvam – you; *niyatam* – what is to be done; *karma* – action; *kuru* – do; *hi* – because; *akarmaṇaḥ* – (when compared) to inaction;

karma – action; *jyāyaḥ* – superior; *akarmaṇaḥ* – due to inaction; *te* – your; *śarīrayātrā* – maintenance of the body; *api* – even; *ca* – and; *na prasiddhyet* – would become impossible

> Do action that is to be done because action is superior
> to inaction. Even the maintenance of your body would
> be impossible by inaction.

The word *niyatam* refers to *karma* that is enjoined by the *śāstra*. By telling Arjuna to do those actions that are to be done, Kṛṣṇa was not suggesting that the *śāstra* would always tell him what was to be done. There are, of course, many situations that the *śāstra* does not cover. But because every situation is a part of the given universal order, the situation itself dictates what is to be done. Thus, you need not be told that a particular action is to be done at a particular time. Given the situation, what is to be done becomes very obvious.

The *karma* that is obvious in a given situation, that which is proper, is also *niyata-karma*. It is *niyata* either by the order of *dharma* or because it is enjoined by the *śāstra*. In any case, it is the *karma* that must be done – daily, occasionally, whenever. Kṛṣṇa told Arjuna to perform action because it is definitely superior to doing nothing. If you do not know the *ātmā* and do not do *karma* either, nothing will be accomplished. Instead, all that will happen is that the body will become sick and the *antaḥ-karaṇa*, the mind, will become even sicker. Thus, doing *karma* is definitely superior.

The word '*śarīra-yātrā*' in the verse, refers to the journey of the living body. From birth onwards, it has been journeying. Even though it reaches certain stages, there are many more stations to travel to, like a train that has not yet reached its destination. The journey of living, Kṛṣṇa says here, does not take place if actions are not performed. You simply cannot live your life. Even mere survival is not possible. And by merely surviving, you are accomplishing nothing.

Life is not for mere survival

Even a frog manages to survive. Every living organism has the instinct for survival and it does survive for as long as it can. Since anyone and anything can survive, survival is not considered to be a human accomplishment. Life, human life especially, is not just for surviving; it is for some accomplishment. This is why the four fold *puruṣārthas*, human ends, security, *artha*; pleasure, *kāma*; righteousness, *dharma* and liberation, *mokṣa*, are mentioned in the *śāstra*. Since there are these ends to be accomplished, we have various desires that impel us to attempt to fulfil them.

To just survive, one must at least eat. There is a Swami who is said to be such a great *sannyāsī* that he does not use his hands even for eating. However, he does open his mouth so that someone else can put the food in! Obviously, he does not understand that opening his mouth is an action and closing it is another action, to say nothing of chewing, swallowing, and preparing for the next mouthful. This same Swami will not talk either. He does nothing and people call it *naiṣkarmya*, which it is not.

Even eating is not possible if you do no action and, to live, you have to get your food somehow. If you will not use your hands to eat, someone else has to put the food into your mouth. When others have to cook your food and put it into your mouth, there is action. Earning the money to buy the food and materials needed to prepare it is also action. Since survival cannot possibly be without action, do what is to be done by you.

By telling Arjuna to perform action, Kṛṣṇa was telling him not to be afraid of action. Arjuna's problem was that his *karma* was the cause of his being bound. When you do *karma*, you produce *puṇya* and *pāpa* and, because of this, you are born again. Again you will perform *karma*s which again produce *puṇya* and *pāpa*, because of which you will be born yet again. This is why *karma* is said to be the villain in the life of *saṁsāra*. Because *karma* alone is the cause for your being bound, you conclude that you should not do *karma*.

Karmas are inexhaustible

The cycle of life can be looked at through the model of *karma*, but if we do so, the model must be taken in its entirety. Suppose you say that by not doing any *karma* at all there will be no problem – no *puṇya* or *pāpa* and, therefore, no more birth and death. The cessation of this cycle of birth and death is what is meant by liberation, *mokṣa*. Therefore, by not doing anything, you will accomplish *mokṣa*. Let others study the *Gītā*; you do not need it because, by doing nothing, you can gain *mokṣa*.

To this, Śaṅkara replies elsewhere by asking further questions. He asks, 'What about all the *karma*s standing in your account from previous births, *sañcita-karma*s? Who is going to fulfil them even if you do nothing in this birth? Secondly, when did you decide not to do any more *karma*? Until you were forty years old, all you did was *karma*! What about that *karma*? It also must be fulfilled. Furthermore, can you remain for even the briefest period of time without performing *karma*? When you have the 'I am a doer' notion, you cannot but do *karma*. In fact, you cannot remain for even a second without performing some action or the other. And if you are not occupied with doing right *karma*, it will take you no time at all to do wrong *karma*!

Not doing *karma*, therefore, is nothing but a pipe dream. There is no such thing as gaining *mokṣa* by not doing *karma*. Of course *karma* is the cause for you being bound. No one ever said that *karma* liberates. *Karma* definitely binds the *jīva*. In fact, it is the third strand of a three stranded knot. Ignorance is the first strand, ignorance in the form of the notion, 'I am a doer.' Once this ignorance-born notion is there, you cannot avoid the second strand, desire, *kāma*. If you think that you are small, limited, and mortal, you will want to be big, full, immortal – all these are desires.

Because you do not want to be limited by ignorance, limited by the knowledge that you have limited knowledge, you do not accept ignorance. This means that you want to be free of the limitation of knowledge and ignorance, which is another desire. There is also the desire to be happy, to be free from unhappiness, inadequacy, lack. These desires arise because you do not know that you are already full. When this ignorance is there, desires will also be there and, of course, they will be according to your limited knowledge.

Therefore, even your wants are not very big. You may want this and that, but they are all small wants really. Then, in order to fulfil these wants, you perform *karma*, which produces the *puṇya* and *pāpa* that create new births for you. Given this ignorance-desire-action cycle, you remain bound by *karma*.

This same *karma*, however, while not itself a releasing factor, can assist in one's release if it is done with the attitude of *karma-yoga*, as we have seen. By performing *karma* in this way one is released from the hold of *rāga-dveṣas*, likes and dislikes. Therefore, the same *karma* becomes a means, a *sādhana*. In the next few verses, the *karma* done in this way is being referred to as *yajña*. It becomes *yoga* and one gains *śuddha-antaḥ-karaṇa*, a pure mind. With this pure mind, the person gains the knowledge that is *mokṣa*. This, then, is the order. Beginning with the next verse and ending with verse 16, Kṛṣṇa then talked about *karma* as a means leading to *mokṣa*.

Verse 9

Karma-yoga releases you from the hold of rāga-dveṣas

यज्ञार्थात्कर्मणोऽन्यत्र लोकोऽयं कर्मबन्धनः ।
तदर्थं कर्म कौन्तेय मुक्तसङ्गः समाचर ॥ ९ ॥

yajñārthāt karmaṇo'nyatra loko'yaṁ karmabandhanaḥ
tadarthaṁ karma kaunteya muktasaṅgaḥ samācara (9)

yajñārthat karmaṇaḥ – other than the *karma* performed for the sake of *yajña*; *anyatra* – with reference to other (*karma*); *ayam* – this (person); *lokaḥ* – the one who is enjoined (to do the *karma*); *karma-bandhanaḥ* – one who is bound by action; *kaunteya* –

O Kaunteya!; *tadartham* – for the sake of that (*yajña*); *mukta-saṅgaḥ* – being one free from attachment; *karma* – action; *samācara* – perform

> A person is bound by *karma* if it is not done as *yajña* (i.e., as an offering to Īśvara). For this reason, Kaunteya (Arjuna)! being one free from attachment, perform action for the sake of that (*yajña*).

Yajña is a very important word in the Vedic literature.Even though the word means a sacrificial ritual, in a wider sense *yajña* means every action of one's life is performed as an offering to Īśvara. In an act of giving, there is a giver, something given, and a recipient. In an offering such as a ritual, one more factor is involved–the place of offering, the altar. Thus there is the altar of offering, the recipient who is invoked in the offering, the one who does the offering, and the offering itself.

Generally, in any offering, there is a word like *svāha* or *namaḥ* meaning, 'I offer this salutation.' For example, when we say, '*Namaḥ Śivāyaḥ*,' it means, 'Unto Lord Śivā, I offer this salutation,' and this is an offering. When this expression is repeated over and over again, it becomes a *japa-yajña*. Even the food you eat is an offering, although most people do not think of it as such. If, however, you look upon the digestive system as digestive fire, the food offered into that fire is an offering and the altar of this offering is the digestive process, *prāṇa*, itself. Therefore, before eating, the food is offered to the Lord in the form of *prāṇa*.

Nothing in the creation is looked upon as something separate from the Lord. The Lord is a conscious being, *cetana*.

Only in a conscious being does the activity of digestion take place and the food offered is not separate from the Lord. This is why the fifteenth chapter of the *Gītā* and the *śloka*, '*brahmārpaṇam...*' are repeated before eating. These verses make it very clear that everything is the Lord, including the food we eat, and the one who eats it. Therefore, eating is an offering.

In a fire ritual, the altar is the fire, the turf. The oblation is offered unto the fire. The offerer is called *yajamāna* and the recipient of the offering, *devatā*. Usually, when you offer something to another person, you expect reciprocal treatment. You expect something in return from that person. Giving and receiving gifts during the Christmas season is a case in point. You offer a gift to another, no matter how small, and that person offers you something too. Because giving gifts at Christmas time is a convention, a beautiful convention, you have to offer and a return is expected. It is not the gift you are interested in; it is the care and consideration, the remembrance, of the other person that counts.

All offerings belong to the Lord alone

But when we offer something to a *devatā* like Indra, reciprocity is not a factor. As part of the *yajña* itself I say in so many words that what I am offering belongs to Indra; it does not belong to me.[5]

---

[5] This is the *mantra* that we say when we make an offering to Lord Indra, '*indrāya svāhā indrāya idaṁ na mama* – offered unto Indra, this is now Indra's, not mine anymore.'

In this way, everything is looked upon as a *yajña*, as we shall see in the fourth chapter. The breathing process is a *yajña*. The breath that goes out is called *prāṇa* and the incoming breath when you breathe in is called *apāna*. When you breathe out the *prāṇa* is offered to *apāna* and when you breathe in the *apāna* is offered back to *prāṇa*. In this way, breathing is considered to be a *yajña*.

Those who are committed to the practice of *prāṇāyāma*, control of the breath, are not really doing exercises. They are performing a *yajña*, *prāṇa* being Īśvara, the Lord. In the same way, all exercises and yogic postures, *āsanas*, are considered to be *yajñas*, In fact, each *āsana* has its own *devatā*. Indian music is also a *yajña*. Every defined melody, *rāga*, is considered to have a head, trunk, and feet. Certain Indian paintings depict each *rāga* with the form of a goddess. Thus, even *rāga*s melodies have their own presiding deities.

Any one aspect in the creation can be looked upon as an aspect of Īśvara, and that aspect becomes the presiding deity or *devatā*. Thus, in any given object, you can invoke the total or an aspect of the total. If it is an aspect, it is called *devatā*. Any functionary such as the eyes, ears, nose, and other organs has a presiding deity, *devatā*, which is but Īśvara.

If you look at Īśvara as the material cause of the whole creation, the eyes themselves are Īśvara. And if you look at the Lord as the efficient cause, the Lord becomes the presiding deity for the eyes. Without this appreciation of Īśvara, this *bhakti*, there is no *karma-yoga*. This appreciation is the very attitude that is *karma-yoga*, in fact. Thus, *karma-yoga* is *bhakti-yoga*.

We are told very clearly that there are only two *yogas* – *karma-yoga* and *jñāna-yoga*.

So for the sake of *mokṣa*, there are two possible dedicated lifestyles, *jñāna-yoga* and *karma-yoga*. Either one pursues knowledge to the exclusion of everything else or one performs *karma* with the proper attitude, which implies Īśvara, along with one's pursuit of self-knowledge. *Bhakti*, appreciation of Īśvara, is common to both the *sannyāsī* and the *karma-yogī*. A *sannyāsī*, *jñāna-yogī*, is not without devotion. In fact, this person's entire life is dedicated to the appreciation of Īśvara. He or she wants only to understand what Īśvara is. The knowledge being Īśvara, nothing but Īśvara is there. Īśvara is the very pursuit. Thus, a *sannyāsī* is not a non-devotee.

Because two words, *jñāna-yoga* and *karma-yoga*, are used, it is commonly thought that there are two separate pursuits, the pursuit of knowledge and the pursuit of *karma*. This misunderstanding leads to the introduction of a seemingly third pursuit, the pursuit of *bhakti*. But how can this be? Suppose a *sannyāsī* is one who renounces all action, *karma-yogī* is one who performs all action, and then there is a third person, a *bhakti-yogī*. Does the *bhakti-yogī* not perform *karma*? And if not, what will he or she do for *bhakti*? To worship Īśvara, certain rituals have to be performed.

Whatever the person does to express his or her devotion is an action, a *karma*. This is *karma-yoga*, in fact. All that is being done is is *karma*. 'No, no,' the *bhakta* might say, 'I only sing, *Hare Rāma*.' He or she may think that singing *Hare Rāma* is *bhakti*, but it is an action, a *karma* performed by the organ of speech and therefore called *vācikaṁ karma*. And if, while singing, the person also claps or dances, the *karma* becomes a *kāyikaṁ karma*, an action performed by the limbs of the physical body. Therefore, the *karma* is not only oral, it is also physical. In fact, this kind of *bhakti* can be so physical that it can totally exhaust the person!

Bhakti-yoga is karma-yoga

Bhakti is the recognition of Īśvara and any *karma* done for the sake of recognising Īśvara is *yoga*. Even if you meditate mentally, it is *bhakti* because the Lord is involved. It is also *karma* because you are doing it with your will. Any action that comes of your will and is invoking someone is a *yajña*, a *karma*. Therefore, the expression 'bhakti-yoga' is to be taken as *karma-yoga*, *bhakti* being a common element.

Similarly, *haṭha-yoga* is a discipline which is a *sādhana* or indirect means for *mokṣa*. Any discipline is either for *antaḥ-karaṇa śuddhi*, purification of your mind, or for the integration and co-ordination of the physical body. Because there are a number of disturbances and many kinds of deficiencies possible in a person, various disciplines can be helpful. Any discipline is *yoga* if the purpose is very clear. If not, it can be a problem. Even Karate can be *yoga*, as long as it is not done to make you feel invincible. The purpose is not to kick someone but to gain certain degree of fitness and co-ordination.

When there is commitment to Īśvara everything becomes *yoga*, a means; there is no discipline or activity that we can say is not *yoga* if the Lord is involved. In the fourth chapter we will see how many types of activity there are and that, with these, everything is covered. Who is doing it, the person's attitude, the purpose for which an activity is being done – all these make any activity a *sādhana*, a *yoga*. So it is important to understand that although *yoga* has been divided into many different types, the *śāstra* makes it clear that there are only two in fact, *karma-yoga* and *jñāna-yoga*.

For the *jñāna-yogī* or *sannyāsī*, knowledge alone is *yoga* because the person is absolved from all duties. It is not that the *jñāna-yogī* does not do any *karma* whatsoever; it is just that the person is absolved of all obligatory duties. The *sannyāsī* is a non-competitive person, one who does not compete in the society in any way. Only then is the person freed from all obligatory duties to pursue knowledge. When *sannyāsīs* start incense factories, for example, they have to compete with other incense manufacturers. They have to project the product, proving it to be better than other products. Only a person who does not compete in the society can be called a *sannyāsī*.

There are only two *yoga*s and *bhakti* is common to both of them. All *karma*s become *yoga* if they are done keeping Īśvara in view. A *yajña* is any *karma* which is done for the sake of Īśvara. It can be any ritual, worship, or prayer, each of which involves special *karma* performed only for the sake of Īśvara.

Bringing up a child is also a *yajña* and is an example of an indirect offering to Īśvara. I am here in this creation and the child is in my keeping. The child has been given to me as *prasāda* and is to be brought up by me. This is a proper attitude and is therefore *karma-yoga*. Īśvara is recognised and the order involved is seen to be Īśvara. To see things in this way is not an ordinary situation. A person has to be sensitive so that the order that is Īśvara is as tangible as a wall or a rock. This kind of appreciation is what *bhakti* actually means.

The real meaning of bhakti

Bhakti is not just chanting, although chanting is also *bhakti*. It is the appreciation of Īśvara and the order. This appreciation is what makes you sensitive and gives meaning to your life. Recognising Īśvara is to be able to see more than what meets the eye, more than what the eyes see. *Bhakti* is an appreciation of what is behind and what is in front, the order within the order, seeing everything as Īśvara. And this is also exactly what is meant by *karma-yoga*.

By any *karma*, you are either directly or indirectly related to Īśvara. *Karma* involves role playing. Something is expected of you. This action is to be done by you because you are placed in this situation. Therefore, you do it. This is how Īśvara's *karma* works. Otherwise, why are you in this place at this time? Why are you not elsewhere? There is a meaning here. You are in this place at this time because there is something to be done by you. This is the law of *karma*.

You see that there is a meaning and that the situation is not a random one. Everything seems to have a cause and an effect. There is no randomness in the creation. To use Einstein's words, the Lord does not play dice. Even if he did, being omniscient, he would know exactly how they were going to fall. Otherwise, he would not be Īśvara. Therefore, he has no need to play dice. Situations do not happen randomly. They happen because they have to happen. If this is understood, you will find that everything, even relationships, becomes meaningful.

To worship the Lord by doing what is to be done by you definitely requires that you see more than the eyes can see. You have to appreciate what is beyond the hands that perform the action, not merely the desire but what is behind the desire. You should appreciate that the desire itself is born of Īśvara. This kind of appreciation is *bhakti*. In this way, the performer of action worships the Lord indirectly.

So, there is a two-fold *yajña*, direct and indirect. When you perform a *karma*, a *yajña* in the form of a prayer, there is a direct relationship between Īśvara and you. You either invoke Īśvara in the form of a *devatā*, a deity, or you invoke him as the Lord straightaway. Either way, there is a *bhakta*, a devotee, and there is a *yajamāna*, one who performs the *karma*. You can do the *karma* yourself or it can be done by someone else, by proxy, like when you ask a priest to conduct a ritual on your behalf. Either way, the result comes to you alone, the *yajamāna*.

Direct and indirect *yajñas*

Karma that invokes a *devatā* or Īśvara directly becomes a direct *yajña*. Any other *karma*, done with an awareness of Īśvara, becomes an indirect *yajña*. Because the *yajña*, direct or indirect, is done for the sake of Īśvara, Īśvara is also called *yajña*.

This section of the *Gītā* provides a beautiful description of *bhakti* that converts *karma* into *yoga*. Everything can be seen here, the order, the ecology, and so on. At every level, there is ecology – the ecology of thought, the ecology of *karma*, the ecology of action. 'Ecology' is an excellent word having brought into light certain understanding that did not exist previously. 'Ecology' is now a commonly used word because there is necessity for it, pollution now being a recognised problem.

Ecology is recognised here at different levels. All the *devatās*, the elemental forces, are doing their jobs and should not be disturbed. Because you are a conscious being with a free will, even the ecology of the divine forces can be disturbed by your actions. If you are abusing your free will, you are disturbing the ecology of *dharma*, which is going to affect all humanity, whatever is disturbed is not going to remain without producing undesirable results.

There is an order and, wherever there is an order, there is ecology. Here, Kṛṣṇa is talking at the *dharma* level. *Dharma* alone should govern your free will. Once freedom is given to you, you can do whatever you want. There is no hindrance whatsoever. If freedom can be hindered, it is not freedom. Therefore, because you have a free will, you can commit homicide and even suicide!

Since there is the possibility of abusing freedom at different levels, there should be an ecology with reference to the freedom given. It seems that the only ecology we are concerned about disturbing is the ecology of the flora and fauna. This attitude comes from human selfishness. We tend to think only about how we are going to be affected by this or that, but there is so much more to ecology than this. Ecology is the very awareness of one's actions and how they have an ever widening circle of reactions. When a stone is thrown into clean water, it does not just drop to the bottom. It creates ripples, which keep on widening and widening into bigger and bigger circles, until finally, they lash upon the shore. Similarly, any action creates extended circles of response.

Disturbing the order

Any action that disturbs the order, the *dharma*, will definitely bring about disorder, *adharma*. Because you are given freedom, your freedom should be controlled by *dharma*. If at all there is a control, it is conformity to *dharma*. And if you do not conform to *dharma*, you will cause an ecological disturbance at the *dharma* level, resulting in various conflicts and problems.

In this section of the *Gītā*, you will find how the universe moves within an ecology. It moves in a certain order and any disturbance in that order is a disturbance to you and to everyone else. Awareness of this fact is what makes a person a *karma-yogī*.

Karma-yoga must be clearly understood. Because it is not an ordinary attitude, it takes a lot of maturity, awareness, and sensitivity. To simply say that one should love God is just so much Sunday talk. It means nothing. How can people who are not able to love their own mothers or those who care for them, love God? You do not even know who this God is or whether he exists.

Bhakti is no joke. You must have a heightened awareness of the whole at the level of the manifest. This heightened awareness is *bhakti* and is what makes you a *karma-yogī*, as we shall see later in this group of verses.

Arjuna was told by Kṛṣṇa to take to *karma-yoga* and he was also told that *karma*, action, binds the person who performs action. Thus, there seems to be a problem here. Action, implying a doer, brings to the doer the results of the action. The results of action are either seen, *dṛṣṭa,* or unseen, *adṛṣṭa*. Seen results are those you see immediately, in this life itself. You can relate directly to them. When you boil water, for example, the boiled water is a result that is seen immediately.

The same actions can also bring about unseen results, those that are not seen by you now, but will come either later in this life or in the hereafter. A prayer or a ritual is a *karma* that brings about an unseen result. For example, *putrakāmeṣṭi,* the name given to a ritual performed for gaining a son, produces result in this life only. How it happens is not known; only the outcome is seen. The connection between the ritual and the result not being seen, the result is called *adṛṣṭa*. That actions produce both seen and unseen results is unfolded by the *śruti*.

How action binds the person

In this way, we see that action does indeed bind the person. It keeps the doer going all the time. Whether the result is good or bad, *puṇya* or *pāpa*, the doer is always there as a *saṁsārī*. For one who can discriminate between the real and unreal, even a good result is a shackle. A good result may mean that a particular situation is a little more comfortable, but it is not going to completely change the person in terms of his or her sense of limitation centred on the I.

A person can become the president of a country because of some *puṇya*, not merely because of his or her qualifications.

You may say it is a fluke or chance, whereas we attribute it to some good *karma*. Even though a highly qualified person may repeatedly contest the presidential elections, he or she may never win. For the highly qualified person, the unseen result of winning a presidential election may not be there, whereas for a lesser-qualified person it is.

And even if you do become the president, there will still be problems. Perhaps you think your nose is too big and, having to be constantly in the public eye, you feel you should undergo surgery! Like this, some problem or other is always going to be there. Simply by becoming a powerful person in society, no one is going to alter his or her sense of limitation centred on the I. Therefore, even *puṇya*, good results, are a shackle, a golden shackle. Whether one's shackle is made of gold or iron, it is still the same.

A discriminating person knows that both *puṇya* and *pāpa* are the causes for bondage, the cause for *saṁsāra* continuing. *Karma* does not cause *saṁsāra*; it perpetuates it. There is no need to cause *saṁsāra* because it is already there. Since *karma* perpetuates *saṁsāra*, instead of releasing you from it, 'Why should I do *karma*?' becomes the question.

In this verse, Kṛṣṇa also acknowledged that *karma* is the cause for continued bondage, *bandha-hetu*. There is no doubt about it if *karma* is done for reasons other than *yajña*. Here, *yajña* does not refer to the ritual itself but to the one for whose sake it is done, Īśvara. By saying that *yajña* is Viṣṇu, the one who is all-pervasive, the *śruti* makes it clear that *yajña* is the Lord. Similarly, in verse 24, chapter 4 of the *Gītā*, everything is seen to be Brahman, the Lord.[6] The one who performs the ritual is the Lord. The place where it is performed, the oblation itself is the Lord. The *mantras*, ladles with which the oblation is offered, and so on, are the Lord and so is the result. This means that there is nothing to gain. Everything belongs to Brahman because everything is Brahman

How action becomes yoga

Kṛṣṇa said here that *karma* only binds a person when it is performed without recognising the Lord. When *karma* is done for the sake of one's *rāgas* and *dveṣas*, without considering the *dharma* as Īśvara, then it is bondage. One gains only the results known as *puṇya* and *pāpa*, those that come from performing *kāmya-karma*, actions done for the sake of one's likes and dislikes. Only in this way can it be said that *karma* binds. It is true that if *kāmya-karma* is done keeping *dharma* and *adharma* in view, no *pāpa* is incurred. However, only when *karma* is done for the sake of *antaḥ-karaṇa śuddhi* does it become a means for *mokṣa*. Only then is it *yoga*.

Karma becomes *yoga* if it is *yajña* done for the sake of Īśvara, as propitiation to him or for *antaḥ-karaṇa śuddhi*. If this is not the case, then even worship, prayer, and so on, become *kāmya-karma*, performed to fulfil one's *rāgas* and *dveṣas*. There is nothing wrong in doing this, but one should know that performing *karma* in this way is bondage. Therefore, Kṛṣṇa said, do *karma*

---

[6] ब्रह्मार्पणं ब्रह्महविर्ब्रह्माग्नौ ब्रह्मणा हुतम् । ब्रह्मैव तेन गन्तव्यं ब्रह्मकर्मसमाधिना ॥ (गीता ४.२४)

brahmārpaṇaṁ brahma havirbrahmāgnau brahmaṇā hutam
brahmaiva tena gantavyaṁ brahmakarmasamādhinā (Gītā 4.24)

properly, for the sake of the Lord, as a *yajña*, propitiation. And how should this *karma* be done? By being free of attachment. What binds you to *karma* are your *rāga-dveṣa*s alone. *Karma* itself does not bind you. For a *jñānī*, a wise person, there is no problem at all. *Karma* does not bind the person. And for a *yogī*, one who is not controlled by his or her *rāga-dveṣa*s, *karma* is an indirect means for gaining the knowledge that is *mokṣa*. Thus, Kṛṣṇa told Arjuna that, whether he looked upon himself as a *jñānī* or a *yogī*, there was no problem.

You find that your previous *karma*, *prārabdha*, has brought you to a given situation. With reference to action itself, you simply have to do what is to be done by you. Another aspect of *karma-yoga* concerns your response to the results of action. You have certain likes and dislikes and, in keeping with *dharma*, you fulfil them. At the same time, you are prepared to accept the results of your action as *prasāda*. In this way, your response to the results of action is also *karma-yoga*.

The action mentioned by Kṛṣṇa in this verse was not meant for fulfilling Arjuna's *rāga-dveṣa*s. It was action to be done simply because it was to be done. Arjuna said he did not want to fight because he did not want the kingdom. Since *rāga-dveṣa*s were not involved, why should he fight? Kṛṣṇa's response was that the matter was no longer in Arjuna's hands and that what was to be done by him must be done. *Rāga-dveṣa*s have to subserve *dharma*. What is to be done, we have to do, without being dictated to by a utilitarian attitude.

Actions are almost always dictated by a utilitarian attitude, what will I get out of this? How much will I get and so on?

But, Kṛṣṇa is saying that if something is to be done by you and you do not want to do it, you better do it anyway! In this way, action becomes a *yoga*. Kṛṣṇa is talking about a *karma-yogī* here, one who is qualified to do *karma*. The *jñānī* is not being addressed at all. For the *jñānī* there is no problem. Because the person knows that he or she is not the doer, there is nothing to be done. The *karma-yogī*, on the other hand, still thinking that he or she is the doer, continues to perform action until knowledge is gained.

Verse 10

Kṛṣṇa explains why karma is to be done

सहयज्ञाः प्रजाः सृष्ट्वा पुरोवाच प्रजापतिः ।
अनेन प्रसविष्यध्वमेष वोऽस्त्विष्टकामधुक् ॥ १० ॥

sahayajñāḥ prajāḥ sṛṣṭvā purovāca prajāpatiḥ
anena prasaviṣyadhvam eṣa vo'stviṣṭakāmadhuk (10)

purā – in the beginning; *prajāpatiḥ* – the Creator; *sahayajñāḥ* – along with (*yajña*); *prajāḥ* – human beings; *sṛṣṭvā* – having created; *uvāca* – said; *anena* – by this (*yajña*); *prasaviṣyadhvam* – shall you multiply; *eṣaḥ* – this; *vaḥ* – for you; *iṣṭa-kāmadhuk* – the wish-fufilling cow; *astu* – may (this *yajña*) be

> In the beginning, the Creator, having created human beings along with *yajña*, said: "By this (*yajña*) shall you multiply. May this (*yajña*) be a wish-fulfilling cow for you."

Prajāpati means the Creator, the Lord of all beings, called Brahmāji. The statement, 'In the beginning, the Lord said,' refers to the Veda. The Veda is a body of knowledge considered not to have been written by anyone. Instead, it is looked upon as knowledge revealed to the ancient sages, *ṛṣis*, by the Lord. What the Lord said, then, is in the Veda and what he said is for the sake of the human beings he has created. Animals, being programmed, do not need the knowledge contained in the Veda. Along with human beings, the Lord created *yajñas* and enjoined everyone to perform the rituals and other *karmas* found in the Veda.

Vedic rituals cover all phases of life. Even before a child is born, a ritual is performed. The Sanskrit word for wife is *patnī* and for husband, *patiḥ*. The letter '*i*' in *pati* is replaced by '*n*' and the feminine suffix '*ī*' is added to form the word *patnī* meaning wife. The *Pāṇini-sūtra*[7] that describes this grammatical rule states that the substitution is only done when a woman is connected to a man for the purpose of doing *yajña*, meaning a Vedic ritual. A man marries for this reason since, without a wife, he cannot perform certain rituals enjoined by the Veda.

Most Vedic rituals require one's wife, *patnī*, to take part. Although the husband, *pati*, actually performs the ritual, he cannot do so without his wife's permission. Nor can he perform it without her. Therefore, the marriage itself has a religious purpose. The very taking of a woman's hand in marriage, accepting another

---

[7] पत्युर्नो यज्ञ संयोगे । ४.१.३३

patyurno yajña saṁyoge (4.1.33)

person into one's life, is religious. The woman herself need not perform any Vedic ritual because she naturally receives half the results of the rituals that her husband performs. And the results of any sins the husband may perform belong to him alone. Thus, she wins, hands down!

Although the wife is not required to perform rituals, she has specific duties related to them, such as preparing certain food. In this way, there is a sharing of responsibility–the husband performs the rituals and the wife gives her permission and attends them. Because she enables him to be qualified to perform the rituals, she is called *patnī* meaning that she is connected to *yajña*. Thus, inherent in the grammar of such words as *patnī* is the Vedic attitude about marriage.

There are Vedic rituals performed for the consummation of the marriage, for impregnation. Again a Vedic ritual is done during the seventh or eighth month of pregnancy, for the safety of mother and child. When the child is born, the ritual called *jātesti* is performed by the parents on the child's behalf because the baby cannot do it. Then there is a naming ritual, *nāma-karana*, which is similar to the Christian christening ceremony. During the first year of the child's life, there is a ritual during which the baby's ears are pierced. This is also said to have some acupuncture value. A ritual for removing the hair may be performed at the same time or later. In the eighth year or the twelfth year, depending on which group the child belongs to, another ritual is performed for initiation into the Veda. A *mantra* is given and the child is referred to as one who is twice born, the second birth being the result of the initiation ceremony. From this time onwards, a male child is to perform certain daily rituals and when he marries, as we have seen, certain other rituals also are to be performed.

Thus, in the Vedic vision, a child is born of rituals and is maintained by rituals. Certain rituals are performed three times daily – at dawn, at sunset, and at noon, when the sun is directly above one's head. This is direct propitiation, as we have seen, all other activities being indirect propitiation. In this way, everything is a ritual, including eating. Only after six morsels of food are given to the Lord does one begin eating. There is another ritual at the end of the meal, using water and a *mantra*. Bathing is also a ritual. A boy who has been initiated into the Veda has to do certain rituals from the time he gets up in the morning until he goes to bed at night; he has to remember certain chants in order to do the required rituals. Throughout his life, this continues.

Commitment to the Veda is a life of yajña

There are yet other rituals, quite a few in fact, that must be done on special occasions. One's entire life is a *yajña* and the person is called a *vaidika*, one who is committed to the Veda. To be a *vaidika* is no joke! It means that the person has to perform all the enjoined rituals–in other words, to live a religious life. This is what Lord Kṛṣṇa meant here when he said that when he created human beings he also created *yajñas*.

Prasava, meaning growth, is an interesting word here. You begin your life with just yourself – *aham*, I, myself. When you get married, there are two of you, because of which there can be no end of growth! Thus, the singular becomes dual and then plural – three, four, or more. So, Kṛṣṇa said that by *yajña*, 'May you grow, increase.'

Whenever the word 'said' is used, as it is in this verse, there is always an intention involved. Thus, to understand a sentence, one has to see the intention. By giving human beings the rituals that are in the Veda, the Lord intended for us to grow. 'Let this *yajña* be for you,' he said. 'Let it be the cow that yields anything you desire. Let it be your wish-fulfilling cow.'

The cow Kṛṣṇa was referring to was certainly not our ordinary milk giving cow! This particular cow called *Kāmadhenu*, belonged to the well-known sage, Vasiṣṭha. One day, Viśvāmitra, the king, came to the forest where the sage lived. The king was accompanied by a huge retinue, all of whom were hungry. Finding Vasiṣṭha's hut, they went inside and asked him for food. Within five minutes, food was served to them. When the king asked Vasiṣṭha how this had been possible, the sage replied that he had a cow in the yard. 'What does a cow have to do with all this wonderful food?' the king asked. 'The cow gives everything,' Vasiṣṭha replied.

The king then asked Vasiṣṭha to give him the cow. Vasiṣṭha told the king that he could give him the cow, but it would not be of any use to him because it would yield only to one who is a *brahmarṣi*, and the king was a *kṣatriya*. The story is a metaphor, based on the real meaning of the word *brahmarṣi*, one who has the knowledge whereby everything is gained. Vasiṣṭha had this knowledge and Viśvāmitra did not. By knowing the whole, Brahman, as oneself, everything is as well-known. Having this knowledge, the person has everything because he or she is everything.

Vasiṣṭha's wish fulfilling cow, *Kāmadhenu*, stands for knowledge. So Kṛṣṇa is saying here – let the knowledge of Brahman prove to be a *Kāmadhenu*; let it fulfil all your wishes.

Definition of a *brāhmaṇa*

When you have no wishes, you do not need any wishes fulfilled. Being full and complete means you have no wishes. But to know that you are full and complete you must be a *brahmarṣi*, meaning you must be a knower of Brahman, a *brahma-jñāni*. There is an *Upaniṣad* called *Vajrasūcikopaniṣad*, *vajrasūcī* meaning a diamond needle, one that pierces and thus defines. A *brāhmaṇa* is defined in it as follows – a *brāhmaṇa* is one who has *brahma-jñāna*, knowledge of Brahman, and everyone else is an *abrāhmaṇa*.

The wish fulfilling cow will only yield to one who knows Brahman. Therefore, the cow would have been useless to the king. All he would have received from it would be a kick! This made the king very angry – of course, a typical *kṣatriya* response. He vowed that he would become a *brahmarṣi* in order to get the cow, for which he performed enormous austerities, *tapas*. As long as he continued to be angry, he did not become a *brahmarṣi*. In fact, as long as he wanted to become a *brahmarṣi*, he did not become one. Eventually, having given up wanting to become a *brahmarṣi*, he got the knowledge that made him a *brahmarṣi*.

In the Veda, the Lord said, 'Let *yajña* give you everything; let it be your wish fulfilling cow.' *Yajña* is a prayer, as we have seen, and as *yoga* it gives you *antaḥ-karaṇa-śuddhi*, purification of the mind, and then *jñāna*, knowledge. *Mumukṣus* want to know and for this they employ various means, various disciplines, all of which are *yajña*.

The wish fulfilling cow is also said to be available in Indra's world. So, when you go there, please make sure that you see it. Just as when you go to Agra, you cannot come back and say that you did not see the Taj Mahal, so too, when you go to heaven, you had better look for *Kāmadhenu*.

Verses 11-13

Propitiating and acknowledging the cosmic forces as devatās gives the highest good

देवान्भावयतानेन ते देवा भावयन्तु वः ।
परस्परं भावयन्तः श्रेयः परमवाप्स्यथ ॥ ११ ॥

devān bhāvayatānena te devā bhāvayantu vaḥ
parasparaṁ bhāvayantaḥ śreyaḥ param avāpsyatha (11)

anena – with this; *devān* – the deities; *bhāvayata* – propitiate; *te* – those; *devāḥ* – deities; *vaḥ* – you; *bhāvayantu* – may propitiate; *parasparam* – one another; *bhāvayantaḥ* – propitiating; *param śreyaḥ* – highest good (*mokṣa*); *avāpsyatha* – you shall gain

Propitiate the deities with this (*yajña*). May those deities propitiate you. Propitiating one another, you shall gain the highest good (*mokṣa*).

Previously, the Lord had said, 'With this *yajña*, may you all grow.' In this verse, Kṛṣṇa told Arjuna how, by performing the daily rituals enjoined by the Veda, the various deities or aspects of the Lord are propitiated.

The sun is a blessing, no doubt, but if you look at it as just a ball of fire, it is not a deity, a *devatā*. It is purely an inert blessing. However, if you look at the sun as a *devatā*, you are recognising that it is non-separate from Īśvara. So too with the other deities – water, Varuṇa; air, Vāyu; fire, Agni; and earth, Pṛthivī. Space, Akāśa, is also a *devatā*, as is time, Kāla. Thus, there are any number of *devatā*s whose blessings you partake of every day.

There is ecology at the level of your understanding with reference to free will, which is where the order that is Īśvara is to be appreciated. Daily *yajñas* imply your oblations, propitiation, to all these *devatā*s, who are Īśvara in the form of various forces. May you propitiate them and, thus propitiated, may they bless you. You perform your daily duties and prayers and let the cosmic forces bless you. Let them bless you and you propitiate them. May you not disturb the cosmic ecology by not doing what is to be done.

A recognition, a sensitivity, is involved here. By recognising the cosmic forces, you do not take things for granted. This is why children in India are told that they must get up before the sun rises. A child might think, 'So what if the sun rises? Let it rise! Why should I get up?' But they are told that they must rise in time to welcome the sun. The sun is a blessing and when a blessing comes, you should not be sleeping; you should be wide-awake for its coming.

A man had been meditating for twenty years. The Lord was pleased with his meditation and appeared before him. Unfortunately, the man was asleep at the time! This happens in meditation sometimes. And so the Lord came and went.

The person had to meditate another twenty years before the Lord came again! But, here, in the form of the sun, the Lord comes every day. So, you should not be under the sheets when he comes. You should get up to receive the blessing that is the Lord. This kind of appreciation is what ecology is all about. There is no ecology other than your own understanding. You have to understand; otherwise, there is no ecology. Ecology is only for the person who understands.

Yajña requires sensitivity

There are those who say that if you have seen one redwood tree, you have seen them all. Ronald Reagan said this when he was the Governor of California. Because timber companies were destroying all the redwood trees, he was asked to put an end to the destruction. Reagan's response was that they would keep just a few trees so that people could see them. He did not see why anyone would want to preserve these hundred year old trees. This represents a particular level of understanding and at this level there is no ecology, only economy. And in the long run, there is no economy either!

Ecology is an appreciation that is in your head–in other words, in the eyes of the beholder. It is not beyond the eyes. It does not exist outside. If you do not see it, it is not there. This, then, is ecology. Appreciation of Īśvara is also ecology but at a deeper level. Īśvara is appreciated as the cosmic forces and is thereby propitiated. One of the forms of propitiation is daily prayer. Therefore, may you appreciate Īśvara in your prayers as the forces, the deities, and let them bless you. May you all grow by doing what is to be done.

There is a mutual respect here. The deities bless you and you propitiate them. You offer them your oblations and they offer you their blessings – in the form of rain, energy, health, and so on. In this way, may you gain *mokṣa, param śreyaḥ,* characterised by knowledge, in due course, step by step, not directly, not immediately, but by *antaḥ-karaṇa-śuddhi,* by preparing the mind, purifying it, for the knowledge.

If you die while pursuing knowledge, without having gained it, it is said that, at the very least, you will gain heavenly enjoyments, *svarga.* Therefore, there is no loss. *Svarga* also stands for better births, meaning that in your next birth, you will go further along towards *mokṣa.* This interpretation is more relevant since the *Gītā* is *mokṣa-śāstra,* not *svarga-śāstra.*

Then, Kṛṣṇa said:

इष्टान्भोगान्हि वो देवा दास्यन्ते यज्ञभाविताः ।
तैर्दत्तानप्रदायैभ्यो यो भुङ्क्ते स्तेन एव सः ॥ १२ ॥

iṣṭān bhogān hi vo devā dāsyante yajñabhāvitāḥ
tairdattān apradāyaibhyo yo bhuṅkte stena eva saḥ (12)

devāḥ – gods; *yajñabhāvitāḥ* – propitiated by *yajña*; *iṣṭān bhogān* – desirable objects; *vaḥ* – to you; *dāsyante* – will give; *hi* – therefore; *taiḥ dattān* – given by them; *yebhyaḥ* – to them; *apradāya* – without offering; *yaḥ* – the one who; *bhuṅkte* – enjoys; *saḥ* – that person; *stenaḥ* – thief; *eva* – indeed

The deities, propitiated by *yajña,* will give you desirable objects. One who enjoys objects given by them without offering to them in return is indeed a thief.

The gods here mean Īśvara in the form of deities who are propitiated by your *yajñas*, your prayers and rituals. They spread before you all desirable enjoyments. Whatever is desirable, they give to you. Thus, for those whose predominant commitment is *yajña*, there will be conducive situations for growth.

Hence, for a person to be able to live a life of *dharma*, you require a society where *dharma* is predominant. It is not that you cannot do it otherwise, but it is difficult. Take life in modern day India, for example. Even to buy a railway ticket, the agent must be bribed. There is simply no other way to purchase a ticket. Because of the melting pot environment created by too rapid an industrialisation following independence, the society is undergoing some rather drastic changes and people's desires have become manifold. The changes have come from the top and there is no foundation, leaving the society top heavy without the roots that proper growth requires. Growth should be like that of a tree. First the roots are established and then the tree grows from there.

A person who wants to live a life of *dharma* will have problems in some parts of the world because he or she does not want to bribe people. Only where there is some *dharma* in the society is it easy to live such a life. To propitiate the *devatās* means to follow *dharma*. By living a prayerful life, you create a conducive atmosphere. And when the majority of people live this way, then the whole society will be conducive to the growth of *dharma*.

Karma-yoga as yajña

The *devatās* will do their jobs whether you propitiate them or not, but when you go against *dharma*, you disturb the order and you are the sufferer. Therefore, everyone must do his or her job. The *devatās* do their jobs and you do yours according to the order of *dharma* given in the Veda.

Animals, trees and other plants are programmed and therefore do not require the Veda. People, on the other hand, do need it because they have to conform to the order, for which they need the understanding that the Veda provides. It is said that if you do not disturb the order, the *devas* do not get disturbed. Thus, ecology of the universal order means there is no disturbance at the level of cosmic forces, the level of *devatās*.

When the sun, water, fire, air, and earth do their respective jobs, what do you get? A delicious Thanksgiving dinner on your plate! In this example, food stands for the various enjoyments, all of which come to your plate as blessings of the deities, cosmic forces, natural laws, and so on. For us, these are not simply nature; they are Īśvara.

In this verse, a person who enjoys the results that are given by Īśvara, without having offered anything, is likened to a thief. Because you are continuously receiving from the cosmic forces, which are nothing but aspects of Īśvara, you should give them something in return. You can only do this by remembering Īśvara, by offering an oblation or a prayer. This is real thanksgiving. Thanksgiving is not something that happens once a year; it goes on all the time.

Although the deities do not need anything from you, you need to respect them and this respect is given in the form of a prayer. The prayer is a recognition of all these forces and makes you a sensitive person. You are not just seeing what the eyes see or hearing what the ears hear. You are going beyond them. This kind of a life is not an ordinary life; it is a profound life. Not giving back to the deities in the form of remembrance makes you a thief.

A thief does not say, 'Thank you.' He or she just takes what belongs to another and runs away. Therefore, a person who does not remember the *devatās* is no different from a common thief. One who takes money from someone and does not return it is also a cheat. This thief who is also a cheat runs away and begins operating from another place so as not to be found out.

Here, the *devatās* do not seem to come looking for you. They are all in your appreciation; otherwise, they simply do not exist for you. Still, they operate constantly. The very air you breathe is Īśvara. The work of the *devatās* is always done and can be recognised by you. And if you do not recognise them, you are a cheat because you take from them and do not give them what is to be given in return.

What we return to the *devatās* is our recognition, which is what is called *yajña*. We perform the *yajña* as a return, as a thanksgiving. It is not for anything else. The *yajña* itself brings about an *antaḥ-karaṇa-śuddhi*, because of which the person can give thanks. By giving thanks, by recognising everything as Īśvara, we will definitely gain *antaḥ-karaṇa-śuddhi*.

A person who respects the cosmic forces is not an ordinary person. He or she no longer goes by *rāga-dveṣa*s but goes beyond them. Otherwise, there would be no recognition or thanksgiving. On the other hand, a person who performs *karma* to satisfy his or her mind and senses alone does not offer oblations, not even water or a simple twig. Such a person is a thief and a cheat. He or she does not give the cosmic forces their due.

In the next verse, Kṛṣṇa describes these two types of people:

यज्ञशिष्टाशिनः सन्तो मुच्यन्ते सर्वकिल्बिषैः ।
भुञ्जते ते त्वघं पापा ये पचन्त्यात्मकारणात् ॥ १३ ॥

yajñaśiṣṭāśinaḥ santo mucyante sarvakilbiṣaiḥ
bhuñjate te tvaghaṁ pāpā ye pacantyātmakāraṇāt (13)

yajña-śiṣṭāśinaḥ santaḥ – those who eat, having first offered the food to the Lord; *sarva-kilbiṣaiḥ* – from all impurities; *mucyante* – are released; *ye tu* – whereas those who; *ātma-kāraṇāt* – for themselves (only); *pacanti* – cook; *te* – they; *pāpāḥ* – sinners; *agham* – *pāpa* (sin); *bhuñjate* – eat

> Those who eat, having first offered the food to the Lord, are released from impurities, whereas those sinful people who cook only for themselves eat *pāpa* (sin).

Karma-yoga is presented as *yajña* in this verse. We have seen how all actions are *yajñas*, whether they are in the form of rituals, prayers, or performing one's duties to others, more of which we shall see in the next chapter.

Since Īśvara, the Lord, is to be recognised in the form of the various cosmic forces or elements, these forces are viewed individually and are called *devatās* or *devas*, meaning deities.

Thus, it is said, may you propitiate the *devas* and let them bless you. This means that you let them do what they have to do and you do what you have to do. In this way, since there is nothing outside of Īśvara, the natural forces are not looked upon as mere inert forces. Everything is within Īśvara, the conscious being, *cetana-vastu* even when one is under the spell of dream.

In a dream we see both living beings and inert objects. The mountain seen in a dream is inert, *jaḍa*. The sun and its rays are also *jaḍa*. Everything seen is *jaḍa*, in fact, and not *cetana*. But the difference between the inert and the conscious, *jaḍa-cetana-bheda*, is only within the framework of what is perceived by you as the subject of the dream. If, having perceived the dream objects, you shift your perception to the person who is dreaming, the creator of the dream, then you will see that there is no world outside of the dreamer.

If the dreamer is a conscious being, the dreamt world is non-separate from the dreamer because he or she is both the maker, *nimitta-kāraṇa*, of the dream world and the material, *upādāna-kāraṇa*, for it. Therefore, from the dreamer's standpoint, there is nothing inert or conscious. Everything is the dreamer alone.

Similarly, from the standpoint of Īśvara, the cosmic forces are recognised as being non-separate from Īśvara because there is nothing outside of Īśvara. They are not simply taken to be *jaḍa*.

Even though they look as though they are *jaḍa*, they are all *devatās* from the standpoint of Īśvara. In this way, the sun becomes a *devatā*, as does the air, fire, water, and the earth.

Acknowledging Īśvara in this way, recognising his many aspects in the form of *devatās*, one performs various rituals and prayers, which are also actions. There are various actions that are to be done, including the daily rituals, *nitya-karma* and rituals performed on certain occasions, *naimittika-karma*, stipulated in the Veda as part of its vision. *Nitya-karma* and *naimittika-karma* are to be performed, without exception, until one takes *sannyāsa*, that is, until one renounces everything.

Whatever results you receive from the actions you perform are blessings given to you by the *devatās* who are doing their jobs. If you acknowledge these *devatās* and give them their due, you become a person who is not a thief or a cheat, as Kṛṣṇa said in the previous verse. Here, in the present verse, he contrasted the person who is not a thief with one who is.

One cannot help but perform certain harmful *karma* as one lives one's daily life. Life does live upon life. If freedom or free will were not there, nothing would be sinful, strictly speaking. There would be no wrongdoing, no *pāpa-karma*. But because one has to eat and must fulfil certain minimum requirements in order to survive, there is naturally going to be some kind of injury, *hiṁsā*, done. Some plants, animals, and bugs will be destroyed. In this way, many non-human living beings are destroyed everyday and this destruction produces certain untoward results, called *pāpas*, which keep on gathering every day.

How are you going to eliminate these results? Knowingly or unknowingly, a lot of *pāpas* are incurred and you gather results that are undesirable, which in turn result in some kind of unpleasantness, *duḥkha*, for you. To neutralise these results, then, there are different types of *yajñas* – *yajñas* to the deities, to one's ancestors, to one's fellow creatures, to the *ṛṣis* who have given us this knowledge, and so on. These *yajñas* are to be performed daily and are contained in one ritual.

The *yajñaśiṣṭāśinaḥ*, in this verse, refers to those who eat, after having first offered the food to the Lord, in other words, those who partake after having paid their dues. While people in India today may not perform all the enjoined *yajñas* very methodically, they always offer the food to the Lord and only then do they eat.

The ritual itself is not what is important; it is the attitude, the *bhāvanā* that counts. Food is cooked and offered to the Lord, the attitude being that only what is left over *yajñaśiṣṭa*, is to be eaten, which is what is meant by *prasāda*. It is a blessing from the Lord. Those who eat only *prasāda* do not eat food; they eat only *prasāda*. Having offered the food to the Lord with a prayer, such as the chant *brahmārpaṇam...*, the food itself becomes *prasāda*. Thus it is said, that those who offer food to the Lord and then partake of what is left over are released *mucyante*, from all the little *pāpas*, *sarvakilbiṣas*, that have been gathered daily because of having performed some injury or the other in the process of survival.

Merely by grinding something, washing the floor, spraying detergent, or walking, we are continually killing something.

This killing is often done deliberately for our own welfare. In fact, we could not live if we did not do it. The bugs that we kill want to live, but we also want to live. Co-existence not being possible, the bugs must be destroyed. This act of destruction involves some sin, some *adharma*, which, as Kṛṣṇa points out in this verse, can only be neutralised by daily prayer, not by anything else.

Freedom from the results of one's actions

Or the verse can be taken another way – having become purified by the knowledge, you will be liberated from all *puṇya* and *pāpa*. No one releases oneself from *puṇya* and *pāpa* without having the knowledge. Thus, the statement, *sārva-kilbiṣaiḥ mucyante* can be taken to mean 'from all *karma*s they get released.'

The word *santaḥ* can be taken together with the word *yajñaśiṣṭāśinaḥ*, meaning 'being ones' who are *yajñaśiṣṭāśinaḥ*, or it can be taken as a separate word meaning 'the saintly people, *sat-puruṣāḥ*, the wise.' In that case it is an adjective to the word *yajñaśiṣṭāśinaḥ*. They become wise because of a life of prayer, which gives them the mind necessary to know.

In the second line of the verse, Kṛṣṇa described those people who are given to *pāpa-karma*s, actions based on *adharma* rather than *dharma*. They do not recognise *dharma* and *adharma* at all; they recognise only what is convenient to them. Their pleasure and security alone are important. They simply do not see anything more than that. While the *yajñaśiṣṭāśinas* get rid of the sins gathered, these people just go on gathering them. Because they do not offer the food they eat to the Lord, it is said that they eat *pāpa*, meaning that when they eat, they eat only sin.

Sin, here, must be understood in the Indian context. Every *karma* has its own result. An action is sinful only in the sense that it results in some unpleasantness, *duḥkha*, for the person who performed the action. Similarly, a good action simply means that it produces a result that gives you some pleasure, comfort, and so on. There is no accurate English translation for the Sanskrit words *pāpa* and *puṇya*. So as not to confuse them with the totally different concept generally associated with the word 'sin' in other contexts, it is preferable to retain the Sanskrit words themselves. Sin, in the Indian context, is always quantified.

Even in the realm of traffic violations, there are quantifiable differences, a driving violation being more serious than a parking violation. A parking violation may simply involve a fine to be paid or your car may be towed away and may be costly to retrieve. But you do not have to keep on paying. It does not affect your insurance premium like a driving offence can. Like the laws governing traffic violations, the law of *karma* means that the result of any action is appropriate to the action performed.

According to the *karma* performed, there is both a seen and an unseen result. If the unseen result is undesirable, it is called *pāpa*. This is how it is. Those who cook and eat only for themselves and not as an offering to the *devatās* eat only *pāpa*, whereas those who eat only after offering the food to the Lord get rid of any sins, any *pāpas*, they might have collected through other actions.

Karma has to be done; it keeps everything going. The great cosmic wheel is constantly turning and, because you are a doer, one who enjoys a free will, you are a cog in it. You can do and you need not do. A tree does whatever it has to do because that is how a tree is made. An animal also does exactly what is expected of it because it is made to do so. In this way, all non-human living beings do what they do because they are programmed in a certain way. The human being, however, is one whose action is performed by will. Therefore, there is choice in action. One may perform an action, not perform it, or perform it differently.

Verse 14

The cosmic wheel keeps going because
of karma alone

अन्नाद्भवन्ति भूतानि पर्जन्यादन्नसम्भवः ।
यज्ञाद्भवति पर्जन्यो यज्ञः कर्मसमुद्भवः ॥ १४ ॥

annādbhavanti bhūtāni parjanyād annasambhavaḥ
yajñādbhavati parjanyo yajñaḥ karmasamudbhavaḥ (14)

bhūtāni – living beings; *annāt* – from food; *bhavanti* – are born; *parjanyāt* – from rain; *anna-sambhavaḥ* – food is born; *parjanyaḥ* – rain; *yajñāt* – from *yajña*; *bhavati* – is born; *yajñaḥ* – *puṇya*; *karma-samudbhavaḥ* – born of action

Living beings are born of food; food is born of rain; rain is born of *yajña* (*puṇya*); and *yajña* (*puṇya*) is born of action.

The expression 'born of food' cannot, of course, be taken literally, since nothing is actually born of food. It refers instead to the food eaten by the person. In Śaṅkara's commentary on this verse, the word *bhuktāt* is added to the word *annāt*, meaning from the food eaten and assimilated.

From the food eaten all living beings, with various bodies, are born. The food eaten by the parents is converted into the causes for conception of the being, the blood, seed, and so on. Therefore, conception itself is because of food and food, being the material for it, is the material cause for the anatomical aspects, the physical aspects, of the body.

Kṛṣṇa then went on to say that the food itself is born from rain. If there were no rains, there would be no food. The entire earth would be a desert, and sand would be the only food. The rain, in turn, Kṛṣṇa said, is born of *yajña*, your daily prayers acknowledging the blessings of the *devatās*.

It is true that if you do not perform *yajña* rain still comes, but it may not come at the right time or in the right quantities. Later, Kṛṣṇa said that the rain always does its job and, unless you are offering daily prayers, you are not doing yours. It is not uncommon for a person to think that since everyone else is doing it, he or she need not do it, like in chorus singing. If one person does not sing at a given time, nothing is lost because most of the others are singing. Even if one person commits a mistake, it goes undetected because the others are not making the same mistake. Only if everyone were to commit the same mistake at the same time, would it become evident.

Therefore, chorus chanting always sounds perfect even though, individually, there may be problems.

Here, too, some people offer their prayers and the rain is enjoyed by everyone. However, Kṛṣṇa likened one who does not do it, to a thief. It is not that the rain will not do its job. It is the recognition of the cosmic forces as Īśvara that is important here. When you perform *yajña* as, when you do your duties, your prayers and so on, then the *devatās* bless you. For example, the sun has always been said to produce the rain since it evaporates ocean water, which then forms into clouds. And when you do your daily *devatā-yajñas*, all the accrued *adṛṣṭa*, unseen results, go to the appropriate deity, the sun here. Then from the sun, the rains come. This is another way of saying that you invoke the forces and the forces bless you. The rains come – at the right time, to the right place, in the right amounts.

The unseen result, *adṛṣṭa*, is what is meant by *yajña* here. A prayer does not produce a tangible result immediately. It produces an unseen result, which, in turn, produces the tangible result later. Without *karma* you can produce neither seen nor unseen results. We know that the seen result of boiled water cannot be produced without the action of heating the water. Similarly, an unseen result is one that is produced by the action of prayer. This action is what keeps the natural forces, the cosmic ecology, going.

When it is said here that *yajña* is born out of *karma*, *yajña* is not referring to a ritual because a ritual itself is a *karma*.

To clarify this point, Śaṅkara said in his commentary to this verse that *yajña* is *adṛṣṭa*, the unseen result. The *adṛṣṭa* is born out of *karma* and is what produces the result. Only in this way, then, can it be said that *yajña* is born of *karma*.

Verse 15

***Karmas (rituals, prayer etc.) come from the
Veda and the Veda from all-knowledge Īśvara***

कर्म ब्रह्मोद्भवं विद्धि ब्रह्माक्षरसमुद्भवम् ।
तस्मात्सर्वगतं ब्रह्म नित्यं यज्ञे प्रतिष्ठितम् ॥ १५ ॥

*karma brahmodbhavaṁ viddhi brahmākṣarasamudbhavam
tasmāt sarvagataṁ brahma nityaṁ yajñe pratiṣṭhitam* (15)

karma – ritual; *brahmodbhavam* – born of the Veda; Brahma – the Veda; *akṣara-samudbhavam* – born of the imperishable Īśvara, the Lord; *viddhi* – may you understand; *tasmāt* – therefore; *sarvagatam* – all-pervasive; Brahma – the Veda; *nityam* – always; *yajñe* – in *yajña*; *pratiṣṭhitam* – abides

May you understand *karma* (ritual, prayer, etc.) to be born of the Veda and the Veda to be born of the imperishable Īśvara. Therefore, the all-pervasive Brahma (the Veda)[8] abides always in *yajña*.

By *karma*, Kṛṣṇa was referring here to the Vedic rituals, *vaidika-karma*. These rituals, *yajñas*, are to be understood as

---

[8] The Veda is called '*sarvagataṁ brahma*' here, because it reveals everything.
सर्वार्थप्रकाशकत्वात् ब्रह्म = वेदः सर्वगतम् । (शङ्कर भाष्यम्)

coming from the Veda itself, called Brahma in this verse. Although Brahma or Brahmāji is also the name given to the Creator in the trinity, here it refers to the Veda as the cause for *karma*.

Brahma is the Veda that reveals the nature of the *karma* and, therefore, becomes its cause. One would not know of the rituals otherwise. Thus, it is said that *karma* is born of the Veda. And how do we know that the Brahma is Veda and not the absolute *param-brahma*, Brahman, the ultimate truth? The verse says that *brahma* is born of *akṣara*, the imperishable, that which never dies, which is never born. Therefore, *brahma* cannot be this absolute Brahman. That Brahma means Veda is confirmed by any Sanskrit dictionary.

The Veda comes from that imperishable Brahman. It is also said that the Veda is born as effortlessly as breathing. The Veda is something that reveals the four human pursuits, *puruṣārthas* – security, *artha*; pleasure, *kāma*; righteousness, *dharma*, and liberation, *mokṣa*. Because it reveals everything that a person requires, the Veda is considered to be omniscient, *sarvajña*.

The Veda is said to be revealed by Īśvara because knowledge cannot be created. Knowledge always is, but it is covered by ignorance. If knowledge were created, the place of creation could only be one of ignorance or no ignorance. If knowledge is created on ignorance, does the ignorance remain? Can knowledge be created on a foundation of ignorance? Or, in the wake of knowledge, does ignorance go?

And what is this knowledge that is created? If you discover something, is it something that is already there or do you create something and then discover it? To create something, you must know it already. You do not create knowledge. Knowledge is already there because it is knowledge of a fact. There is a certain reality, a fact, and the knowledge of it is as true as the reality, as true as the particular fact. Therefore, knowledge is nothing but realisation of facts.

This means that knowledge is always of what is, what is possible, and so on. Everything is only 'what is.' The future is also 'what is.' The future as a possibility 'is.' This 'what is' is what we call-knowledge.

For Īśvara, all-knowledge is always there. In fact, all-knowledge is what is meant by Īśvara, the Lord, omniscience. If all-knowledge is there, is Īśvara a conscious or an unconscious being? A being is always conscious; an unconscious being is not a being at all. That Īśvara, whose being is consciousness, has omniscience and this omniscience exists ultimately in the consciousness.

The *jīva*, the individual, who is related to Īśvara, is also a conscious being. And what is the nature of that conscious being, the individual? Is 'conscious' an adjective to 'being' or is being consciousness? Is there a being other than consciousness? If so, what is that being? How do you recognise it?

The being is consciousness; consciousness is being. Therefore, all-knowledge exists in the conscious being, in the being that is consciousness. This being the case, why do I not have it?

Because of ignorance alone. Ignorance covers the knowledge. Thus, whenever any knowledge is gathered, it is simply a matter of scraping off ignorance. We are just so many scrapers, 'scraping through' all the time. Scraping off ignorance is what we call getting knowledge. And, with reference to knowledge of the empirical world, we do not scrape very well!

One can scrape well only with reference to *ātmā*. Everything else remains either unscraped or a little scraped. It is as though you see some spots on something and then, scraping away at them, you gain a scrap of knowledge. A thesis may be written on one of these spots for which the person receives a Ph.D. degree. Then, afterwards, someone else comes along and again covers up what was scraped off by proving that the previous person did not really scrape at all. So, this person also gets a Ph.D. This scraping process can continue only because there is no bottom line, no last word, in any empirical field.

Only in the self is a total scraping possible because you are talking about the whole that has no parts. Any part always has further parts, which have further parts, ad infinitum. This is the nature of empirical reality, whereas *ātmā* is the partless whole. Thus a total scraping is possible with reference to oneself, the *ātmā*. All this is by the way, given the focus of our present discussion.

The conscious being has all-knowledge and this knowledge is covered by ignorance, *ajñāna*. Because of this *ajñāna*, people are *saṁsārīs*, limited beings given to various problems. Nevertheless, knowledge is always there. It was never created. Ignorance also is not created. All that is created is error, opinion, belief, unreasonable statements, any speculative form of knowledge, and so on. For example, sitting in an easy chair, one can continue to write about God. Error, of course, is not created deliberately. But it is born of a given intellect, with all its limitations, whereas knowledge is never born, never created.

Thus, the Veda is a body of knowledge that is not attributed to a given author. There is no founder. It is not historical and, therefore, we accept it as revealed. There is a 'Veda as history' argument propounded by some, but according to the tradition it is not valid because, for something to have its basis in history, it has to have been born of a certain intellect. And whatever is born of a given intellect has all the limitations of that intellect.

Knowledge is not born of a given intellect; it is something that is uncovered and handed over. All we can say about the Veda is that it is a body of knowledge that is revealed. And as a means for one to gain the knowledge, as a *pramāṇa*, it works. Its very words are the *pramāṇa*, *śabda pramāṇa*.

A *pramāṇa* can produce two types of knowledge – indirect or mediate knowledge, *parokṣa-jñāna*, and direct or immediate knowledge, *aparokṣa-jñāna*, depending upon the subject matter to be known. If the *pramāṇa* talks about a heaven, the knowledge is purely indirect knowledge. When you have faith, *śraddhā*, in the *pramāṇa*, the knowledge is indirect. Otherwise, you simply accept what is said, which is only a belief, not knowledge.

Similarly, when the *pramāṇa* says there are *devatās*, it is indirect knowledge. For instance, when the Veda talks about a ritual that invokes a particular *devatā* that will produce certain result, the knowledge is indirect. When you perform the ritual and it produces the expected result, you understand that it has been verified that it works. Homeopathy and ancient systems of medicine that have not been scientifically validated are other examples of indirect knowledge. In other words, the only proof that something works is because it works!

All we know about the rituals enjoined by the Veda is that they work, for which there is statistical proof. This applies to all scriptures in the world. This prayer may work or that prayer may work. You can dismiss an African tribesman as a heathen, but when he dances for rain, the rains, I am told, often come! Therefore, we say that his rituals work. God understands his mumbo jumbo as well as he understands ours. In fact, for God, there is no such thing as mumbo jumbo. For him, everything is meaningful. Even if you blabber, he picks up your intention.

However when the Veda talks about what is, it does not lend itself to speculation. It talks about you, the self, 'I,' which is already an evident being. If there is confusion about that being, the resolution of that confusion is immediate knowledge, direct knowledge. Because this knowledge is direct knowledge, there is no comparison possible between what the Veda says and what any other revealed body of knowledge says, unless, of course, they are both saying the same thing.

If both revealed bodies of knowledge have the self as their subject matter and are saying that the self is the whole, then they are saying the same thing. This knowledge, the knowledge about the reality of the self, does not belong to any territory and is what we call Vedanta.

The strength of the Veda

In the vision of the Veda, the self is the whole and there is nothing beyond it. If this fact is recognisable then it is not unreasonable. Because it is reasonable, everything contrary to it becomes unreasonable. That the self is self-evident and is the whole cannot be denied or negated, whereas everything else can be. Therefore, any scripture that makes this statement of fact, regardless of the language it is written in or the people who claim it as their own, is Vedanta.

This knowledge, this Veda, is born of Īśvara alone; it is not founded nor does it have a historical basis. Therefore, it does not have in it the problems of a given intellect. It is simply handed over from one generation to the next. That it has no beginning, no history, that it was not born of a given intellect, should not be considered its weakness; it is, in fact, its strength.

Another important point is that the Veda does not belong to anyone. No individual or culture can claim it. It is simply a body of knowledge belonging to humanity at large. This knowledge is here, in the world, for all people. The fact that it is maintained in a particular geographical area does not mean that it does not belong to humanity. To think otherwise, leads to the notion that the knowledge has been given to a particular person and, therefore, all wisdom comes through that person. Such notions generate all sorts of expectations and disappointments, the results of which are evident everywhere. Kṛṣṇa said that the Veda comes from the imperishable, the Lord, Īśvara.

Because it is born of Parameśvara, the Lord, the Veda is said to abide in the *yajña*. How is this so? The ultimate cause, Brahman, is all-pervasive and also imperishable. From this Brahman alone, the ultimate cause of everything comes Brahma, the Veda, and from the Veda comes the *yajña* as well as its result. From the result alone comes the rain and from the rain comes the food. From the food come all living beings. The beings do *yajña* and out of *yajña* come the rains and all other results, which in turn lead to more *karma*. This, then, is the cycle, the *cakra*.

Brahman is all-pervasive because it is both the efficient and material cause. And no effect can be away from its cause. Out of this all-pervasive Brahman, the Veda is born and the cycle described above is set in motion. In this way, everything is born out of *paraṁ-brahma*. Thus, it is said that Brahman is in the *yajña*, *yajña* being born from the Veda and the Veda being born directly from Parameśvara, the Lord. Or, as Śaṅkara puts it, being born of the Veda, *yajña* is non-separate from the Veda and thus very much in it. And the Veda is non-separate from Īśvara. Therefore, when you perform the *yajña*, you are naturally in tune with Parameśvara. You also are not away from the Lord. The *yajña* is looked upon as being immediately connected with Parameśvara. *Yajña* is a revelation of Īśvara and, by performing this *yajña*, which is a *karma*, you are propitiating the *devatā*s that are Parameśvara. And what happens if you do not perform such *karma*?

Verse 16

There is a mutual benefit inherent in the
order already set to motion

एवं प्रवर्तितं चक्रं नानुवर्तयतीह यः ।
अघायुरिन्द्रियारामो मोघं पार्थ स जीवति ॥ १६ ॥

evaṁ pravartitaṁ cakraṁ nānuvartayatīha yaḥ
aghāyurindriyārāmo moghaṁ pārtha sa jīvati (16)

pārtha – O Pārtha (Arjuna)!; *yaḥ* – the one who; *iha* – here in this life; *evam* – in this manner; *pravartitam* – already set in motion; *cakram* – the cosmic wheel; *na anuvartayati* – does not follow; *aghāyuḥ* – one who lives in sin; *indriyārāmaḥ* – one who is given (only) to sensory pleasures; *saḥ* – that person; *mogham* – wastefully; *jīvati* – lives

A person who does not follow here in this life, this cosmic wheel that is already set in motion, in this manner, and lives in sin given only to the pleasures of the senses, lives wastefully, Pārtha (Arjuna)!

If you perform *yajña*, the *devatā*s are pleased and you work in harmony, according to the order, referred to here as the cosmic wheel, *cakra*. There is a mutual benefit here that is inherent in the order that is already set in motion.

The whole universe, the whole planetary system, operates by mutual attraction. Every planet, the sun, the moon, and the earth move in their respective orbits because of the force of attraction that keeps the whole system going. Otherwise, it would collapse. When you look into any nucleus, you find that the motion of the particles operates in the same way. Similarly, certain proteins attract certain other proteins. Structurally, they are all attracted to each other. Certain bugs attack only certain things, all because of protein structures. In this way, the entire cosmos is nothing but a force of attraction operating in a most intelligent manner.

Living beings, who are not mere physical entities, are conscious beings mutually related to the *devatā*s. Since this is how the order is set up, you recognise them, acknowledge them. The *cakra* spoken of here is much more than a cosmic wheel. It not only includes the physical world, it includes everything. This *cakra*, this order, is set up as it is by Īśvara, the efficient and material cause of it all.

Seeing beyond the sense organs

Aghāyuḥ is a person whose life is nothing but *agha*, *pāpa*, sin. In this verse, such a person is also called *indriyārāma*, meaning one who lives only at the level of the sense organs and therefore does not perceive anything beyond the eyes, nose, and ears. The origin of these functionaries is never questioned by such people. The eyes are there and, therefore, they feast. These are people who are given to sensory pleasures alone. Those who live in this way, who do not follow the *cakra*, the wheel that is the order, live wastefully, Kṛṣṇa says here. Everything that is given to these people lays waste. Such people waste their lives and live without any purpose, drifting along without anchor or roots. The depth and understanding that a human being is supposed to have is not there for an *indriyārāma*.

Whenever there is this kind of criticism in the *Gītā*, its purpose is only to direct your attention to what is to be done. You are to push this wheel, this *cakra*. Knowing that you are a cog in it, someone who is important in maintaining the order, do what you have to do. By doing so, it keeps going. To think that by not doing what you have to do, the order will not be disturbed, is not proper, as the following story demonstrates.

There was once a king who thought that his citizens were all excellent people, but his chief minister, a very intelligent man, could not agree with him. He knew that while, by and large, they had a good kingdom, there were probably some thieves among them. They simply did not hunt down every last one of them. There are always some petty thieves around, even if they only pick their own pockets for practice. Knowing this, the minister could not concur with the king that every citizen was upright.

To prove who was right, the king or himself, the minister erected a huge tank with a ladder to the top. He issued a decree that every citizen was to deposit one ounce of milk into this tank. Dutifully, the people all lined up to add their milk to the tank. When they had all done their duty, the minister said to the king, 'Let us go and see whether the milk in the tank is pure or whether it is somewhat watered down.' What they found was not pure milk nor even thin milk; only water was there without so much as a trace of white in it!

The king then asked the minister whether he had asked the people to put milk or water into the tank. The minister confirmed that he had said milk. 'But how can this be?' the king asked. The minister then explained to him that each person, thinking that his or her water would make no difference in so much milk, opted not to give any milk at all. This only shows, if you think that you do not need to do what has to be done because everyone else will do it, and if that is the thinking of everyone, then everything comes to a halt. And, if all but one person does do what is to be done, the one who does not do it and who partakes of the benefit becomes a cheat.

Ecology always starts with you

This is true in any system, be it a small community, a factory, a society, the world, or the entire universe. The same psychology, the same law, applies and is all that ecology is about – live, and let live, and recognise what the contribution is. This is what makes a person sensitive. Such a person is not an ordinary person and it is here that one's attention is to be drawn.

Ecology starts with one person and that person is you. It never starts with someone else. If you start with yourself, there is no problem. Whenever you count, count yourself first. Counting yourself first is not selfishness, as we shall see.

Verses 17&18

**There is nothing to be done for the one
who ever delights in the self**

यस्त्वात्मरतिरेव स्यादात्मतृप्तश्च मानवः ।
आत्मन्येव च सन्तुष्टस्तस्य कार्यं न विद्यते ॥ १७ ॥

*yastvātmaratireva syād ātmatṛptaśca mānavaḥ
ātmanyeva ca santuṣṭastasya kāryaṁ na vidyate (17)*

tu – whereas; *yaḥ mānavaḥ* – the person who; *ātma-ratiḥ eva* –
delights in the self alone; *ātma-tṛptaḥ ca* – and is satisfied with
the self; *ātmani eva* – in the self alone; *santuṣṭaḥ ca* – and is
contented; *syāt* – would be; *tasya* – for him; *kāryam* – work to be
done; *na vidyate* – does not exist

> Whereas, for the person who is delighted in the self,
> who is satisfied with the self, contented in the self
> alone, (for him) there is nothing to be done.

If *karma* has to be done in order to keep the cosmic wheel
going, does everyone have to perform it? And since some
people do gain *mokṣa*, does it mean that *karma* becomes the
way to *mokṣa* and knowledge has nothing to do with it? Kṛṣṇa
had already said that *karma-yoga* does not produce *mokṣa*
directly. Therefore, he had to address this doubt here.

If *karma* were the means for *mokṣa*, then everyone would
have to do *karma* only as a *yoga*. But *karma-yoga* is not the means
for *mokṣa*, let alone the only means; it is the means for *antaḥ-
karaṇa-śuddhi*, purification of the mind. *Jñāna* is the only means
for *mokṣa* meaning that there is no *kartavya*, there is nothing

that 'has to be done.' If knowledge is the means for *mokṣa* and the person gains that knowledge, then there is nothing else for him or her to do. There is no *kartavya* because the person is not bound by any *karma*, knowledge having destroyed the doer. Without the doer, no action is done.

Knowledge destroys doership completely. If someone is addressed as a doer, who is it that responds? Only a person who takes himself or herself to be a doer. The one who is not a doer is not addressed at all and therefore, of course, does not respond. 'Whereas' in the present verse is to distinguish the non-doer from the doer. Śaṅkara calls the non-doer *sāṅkhya* here, meaning one who has self-knowledge, a *sannyāsī*. Such a person is a *sthitaprajña* as we saw in the second chapter. For this person, there is no doubt, error, or vagueness with reference to 'I' the *ātmā*.

In order to become happy in oneself with oneself, a person has to become steadfast in the knowledge of *ātmā*. This is not possible for a person who looks upon *ātmā* as a *saṃsārī*, a limited, sorrowful, sinful person. The moment such a person thinks of himself or herself, he or she is unhappy because *ātmā* is looked upon as a doer, an enjoyer, as one who has limited knowledge, an imperfect person, a sinner, and so on. Because one cannot be happy in the *ātmā*, the person has to look towards something other than the self and must manipulate the world or the mind in order to gain even a small degree of happiness.

An enjoyer, *bhogī*, manipulates the world and a *yogī* manipulates the mind. A *bhogī* is one who looks upon the world as something to be enjoyed and who goes about manipulating situations, manipulating the world, to create conducive situations wherein he or she can discover a moment of joy. The situation thus created pleases the person – but only for the time being, whereupon the process of manipulation must begin again.

A *yogī* on the other hand, is one who does not manipulate the world. Such a person is concerned only with his or her thoughts, contending that the pleasurable mental disposition picked up by the *bhogī* through manipulating the world can be created straightaway in the mind. Thus, the *yogī* goes about manipulating the mind, whereas the *bhogī* goes about manipulating the world. There is yet another person, the *rogī* who is so diseased that he or she cannot manipulate the world, much less the mind. Such a person cannot keep himself or herself in good humour because of the pain of illness. Nor is the person healthy enough to manipulate the world.

'Becoming' is a problem

Yogic postures, *āsanas*, breath control, *prāṇāyāma*, and so on, all create certain conducive situation wherein the *yogī* can pick up a moment of joy. The *bhogī*, of course, manipulates the world for enjoyment, and the *rogī* is unable to do anything in order to enjoy. The point here is that all three of them look upon the *ātmā* as something that has to become something. This 'becoming' creates a lot of problems. Any becoming is unbecoming because it always requires yet another becoming. So, becoming is nothing but continuous becoming. Before becoming, there are nothing but problems. While becoming, there is a lot of pain, and after becoming, the person has to become something else again. Therefore, the problem is never solved.

A person who looks upon the *ātmā* as imperfect is always in trouble and is a *saṁsārī*, whereas the person described in this verse, an *ātmarati*, is one who always revels in the *ātmā*. The joy that revelling in the *ātmā* implies, does not require anything other than oneself. No object, no situation, no person, is required for the happiness of such an *ātmarati*. This means that the self cannot be imperfect, that it is the very essence of happiness and fullness.

If the essence of *ātmā* happens to be fullness, *pūrṇa-svarūpa*, and if this is known to the person, then he or she is one who is steadfast in the knowledge of oneself, *ātmā-jñāna-niṣṭha*. In order to be happy with oneself, one has to have knowledge, *jñāna* of *ātmā* as fullness. Generally, one who picks up a moment of joy does so with reference to some object or situation, either outside in the case of the *bhogī* or inside in the case of the *yogī*. The only difference between the two is that the *yogī* does not require any tools except oneself or herself. A *yogī*'s raw material is an agitated mind. If this is there, *yoga*, which is a discipline, can be practised. If the mind is not agitated, *yoga* is not required at all. Thus, the *yogī*'s joy is also with reference to an object, the mind, even though it is not available to the senses.

In order to be a person whose joy is in the *ātmā*, one has to be awake to the *ātmā*. The person who is steadfast in the knowledge of oneself, an *ātmā-jñāna-niṣṭha*, is one whose happiness is within oneself and not in internal or external objects.

Kṛṣṇa also described this person as *ātma-tṛpta*, one whose satisfaction is in oneself. Nothing more is required for a person to be satisfied.

Everyone wants to be satisfied. 'This is not satisfying at all!' we say. And then we continually seek situations that will satisfy us. An *ātma-tṛpta*, however discovers joy in the *ātma*, in the self, and thereby satisfies himself or herself with the self alone. Generally, we satisfy ourselves with something else, but here, with the knowledge of the *ātma*, the person is satisfied with oneself.

Happiness is with the self alone

People pick up a moment of happiness when an external object desirable to them is gained. Whereas, for the *ātma-jñāna-niṣṭha*, not being dependent on the gain of any external situations or objects, happiness is with the self alone. This means that such a person is free from any longing to be secure, to be happy, and is therefore a *sarva-karma-sannyāsī*, a *jñānī*, one who looks upon himself or herself, not as a doer or an enjoyer, but as pure consciousness, that is *ātma*. For this person, there is no *karma* to be done. He is happy with himself, *ātmani-eva santuṣṭaḥ*.

For a person who already has this knowledge, the Veda, with all its enticing words, is as useful as a well when the well itself is under water. The wise are in no way enjoined by the Veda to do anything. This is an important point of clarification, since the Veda prescribes daily and occasional rituals in such a way that people think there is no way for anyone to escape them.

It is true that everyone performs action, even a *jñānī*. But the *jñānī* does not look upon himself or herself as a doer. For such a person, there is no doership and, therefore, the Veda does not enjoin any action. The *jñānī* is not even addressed, in fact. Only the *ajñānī*, one who looks upon himself or herself as a doer, is addressed. It is like calling someone by name, 'Rāma, please come here!' Only Rāma will come. Kṛṣṇa will not come, nor will John. Similarly, it is only the *ajñānī*, the doer, who is being addressed by the Veda – 'Oh! Doer, please perform this action.'

Only the person who looks upon himself or herself as a doer is bound by *karma*. Thus, *karma-yoga* is not meant for a *jñānī* but for the ignorant, the *ajñānī* alone. *Karma-yoga* is enjoined for the ignorant because, without it, you cannot acquire the knowledge. Thus, *karma-yoga* becomes the indirect means for gaining the knowledge that is *mokṣa*.

Here, a doubt may arise. If knowledge of *ātmā* can only be gained by an enquiry into the *pramāṇa* that gives this knowledge, why should I bother about *karma-yoga*? After all, *karma-yoga* is not the means for knowledge; it is only the means for *antaḥ-karaṇa-śuddhi*. But can you enquire into the *pramāṇa* and gain the knowledge if your mind is not prepared? The *antaḥ-karaṇa*, the mind, is where the knowledge has to take place. Thus, preparing the mind is necessary and is accomplished by *karma-yoga*. This is why Kṛṣṇa kept telling Arjuna to perform action, *karma-kuru*. And again this is why he told him that both the lifestyles, *karma-yoga* and *sannyāsa* or *jñāna-yoga* are meant for *mokṣa*.

The ritual of *sannyāsa* can be performed for the sake of knowledge, but it does not mean that, simply by taking *sannyāsa* you will achieve *naiṣkarmya*, actionlessness. Without knowledge there is no *naiṣkarmya*. Throughout the *Gītā* this was Lord Kṛṣṇa's contention.

The next verse describes the person who knows that he or she is not a doer.

नैव तस्य कृतेनार्थो नाकृतेनेह कश्चन ।
न चास्य सर्वभूतेषु कश्चिदर्थव्यपाश्रयः ॥ १८ ॥

naiva tasya kṛtenārtho nākṛteneha kaścana
na cāsya sarvabhūteṣu kaścid arthavyapāśrayaḥ (18)

tasya – for that person (who revels in the self); *iha* – here in this world; *kṛtena* – by doing action; *arthaḥ na* – there is no purpose; *akṛtena* – by not doing action; *kaścana* – any (purpose); *na eva* – indeed is not; *ca* – and; *asya* – for this person; *sarvabhūteṣu* – in all beings; *kaścit arthavyapāśrayaḥ* – dependence (on any being) for anything; *na* – is not

> For that person (who revels in the self), there is indeed no purpose here in this world for doing or not doing action. Nor does such a person depend on any being for any object whatsoever.

We have seen that *karma* is performed either for a specific result or for *antaḥ-karaṇa-śuddhi*. The person being described in this and the previous verse does not require *antaḥ-karaṇa-śuddhi* because, without it, he or she would not have acquired the knowledge that has made it possible to revel in the *ātmā*.

Suppose the question is asked, 'How do you know the person has *antaḥ-karaṇa-śuddhi*?' Then, the response is, 'because he or she has *ātmā-jñāna-niṣṭha*, firmness in the knowledge of the self.' Then, the next question could be, 'but suppose the person has *ātmā-jñāna-niṣṭha* and does not have *antaḥ-karaṇa-śuddhi*?' Here we have to question ourselves as to – what is it that we really want? Do we want *antaḥ-karaṇa-śuddhi* or *ātmā-jñāna-niṣṭha*? Of course, we want only *ātmā-jñāna-niṣṭha*, which can only be had if the mind is prepared. So, having the knowledge implies *antaḥ-karaṇa-śuddhi*.

Karma either produces a result that is outside oneself, that is, other than oneself, or *karma* is with reference to the person's *antaḥ-karaṇa*. When you require nothing more than yourself, nothing else will benefit you in terms of happiness or security. And if some purpose, some benefit is there in terms of either security or happiness, then you do not know yourself. If you think that there is some benefit to be gained in heaven, it indicates that you do not look upon yourself, the *ātmā*, as fullness. The whole creation being oneself, where is the question of gaining some benefit somewhere? Therefore, for the wise person, no purpose is served by doing *karma*.

Can there be a result without action?

There is another contention to be considered here. It is granted that by performing action, a person with this knowledge does not get a result. But by not doing what is to be done, will there not be an undesirable result? This seems to be our experience. Is it not the same for a wise person?

The Veda says that certain *karma*s are to be performed daily. According to the contention being discussed here, there are certain *karma*s such as breathing for which there is no result. All that happens is that you continue to live, nothing more. It is only when you do not breathe that you have a problem!

This, then, is the contention. There are certain *karma*s that we have to do and by doing them we do not achieve anything. But by not doing them, we attract *pāpa*. When you do not do the prayers, rituals, and duties, which are to be done daily and occasionally, there is a problem, whereas if you do them, there is no problem. Śaṅkara dismisses this argument as meaningless.

'When you perform an action, there is always a result,' says Śaṅkara. There is no such thing as a *karma* not producing a result. You cannot even throw a small pebble into a pond without creating ripples. There will always be a result. Suppose a *karma* done does not produce a result and only when you do not do it, there is a result. You can ask, 'How can an action that I have not done produce a result? If I do not do an action, it will produce neither a desirable nor an undesirable result because nothing has been done. *Karma* done will produce a result and *karma* not done will not. It is as simple as that.

Why, then, is it said that if you do not do these enjoined *karma*s, you will attract *pāpa* and so on? Because if you do not do what is to be done, it will take no time at all for you to do what is not to be done. Therefore, doing *karma* is always better than not doing it because, by not doing it, you will attract a lot of other problems. Sooner or later, laziness will overcome you and you will begin doing improper things. As a human being, you are supposed to be a thinking person, but the thinking itself will be the first casualty. Your capacity for discrimination and enquiry will go, leaving you to ruminate and vegetate.

This kind of problem is not there for the *jñānī*. Everything that has been said is for an *ajñānī* alone. For the *jñānī*, there is nothing to be accomplished or to get rid of because he or she is fullness. The do's and don'ts do not affect such a person. Nor are *dharma* and *adharma* applicable. The *jñānī* is above right and wrong. Does it mean that one can do anything, including murder? Yes, because the person is not a doer. Of course, there is no reason for a wise person to commit murder because there is nothing to be gained.

Doership and knowledge do not co-exist

Behind a murder or any other crime, there is a small person, an *ahaṅkāra*, ego. A person who knows himself or herself to be fullness cannot commit a crime. Crime is only possible when there is fear, greed, anger, and so on, all of which the wise person has already taken care of. An act of crime cannot co-exist along with the knowledge that 'I am the whole.' For a person to commit a crime, there has to be the notion, 'I must do this or that so that I can be somebody.' Such a notion implies an *ajñānī* and is not there for a *jñānī*, which is why it is said that the *jñānī* is above *dharma* and *adharma*, right and wrong, do's and don'ts.

There is no doing or not doing for the *jñānī* in the sense that the person knows that he or she is not the doer.

And when there is nothing for the *jñānī* to do because there is no sense of doership, what is there that he or she cannot do?

A *jñānī* is not dependent on anything or anyone, from Brahmāji downwards including all beings that exist anywhere. When you say, '*indrāya-svāhā* – unto Indra, I offer this oblation,' Indra, the god, becomes the basis for gaining something – some strength, some money, health, power, purification of the mind. Some purpose, *kaścid arthavyapāśraya*, is served. For example, you can say that you are performing this *karma* for the sake of knowledge, for the sake of dispassion, *vairāgya*. In order for this dispassion and knowledge to grow in you, you are offering this prayer. This is all well and good, but it is still *arthavyapāśraya*. There is some *devatā* to whom you offer the prayer. A petition may also be extended to Īśvara to a *devatā*, or to a local village official, the person to whom the petition is offered being the *arthavyapāśraya*.

If I perform an action in order to accomplish something, then that because of which I perform the action also becomes *arthavyapāśraya*. But Kṛṣṇa said, there is no *arthavyapāśraya* whatsoever for a wise person. He or she cannot say, 'I am doing this *karma*, I am invoking Īśvara, for the purpose of gaining knowledge,' because the knowledge has already been gained. For a *jñānī*, there is no Īśvara other than *ātmā*. All that is there is Īśvara alone and that Īśvara has already done everything that is to be done. He has paid off all the person's prayers, which is why the person is called a *jñāni*. This is what we mean by *mokṣa*.

Therefore, amongst all the beings and things, there is nothing upon which a *jñānī* depends for anything. No one is going to contribute to his or her betterment. No one is going to affect the *jñānī*'s fullness in any way, and the fullness that the *jñānī* knows himself or herself to be, is not dependent upon anything. It is oneself and everything else is oneself also.

Verse 19

Performing action without attachment –
one gains the ultimate

तस्मादसक्तः सततं कार्यं कर्म समाचर ।
असक्तो ह्याचरन्कर्म परमाप्नोति पूरुषः ॥ १९ ॥

tasmād asaktaḥ satataṁ kāryaṁ karma samācara
asakto hyācaran karma param āpnoti pūruṣaḥ (19)

tasmāt – therefore; *asaktaḥ* – without attachment; *satatam* – always; *kāryam* – what is to be done; *karma* – action; *samācara* – perform well; *hi* – because; *asaktaḥ* – without attachment; *karma* – action; *ācaran* – performing; *pūruṣaḥ* – person; *param* – the highest; *āpnoti* – attains

Therefore, always perform well the action that is to be done without attachment because, by performing action without attachment, a person attains the highest.

Given what has gone before, what does the first word of this verse, 'therefore,' mean? Kṛṣṇa had just said that, for the wise, there is no *karma* to be done and that by doing *karma* or not doing it, nothing is gained and nothing is lost. Why, then, was Kṛṣṇa now talking about performing action? Arjuna had expected him to say, 'Therefore, Arjuna, do not do anything!'

But could Kṛṣṇa really have said such a thing? No. It is true that he had already established that knowledge could not be gained by doing or not doing action. 'Pursue knowledge,' Kṛṣṇa said, 'but, then, what is to be done, please do it!' This seemingly contradictory statement was based on the fact that, if knowledge is already there, there is nothing for you to do. But until that knowledge takes place, do whatever is to be done by you. The word 'therefore' is connected to the topic ending with the nineteenth verse.

The 'what is in it for me?' attitude

In this verse, Kṛṣṇa also reminded Arjuna that *karma* that is not *yoga*, binds the person. Performing action without attachment refers to the attitude one should have towards the results of one's actions, *karma-phala*. A vulture flying in the sky looks as though it is just gliding along, enjoying the flight, but in fact its eyes and beak are always directed downwards so as not to miss some dead rat or other prey to swoop down upon. No matter how high it soars, a vulture's eyes are always on the prey – hence the expression, 'vulturous.' People are said to have a vulturous attitude when they think that anything they do should bring them something. Because this attitude is so prevalent, people sometimes find it very difficult to understand a person who does things without expecting anything in return. One's likes and dislikes need not constantly dictate one's actions. *Dharma* and *adharma* can as well dictate them. Thus, Kṛṣṇa said to Arjuna, 'What is to be done, please do.'

Through *karma-yoga* alone you can gain the *antaḥ-karaṇa-śuddhi* that leads to steadfastness in the knowledge. Only then can you revel in the *ātma*. Knowledge itself requires no action; it will take care of itself. This is what Kṛṣṇa meant when he said to either pursue knowledge while doing *karma* or take to a life of *sannyāsa*. That this choice is there is without question, but the end is the same for both. Which one is more appropriate for you is all that matters. If you choose the one that is more appropriate for you, you will be the gainer. But if you choose *sannyāsa*, and it is not appropriate for you, then the life of a *sannyāsī* will not bear the fruits that you expect.

In Kṛṣṇa's view, *karma-yoga* was exactly what Arjuna was fit for. So, he tells him to continue doing *karma-yoga* and also to pursue knowledge. Not until all eighteen chapters of the *Gītā* had been taught by Kṛṣṇa did Arjuna finally say, 'I am going to do what is to be done!' He then started the fight and finished it.

By the time the Pāṇḍavas had become victorious, a lot of people had been lost – Arjuna's son, Abhimanyu, Draupadī's five sons, Bhīṣma, Droṇa, Duryodhana and all his brothers, Karṇa, and so many others. Thus, a lot of destruction had been done and Arjuna was very sad. He then asked Kṛṣṇa to teach him again! Arjuna might have said something like, 'Before the war began, long ago, before all the fireworks, we had a dialogue. It was wonderful. Please teach me again because I have forgotten the words. Perhaps the message is with me still, but the words are gone.' Kṛṣṇa replied that although he could not repeat the teaching verbatim, he could go over what he had taught him previously. So, there is one more *Gītā*, called *Uttara-Gītā*, meaning a subsequent *Gītā*.

Arjuna knew that he had to gain this knowledge. In his present circumstances, in the middle of the battlefield, he could only listen. There was no time for him to do a thorough analysis and reflect on everything Kṛṣṇa was telling him. Therefore, it was something he had to work out. This was why Kṛṣṇa told him that he should continue to do *karma* and gain knowledge in the process.

The *śāstra* says that one should do what has to be done with a mind free from the hold of likes and dislikes with reference to the results of one's actions. When one performs action in this way, the mind becomes purified. Only when the mind is prepared can knowledge take place and, through knowledge, one gains *mokṣa*. You will find this point consistently reiterated by Śaṅkara in this *bhāṣya*.

Karma-yoga or any other *yoga* does not directly produce *mokṣa*, as we have seen. To think otherwise is not to understand. First, the mind is to be prepared through *karma-yoga* and then the knowledge can take place. There is an order here and it is this order that Kṛṣṇa was describing in this verse. Then, he continued.

Verse 20

The wise need not give up activity

कर्मणैव हि संसिद्धिमास्थिता जनकादयः ।
लोकसङ्ग्रहमेवापि सम्पश्यन्कर्तुमर्हसि ॥ २० ॥

karmaṇaiva hi saṁsiddhim āsthitā janakādayaḥ
lokasaṅgraham evāpi sampaśyan kartum arhasi (20)

hi – indeed; *janakādayaḥ* – Janaka and others; *karmaṇā eva* – by action alone; *saṁsiddhim* – liberation; *āsthitāḥ* – gained; *api* – also; *lokasaṅgraham* – (of) protecting the people from falling into unbecoming ways; *eva* – merely; *sampaśyan* – seeing the desirability; *kartum* – to perform action; *arhasi* – ought to

Indeed, by action alone, Janaka and others gained liberation. Also, by merely seeing the desirability of protecting the people from falling into unbecoming ways you ought to perform action.

Kṛṣṇa did not say that *karma* is to be done by everyone. *Karma-yoga* is meant for a person who is a *mumukṣu*, who is desirous of the knowledge that is liberation. For a *jñānī*, one who already has the knowledge, there is no *karma* to be done, *kartavyaṁ nāsti*, because there is no doer. The absence of doership is purely in terms of knowledge. The *jñānī* knows that he or she is not the doer or enjoyer of any action. Knowing this, a wise person is not bound by any *karma* nor is he or she enjoined to do any *karma* even by the Veda. Only a *mumukṣu* has to do *karma*, as does the *avivekī*, one who is only interested in fulfilling his or her *rāga-dveṣas*.

It goes without saying that an *avivekī*, a person whose likes and dislikes have to be fulfilled, has no choice. *Karma* definitely has to be done by such a person. And while performing action, he or she has to follow *dharma* and *adharma*, right and wrong. Otherwise, the results of the person's action will be something undesirable, if not immediately, certainly later. A person who has a value for *dharma* need not be a *mumukṣu*, a *vivekī*, but may legitimately fulfil his or her desires, keeping what is right and wrong in view.

A *mumukṣu* also does *karma* but not always to fulfil his or her likes and dislikes. More often than not, such a person does *karma* simply in order to do what is to be done in a given situation. And if one does perform action in order to fulfil one's likes and dislikes, the action is performed and the results of the action, whatever they may be, are taken as *prasāda*, gifts from the Lord.

In this verse, Kṛṣṇa provides further arguments for the performance of *karma*. People who have really given up everything to pursue this knowledge enjoy certain disposition which, according to the *śāstra*, is not gained accidentally. They have earned it by performing *karma* with the proper attitude. Thus, *karma-yoga* precedes *antaḥ-karaṇa-śuddhi*, purification of the mind, which in turn precedes *jñāna*, knowledge. This order is the context for the present verse.

Janaka and others like him, Aśvapati, for instance, are mentioned in the *śruti*. They were all kings and householders. They had offices to keep and were very busy with a variety of activities which were *kartavyaṁ karma*, to be done *karmas*. They were also considered to be wise men who had gained *saṁsiddhi*, another word for *mokṣa*, liberation. They had discovered freedom by living a life of *karma*, a life of activity.

Even though considered by the *śruti* to be wise men and scholars too, Janaka and others were not renunciates; they were house-holders. They acquired wisdom without giving up *karma*. Thus, it is very clear that performing *karma* is not against *mokṣa*, even though it cannot produce *mokṣa*. Only knowledge can be said to 'produce' *mokṣa*, *mokṣa* being an already accomplished fact. In other words, *ātmā*, oneself, is already liberated, *mukta*, and knowledge alone 'makes' one recognise this fact. And to prepare the mind for this recognition, there are a lot of means that one can use. This is the reason for saying that there is nothing equal to knowledge for gaining liberation.

Here, the use of the words 'produce' and 'make' must be properly understood. Because knowledge is always true to a fact, it cannot 'make' or 'produce' anything unless there is a fact. Knowledge of the object 'pot' will only be equal to what is there – a pot. If the pot is a clay pot, it is a clay pot, not a brass pot. By knowledge, you cannot change the nature of the pot. You can only understand its nature. This is the very meaning of knowledge.

Mokṣa is always for oneself. And because the self is already *mukta*, *mokṣa* is always for oneself; it is not for anyone else. And because the self is already *mukta*, *mokṣa* can only be gained by knowledge of the fact that the self is liberated. *Mokṣa* is already accomplished in the self and one can gain this knowledge without giving up *karma*, as Janaka and others like him did.

Karma is only opposed to knowledge when performed purely for fulfilling one's *rāga-dveṣa*s and not for neutralising them. Such *karma* is without any doubt binding in nature. But this is not the *karma* that Kṛṣṇa was referring to here. He was talking about *karma* that is to be undertaken by oneself with an attitude of *karma-yoga*. This *karma* is a *yoga* whereby you gain the kind of mind necessary for the knowledge to take place.

Understanding that one does *karma* to render one's mind fit for the knowledge, you may ask why the wise should continue to do *karma* once the knowledge has been gained. If Janaka and the others had already come to know, should they not have dropped all the *karmas*? No, Kṛṣṇa said. They could continue to do whatever *karma* was there for them to do, according to their *prārabdha*, the result of previous *karma* that had caused their present births.

Once knowledge is gained, any action is spontaneous. Whatever is to take place, will take place. No one is going to stop it. Therefore, if Janaka were to continue being the king, he would be the king. If he were to renounce everything and continue his life as a *sannyāsī*, he would have done so. It all depended on what was stored in his *prārabdha*. Once a person is no longer bound by his or her *karma* or by any *rāga-dveṣa*, the question of performing or not performing *karma* simply does not arise. How the person lives, whether he or she lives a life of activity or a life free from all activities, depends purely on the person's *prārabdha*. One is no longer controlled by likes and dislikes. Even the desire for *mokṣa*, for liberation, is gone, having been fulfilled by the knowledge of the truth of oneself. The doer not being there, there is virtually nothing for a wise person to do. Nor is there anything that such a person cannot do either. What the person will do depends only on what happens within him or her, itself governed by the *prārabdha* that resulted in this particular birth.

Prārabdha-karma is generally accompanied by the free will that a human being has. This free will can interfere with the *prārabdha-karma* in many ways – modifying it, mending it, working against it, and doing anything else to it that free will can do. Given that *prārabdha-karma* and free will go together, every situation is both *prārabdha* based and will based. Where *prārabdha* stops and free will begins, no one can say. There is no way of knowing which one brought you to a particular situation.

In the wake of self-knowledge, however, free will is not a factor. Only then does *prārabdha* alone takes care of your life. If it is in your *prārabdha* to teach, you teach. If you are to sit quietly, then that is what you do and if you have to rule a kingdom, you rule the kingdom, just as Janaka did.

Kṛṣṇa mentioned Janaka here because Janaka was a king who was considered to be a wise man. Being a king meant that Janaka was engaged in a lot of activities. He did not just sit and relax. He was the one whose phone was always ringing, so to speak. Even though he had a lot of people to help him, they were always asking him for advice. They would ask, 'What should I tell this person? What should I tell that person? We do not have any money. Our granary is empty. What shall we do?' But, in spite of all the activities that were involved in ruling the kingdom, Janaka continued to rule because of his *prārabdha*.

Knowing that Arjuna's *prārabdha* was to fight this battle, Kṛṣṇa told him to do *karma*. It was not that Arjuna had decided to fight Duryodhana; he did not even want this war.

He was brought to it by his *prārabdha*. Arjuna was right inside this particular situation, one that warranted certain action on his part.

If Janaka and the others were wise men, they continued to do their jobs because of their *prārabdha* and if they were not wise, they were doing *karma-yoga*. The point Kṛṣṇa is making here is that a person achieves wisdom by doing whatever is to be done and not by running away from it.

Kṛṣṇa might have said to Arjuna, "Suppose you look upon yourself as a wise man. Are you going to say, 'I am a wise man; therefore, I should not do action?' Is there any rule that says that a wise man should not do action?" If a so called wise man, deciding he is wise, does not do *karma*, it means that he is bound by *karma* because he is taking himself to be a *kartā*, a doer. And if he is bound by *karma*, he is definitely not wise!

Wisdom is knowing that *ātmā* is not a doer, *ātmā* is *akartā*. For the person who has this wisdom, there is no mandate to do or not to do *karma*. This in no way means that because you are wise, you will not do *karma*. Not to do *karma* amounts to laziness unless, of course, you take *sannyāsa*, for which certain preparedness is required. The point here is that even if you are a wise person, you can look at the situation you have been presented with and do what is to be done.

Arjuna was a leader

In Arjuna's case, the people had to be protected. Arjuna was a leader whether he liked it or not. Even if he himself thought he was not a leader, people looked upon him as one. Therefore, he had to do what was expected of a leader.

There are three types of leaders. One is the opportunist who becomes a leader to promote a particular cause in which he or she has a personal interest. Community leaders tend to be of this sort. Temples and churches usually get built in this way. A person who is successful in the community comes forward and heads a particular project. However, because others also want to be leaders, problems among various members of the community are inevitable. Thus, when there is an opportunity available, a person who wants power and who has the leisure and resources required, will organise the situation so that he or she becomes the leader. When an opportunist wields power in this way, it is usually an ego trip or in the interest of money. Generally speaking, our societies are led by such people.

The second type of leader, who is even more dangerous, is the idealist. The opportunist has no ideal other than his or her ego and sets sail purely according to the direction of the wind. Such a person can switch political parties simply by crossing the floor. The idealist, on the other hand, is not on a power trip. This type of leader looks upon society as being full of problems that have to be solved by him or her, for which the person has a particular system – political, economic, religious, and so on. Certain religious leaders, for example, tend to think that they alone have the answers and everyone else is a heathen whom they alone must save. In other words, an idealist is one who thinks that the answers can only come through him or her. And such a person can be a real danger to the society. Communists, terrorists, and nationalists are all idealists who make such contentions as, 'My country is the greatest country,' 'My culture is the greatest culture,' 'My religion is the greatest religion,' or 'My political or economic system is the only answer.'

An opportunist can easily be discovered, whereas the idealist converts more and more people to his or her way of thinking. When an idealist talks, there is so much conviction, so much heart and mind being brought to bear on the topic that those who are gullible will go along with whatever is being said. The idealist is one who has sold himself or herself on a particular idea and is prepared to die for it, Hitler being a case in point. His 'blue blood' theory was pure idealism and caused the colossal destruction of millions of people. He really believed he was the one who was born to protect and rule the world and that people of the Aryan race were superior. Once this idea struck him, Hitler had no rest. Nor did he allow others to rest. Under the spell of this idealism, they carried out his atrocious orders. Throughout the history of the world we find that wherever there were idealists, there was war and colossal destruction. Idealism creates religious and political fanatics and these people create havoc, as the history books reveal.

The third type of leader is one who leads, not because he or she wants to lead, but because there are some people following. Such a person lives his or her life always ready to reshuffle one's ideas in order to live according to what is true. The person may not even know that he or she is a leader.

Whether it is to one's liking or not, one becomes a leader. This is the type of leading that makes one a real leader and this was the kind of leader Arjuna was.

Here, Kṛṣṇa said to Arjuna, 'Whether you like it, there are people who look up to you as their leader.' Arjuna was the archer of the age and was looked upon by the people as a trend setter. He was supposed to set an example and was not, therefore, someone who could just walk away from it all. It was not his *prārabdha*.

If Arjuna had been a loner and had wanted to become a *sannyāsī*, Kṛṣṇa would not have talked with him about the appropriateness of *karma-yoga*, and so on. Kṛṣṇa would have agreed to Arjuna's becoming a *sannyāsī*, even though he knew there would be some problems. This, however, was not Arjuna's situation. Being a leader and looked up to by all the people, he had to set a proper example. And if he set a wrong example, the people would follow it. Therefore, to protect the people, Arjuna had to do *karma* even if he considered himself a *jñānī*. That was how his *prārabdha* had set up his situation. And if he was a *karma-yogī*, and protecting the world was his *karma-yoga*, because he was a leader then that was what had to be done.

The question that may arise here is why the world is to be protected. All that is involved here is that you find yourself in a situation with duties to perform. Someone has to be in this particular position and you happen to be that person. If you were not there, someone else would be. There is no choice involved here. Arjuna did not choose to be the son of Pāṇḍu.

He happened to be born into this particular royal family and therefore had certain jobs to do.

So Kṛṣṇa said, 'Whether you are a *jñānī* or a *karma-yogī*, here is a situation for you to do *karma*. This is not opposed to knowledge because you are not a doer.' *Karma* can be done even if you know that you are not the *kartā*. Or, put another way, *karma* is not opposed to knowledge, nor is it a means to knowledge, because by just doing *karma*, you cannot gain *mokṣa*. If you have no *viveka*, *karma* can bind you, whereas it can also be a means for purifying your mind if you make it a *yoga* by a change of attitude.

Verse 21

Kṛṣṇa tells Arjuna why he should do his duty

यद्यदाचरति श्रेष्ठस्तत्तदेवेतरो जनः ।
स यत्प्रमाणं कुरुते लोकस्तदनुवर्तते ॥ २१ ॥

yadyad ācarati śreṣṭhastattadevetaro janaḥ
sa yatpramāṇaṁ kurute lokastad anuvartate (21)

śreṣṭhaḥ – an important person; *yat yat* – whatsoever; *ācarati* – does; *itaraḥ* – the other; *janaḥ* – person; *tat tat eva* – that alone; *saḥ yat pramāṇam kurute* – what he sets as proper; *tat* – that; *lokaḥ* – the world of people; *anuvartate* – follows

Whatsoever an important person does, that alone the other people do. Whatever that person sets as proper, the world of people follows that.

Śreṣṭha here refers to one who is considered to be important by other members of the society, a leader to be reckoned with, like a king, prince, judge, or an officer of some kind. The father of a given household is such a person, a role model. The word *ācarati*, in this verse, refers to what one does in terms of how one lives, how one acts, and reacts to the variety of situations encountered in day to day life.

A person who is looked up to, sets the trend for how everyone else lives. People always look up to someone and whatever that person looks upon as the standard is what they follow. Here the word *pramāṇa* means the measure of what is right and what is wrong. The same word we have used earlier to refer to a means of knowledge. If a king looks upon the Veda as a *pramāṇa*, then most of his subjects will look upon it in the same way.

This is exactly what happened in ancient India when Aśoka and other kings came under the influence of Buddhist monks. Because these kings no longer looked to the Veda as a *pramāṇa*, a lot of people also shifted to Buddhism. Thus, converting people to any new interpretation of Vedic religion was very easy in India in those days. All that had to be done was to convert the king. Whatever became a *pramāṇa* for the king became a *pramāṇa* for his subjects.

Because people generally have neither the time nor the inclination to look into religious matters, they do not stand on their own. They tend to follow someone else and can be easily carried away merely because their leader has set a particular trend. Mao, for example, told the people that if they wanted to be efficient and accomplish their ends, they should read his Red Book every day. In this way, he made a scripture out of it.

In India, too, it is said that by reading a particular verse or chapter every day, you will get this or that. The difference is that Mao's Red Book is not a scriptural authority; it is a worldly authority, a *laukika-pramāṇa*. It is not a Veda, *vaidika-pramāṇa*. Any system or book becomes a *pramāṇa* if you think it is going to solve all the problems of the world, including your own, of course. There are people, for example, who cannot go to the bank or do anything else unless they consult the I-Ching or Tarot cards. This is their *pramāṇa*. In the same way, whatever a leader does, everyone else will do. Whatever he looks upon as his guide book, his *pramāṇa*, others will also look upon as a *pramāṇa*, even if it is the Red Book!

You will find that every revolution has some kind of book behind it. Mein Kampf – My Struggle, was the book Hitler's followers read and were inspired by. It became the *pramāṇa* for them. Hitler's entire ideology is there, including what exactly Aryan rule is, how the Aryan race is bound to rule, and the superiority of the Aryan race. Whatever the *pramāṇa, laukika* or *vaidika*, if it is considered a *pramāṇa* by a *śreṣṭha*, people will follow it.

Similarly, if a king says the Veda is not a *pramāṇa*, then the people will give it up. And if he says it is a *pramāṇa*, the people will look into it. This is why Kṛṣṇa told Arjuna that whether he liked it, he was a leader and if he walked out, he would find that everyone else would also give up. Suppose, however, that Kṛṣṇa had encouraged Arjuna to go and, turning the horses around, drove him to Rishikesh. All the other soldiers would also have turned around. They would have pitched camps there because Arjuna was there. All the subjects would also have gone to Rishikesh. If Arjuna wore a certain type of clothing, everyone would have dressed in the same way. If he wore *rudrākṣa* beads, everyone would have them!

Therefore, Kṛṣṇa said, 'This is how it is, Arjuna. Whatever you do is exactly what others are going to do because you are a *śreṣṭha*, a leader, someone who is important.' Because Arjuna's decision would have far reaching consequences, he had to look at his situation very carefully before he decided anything. Kṛṣṇa also assured Arjuna that he would lose nothing by doing his duty. If he was a *jñānī*, his action would be based on his *prārabdha* and would create no problems for him. And if he was an *ajñānī*, the action was definitely to be done because it was his duty. This was Kṛṣṇa's whole point here.

Verses 22-24

Kṛṣṇa points to himself with reference to the performance of action

न मे पार्थास्ति कर्तव्यं त्रिषु लोकेषु किञ्चन ।
नानवाप्तमवाप्तव्यं वर्त एव च कर्मणि ॥ २२ ॥

na me pārthāsti kartavyaṁ triṣu lokeṣu kiñcana
nānavāptam avāptavyaṁ varta eva ca karmaṇi (22)

pārtha – O Arjuna!; *me* – for me; *kartavyam* – to be done; *na* – not; *asti* – is; *triṣu* – in the three; *lokeṣu* – worlds; *anavāptam* – not yet gained; *avāptavyam* – to be gained; *kiñcana* – anything; *na* – not; *ca* – yet; *karmaṇi* – in action; *eva* – indeed; *varte* – I remain engaged

Pārtha (Arjuna)! For me, there is nothing to be done. In the three worlds, there is nothing to be gained by me, which is not yet gained. Yet, I remain engaged in action.

If one is awake to one's own nature, awake to the self as *akartā* then the state of actionlessness is achieved. Actionlessness does not imply the absence of activity, however, inactivity being impossible as long as one is alive, as we have already seen. A person is always doing one thing or another, whether he or she is a *sannyāsī*, a *karma-yogī*, or simply a *karmī*. Total renunciation of action is possible only in the form of knowledge that I (*ātma*) perform no action – *ahaṁ karma na karomi*.

This knowledge is an awakening. In my presence all activities take place, as will be made clear later. I, myself, do not perform any action. This is not just a volitional or a self hypnotising thought. It is the recognition of a fact. This knowledge alone makes me a renunciate of all actions in spite of my being seen to perform actions. From my own standpoint, there is no action whatsoever. All action is only from the standpoint of the physical body, mind, and sense organs. From their standpoint, there is action, whereas from the standpoint of the self, there is no action at all. This is what is called *naiṣkarmya*, actionlessness.

Whether you have achieved this knowledge of actionlessness, doing *karma* is in no way a problem. In fact, if you have come to know what the self is, then all there is for you is *prārabdha*. Lord Kṛṣṇa knew Arjuna's *prārabdha* very well. If you know the action free-self, whatever your *prārabdha* dictates, whatever the situation warrants, you do. Such *karma* does not bind you at all.

If you are an *ajñānī*, unaware of the fact about the *ātmā*, then *karma* can become a *yoga* for you, neutralising your *rāga-dveṣa*s, likes and dislikes. *Rāga-dveṣa*s cannot be neutralized unless you pay attention to them, which is what *karma-yoga* is all about. Either way, whether you are a *jñānī*, or an *ajñānī*, you can perform action.

Here, Kṛṣṇa talks about himself with reference to action, saying that there was nothing to be done by him, nothing that was not accomplished, nor anything that had yet to be accomplished. The expression, 'in all three worlds,' is meant to cover the entire universe and any others that may exist as well. Kṛṣṇa had no mandate whatsoever, either here on earth, or in heaven, or anywhere else. He was not duty bound in any way.

Only when there is something to be accomplished, is there something to be done. If there is something to be accomplished in order to make myself better, then I must definitely do whatever is to be done. Without doing, I cannot accomplish and without accomplishing, I will not be satisfied. I will be stuck with the desire to accomplish, which is what makes a person a *saṃsārī*. However, for Kṛṣṇa, there was no such thing as not accomplished or to be accomplished because he knew he was everything. Knowing this, everything was accomplished. There was nothing for him to do, *kartavyaṃ nāsti*, because there was nothing for him to gain or lose.

If I want *antaḥ-karaṇa-śuddhi*, I have something to be done, *kartavyam asti*. I have to do *karma* with a *karma-yoga* attitude, *yoga-buddhi*. Only then will my mind become pure enough for the knowledge to take place. And of course I have to do *karma* if I want to fulfil my *rāga-dveṣas*.

Most people have a long list of items to be done in order to fulfil their likes and dislikes and they perform actions for this purpose alone. For such people, fulfilling their likes and dislikes is important because they do not want to be bugged by unfulfilled desires. However, desires, *kāmas*, are no different than bugs; they breed and grow very quickly. Desire bugs do not remain single or childless! They make sure that before they go they have left behind at least a handful and have a definite knack of generating their own species in great abundance.

Desire produces other desires, its nature being to continually perpetuate itself. Like fire that leaves a black trail of charred earth and never says, 'Enough! Don't give me any more fuel. I have burned up so many houses already,' desire too will never complain. This is why desire is described poetically as the 'villain of the piece' of *saṁsāra*. There is no way of having a desire without fulfilling it. Thus, we always have a list of things to be done – *kāryaṁ kartavyam asti*.

The person who understands *ātmā* as the whole is free from those desires that are binding in nature. But this does not mean that such a person does not perform action. Kṛṣṇa, who was no ordinary person, was driving Arjuna's chariot. He was a king, the king of Dvārakā, but he did not consider driving a chariot a mean job. There was dignity in his labour. In fact, he felt honoured when Arjuna asked him to drive the chariot and he happily agreed to do so.

Kṛṣṇa was always doing one thing or another. His entire life had been one of activity even though there was nothing for him to accomplish. From childhood onwards, he had been destroying one demon after another. And if there was nothing else to do, he would pick up his flute and keep everyone else busy singing and dancing. This was Kṛṣṇa, always active. 'Before I came here to drive your chariot, I went as a mediator to Duryodhana,' Kṛṣṇa could have said to Arjuna. 'I played the role of a messenger, in fact. Then I came back and told you what Duryodhana said and now I am driving your chariot. And in response to your request that I teach you, I am doing that too right now.'

Why was Kṛṣṇa always in the midst of action? This he answered in the next verse.

यदि ह्यहं न वर्तेयं जातु कर्मण्यतन्द्रितः ।
मम वर्त्मानुवर्तन्ते मनुष्याः पार्थ सर्वशः ॥ २३ ॥

yadi hyahaṁ na varteyaṁ jātu karmaṇyatandritaḥ
mama vartmānuvartante manuṣyāḥ pārtha sarvaśaḥ (23)

hi – because; *pārtha* – O Pārtha!; *jātu* – ever; *yadi aham na varteyam* – should I ever not engage myself; *atandritaḥ* – without being lazy; *karmaṇi* – in action; *manuṣyāḥ* – human beings; *mama* – my; *vartma* – path (example); *sarvaśaḥ* – in every way; *anuvartante* – would follow

For, should I not ever engage myself in action, without being lazy, Pārtha (Arjuna)! people would follow my example in every way.

Here, Kṛṣṇa told Arjuna that if ever he became inactive, all human beings would follow him in this respect. They may not have followed him in certain other respects, but in this matter of inaction, they would definitely follow him. 'See what Kṛṣṇa is doing?' they would say. 'He just sits. Therefore, we should all just sit, too. What is the use of doing anything? This life of *saṁsāra* is useless; therefore, let us do nothing. No one who performs action ever achieves anything!'

All that is achieved by this line of thinking, of course, is that you become worse. It is like saying that since everyone who underwent any treatment eventually died, I should not undergo treatment of any kind. Or, because everyone who eats has problems at one time or the other, I should not eat. Everyone who talks quarrels with someone, therefore, I should not talk. To decide not to talk simply because when you talk, it causes problems, does not really solve the problem. You may not be talking externally, but you will definitely be talking internally. Previously, you talked to people and now you talk only to yourself! There may be a problem caused by talking, but it will not be solved by not talking.

If I perform no action, I would confuse and destroy people

Kṛṣṇa knew that if he did nothing, everyone would follow him because doing nothing always looks easy. Activity definitely implies certain will. Thus, there is a tendency to go for the convenient or the pleasant and to avoid anything that is painful. People generally think that the most pleasant activity of all is to do nothing. Doing something may imply pain and, therefore, is thought to be unpleasant. So, if people are to do anything at all, it should only be something that is pleasant.

If, however, you keep to this course, life eventually becomes full of painful situations because you have done only the pleasant, leaving undone whatever is painful. In this way, you are left with only the painful. You become a pain to yourself and to everyone else as well. If you keep on postponing the painful, then you will be stuck with the painful alone! The pleasant is done and the painful remains undone. In fact, there need be nothing painful about such activities, providing you do them. Then they are out of your way and you have only the pleasant to do.

Still, people are people; which is the reason Kṛṣṇa, the king of Dvārakā, praised as an *avatāra*, an incarnation of Īśvara, had to set an example and perform action.

Further, Kṛṣṇa continued:

उत्सीदेयुरिमे लोका न कुर्यां कर्म चेदहम् ।
सङ्करस्य च कर्ता स्यामुपहन्यामिमाः प्रजाः ॥ २४ ॥

utsīdeyurime lokā na kuryāṁ karma ced aham
saṅkarasya ca kartā syām upahanyām imāḥ prajāḥ (24)

aham – I; *karma* – action; *na kuryām cet* – if (I) were not to do; *ime* – these; *lokāḥ* – people; *utsīdeyuḥ* – would perish; *ca* – and; *saṅkarasya* – of confusion; *kartā* – author; *syām* – would be; *imāḥ* – these; *prajāḥ* – beings; *upahanyām* – I would destroy

If I were not to perform action, these people would perish. I would be the author of confusion (in the society) and I would destroy these beings.

If Kṛṣṇa performed no action and the people followed him, let them follow, one might say. The problem is that they would destroy themselves in the process. If the people have innumerable likes and dislikes and they do not perform the actions that will fulfil them, what will happen? Because they have no *viveka*, discrimination, they will become insane, which is what destruction means here. There is no destruction for a human being other than insanity.

Everyone, normal and abnormal, is born of ignorance and error. And because there is very little difference between the empirical, the objective, and the subjective, this ignorance and error can lead to madness, there being a streak of madness in everyone. This is why it is said that the line between sanity and insanity is a very fine line indeed. If you see an object, you do not see it as objectively as the object is because there is always certain subjectivity involved in the seeing. So, it is very difficult to distinguish between subjective projection and objective appreciation.

A sane person is one who has some objectivity while an insane person is more subjective. He or she also has this much objectivity, in that an insane person eats bread and not rocks just as a sane person does. The problem is that such a person may feel persecuted, for example, when, in fact, he or she is not. There may be some objectivity, but because there is a lot of subjectivity we call the person insane.

Even a person who is very objective may have some degree of subjectivity. But because the objectivity is more predominant, he or she is called normal. The person may expect that money will provide security, an expectation that cannot be described as very objective. Another indication of subjectivity is when the person does not take people as they are and, instead, projects his or her own fears upon them. Thus, the difference between those we describe as normal and those we call insane is not very much. The insane person is more subjective than objective and the sane person is a little more objective than subjective. Insanity can occur with the increase of one's subjectivity or the decrease of one's objectivity. It does not take much time and is what is meant here by destruction.

Therefore, Kṛṣṇa told Arjuna in this verse, 'If I do not perform *karma*, these people will definitely destroy themselves.' Kṛṣṇa was not talking here about being in charge of all three words. *Lokaḥ* usually means 'worlds,' but here it means 'people.' Kṛṣṇa did not say that if he performed no action in his capacity as Īśvara, all the worlds would fall apart. If this were the case, there would be no problem! We would all gain *mokṣa* because Īśvara turned lazy! This is the kind of translation that can happen if the word *lokaḥ* is not properly understood here.

Kṛṣṇa meant that the people would destroy themselves if they performed no *karma*. He also said that, if he performed no action, he would be the author of confusion. Arjuna thought if he fought this battle, he would create utter confusion in the society and thereby incur sin, which is why he did not want to fight. Now Kṛṣṇa was telling him that, by not fighting,

Arjuna would be creating confusion because the people would also not do what was to be done.

Knowing all this, Kṛṣṇa knew that he himself had to set a good example. Otherwise, he would be the cause of everyone's destruction. The people had to do their *karmas*. Not doing them was not going to help them. They would not be happy not doing what was to be done by them. They may not have been very happy doing *karma*, but not doing it would be far worse. One big *tamas*, mass lethargy, would completely overtake the society.

Previously, Kṛṣṇa had pointed out that when one's *buddhi*, the intellect, is gone, the human being is destroyed–*buddhi-nāśāt praṇaśyati (Gītā 2.63)*. This destruction is not physical; it is *buddhi-nāśā*, destruction of the intellect, the capacity to discriminate between what is and what is not. Here Kṛṣṇa, said that if the people did not do what was to be done, there would be *buddhi-nāśā*, meaning that all reasoning would be gone and they would no longer be human beings. Thus, simply because people always take what an exalted person in the society does as their model, Kṛṣṇa would be the cause of their destruction if he did not perform *karma*.

Verse 25

The wise perform action to bless the world

सक्ताः कर्मण्यविद्वांसो यथा कुर्वन्ति भारत ।
कुर्याद्विद्वांस्तथाऽसक्तश्चिकीर्षुर्लोकसङ्ग्रहम् ॥ २५ ॥

saktāḥ karmaṇyavidvāṁso yathā kurvanti bhārata
kuryādvidvāṁstathā'saktaścikīrṣurloka saṅgraham (25)

bhārata – O Bhārata (Arjuna)!; *karmaṇi* – to action; *saktāḥ* – attached; *avidvāṁsaḥ* – the unwise; *yathā* – just as; *kurvanti* – perform action; *tathā* – so too; *vidvān* – the wise; *lokasaṅgraham* – the protection of the people; *cikīrṣuḥ* – desirous of doing; *asaktaḥ* – without attachment; *kuryāt* – would perform

Bhārata (Arjuna)! Just as the unwise, who are attached to the results, perform action, so too would the wise perform action, (but) without attachment, desirous of doing that which is for the protection of the people.

Previously, Lord Kṛṣṇa had said that he did not really have anything to be done because there was nothing for him to accomplish in all three worlds, meaning here on earth, in the heavens, or in any other world. This was because he knew himself to be everything, *sarva-ātmā*. Because Arjuna saw Kṛṣṇa continually immersed in activity, Kṛṣṇa explained that he performed action to set an example, as we have seen.

Here, in this verse, Lord Kṛṣṇa asked Arjuna to suppose that he, too, were a knower of the *ātmā*, an *ātmavit*. Then he too could say, 'Hey, Kṛṣṇa, in all the three worlds, there is nothing for me to accomplish because I am an *ātmavit*. I know I am everything!' And knowing this Arjuna could then also perform action. He would have nothing to lose. He, too, would perform action for the sake of the people; otherwise, he would be destroying them.

The people did not know whether Arjuna knew or not. They only knew what he did. All they would see was Arjuna not doing what he was supposed to do and would simply conclude that not performing action is preferable.

Once again, Kṛṣṇa was bringing up the argument that the people would follow Arjuna's lead and, because of this, Arjuna should set an example.

Keeping this in mind, Kṛṣṇa addressed Arjuna here as Bhārata, for which there are two meanings. A person born in the family of Bharata may be referred to as Bhārata. Secondly, *bhā* means *brahma-vidyā*, knowledge of Brahman, and *tasyāṁ yaḥramate*, the one who revels in that, the knowledge of Brahman, is called Bhārata. Therefore, Arjuna was Bhārata in this sense also because he was receiving and revelling in the teaching of Brahman. In this verse, *vidvān* means one who has this knowledge and *avidvān* is one who does not, taking the self to be a doer. Taking themselves to be the doer, people are bound to *karma*. They do not even perform action for the sake of *antaḥ-karaṇa-śuddhi*, but with the expectation that, 'If I perform this action, I will gain this result.' This expectation, this attitude, is what is meant by attachment to *karma*.

Action itself is not what people are attached to; they are attached to the results. Because people are interested in results, they undertake certain actions with a combination of enthusiasm, anxiety, and concern. What Kṛṣṇa was saying here is, let the *vidvān*, the wise person, perform action with the same enthusiasm as a person who performs action for the results alone. Thus, the enthusiasm is a common factor between the two, whereas the anxiety and concern are not.

A person who is attached to the results of action thinks, 'Such and such should happen to me.' For this person, there is no *karma-yoga-buddhi* which is *prasāda-buddhi* with regard to results. The terms dictating the action are purely *rāga-dveṣa*s. The *kartavya-buddhi*, the to be done attitude, is not there for the person. When such people undertake activities, there is definitely going to be enthusiasm in anticipation of the results desired. But this enthusiasm will be dampened somewhat by the apprehension one has about getting undesirable results. Because there are no real guarantees that the action will produce the desired results, some anxiety will always be there. And the more enthusiastic a person is with reference to the result, the more anxious he or she naturally becomes. Therefore, for one who does not know oneself as everything, anxiety accompanies enthusiasm and with these, the person performs action.

Attitude in action

Why is it that the wise can undertake action with the same enthusiasm but without the anxiety and concern? This is purely because of a difference in attitude. A wise person performs action simply because it is to be done. How a result comes or whether the expected result comes is not a concern for the wise. When the result comes, it is met with equanimity.

Action is always result oriented. No one can perform an action without expecting a result. Expectation of a particular result alone makes the action meaningful. An action performed without expecting a result is meaningless. An action is always done for some purpose, even if it is *kartavya*, a to-be-done action. Thus, the purpose of any action is always known, whereas whether the purpose is going to be fulfilled is definitely anyone's guess! The results are not in your hands. You can only plan what you will do, then do it, and keep on doing it. But the results of the actions are not within your control. Thus, Kṛṣṇa said here that if Arjuna was an *ātmavit*, a *vidvān*, he would perform whatever action was to be done by him with the same enthusiasm as people who are attached to the results, but without the attachment – in other words, minus the anxiety and heartburn.

One may ask, why does a wise person perform action if he or she is not interested in the result? No one is saying that the person must perform action, but the question is what does he or she lose by doing it. In fact, nothing is lost and there is a lot to be gained in terms of protecting others. It is true that the gain is not for the wise person, but there is nothing wrong with that. Let the others be protected and enjoy the gain. For a wise person who knows he or she is everything, there is nothing to gain, nothing to accomplish.

One who wants to do something is called *cikīrṣu*.[9] The desire spoken of here is to protect the people *lokasaṅgraha*. Those who want to perform action, even though they have nothing to accomplish for themselves, do not want the people to fall into ways that are non-productive and destructive. Therefore, to bless the world, to serve as an example to the world, the wise perform action. What else is there to do for a person who has nothing to do but to set an example, thereby protecting the people? This is why Kṛṣṇa was on the battlefield, in fact, driving Arjuna's chariot.

---

[9] *cikīrṣuḥ-kartum icchuḥ* – one who desires to do.

Kṛṣṇa was definitely taking a risk sitting in the front seat of the chariot. He was the one who would be bombarded. Every arrow would have to cross his head and shoulders before finding its way to Arjuna. Kṛṣṇa could well be hit in the process. Being a charioteer is something like being a tank driver. Even though other men are using the weapons, the driver is risking his life. Thus, Kṛṣṇa was as much as saying to Arjuna, 'I am your driver and, therefore, I am taking a great risk. I have actually given you my neck in fact. Why? For the protection of the order, the *dharma*, and thereby for the protection of the people.'

Dharma itself is not something that has to be protected. To think so would be idealism. In fact, it is the *dharmīs*, the people who follow *dharma*, that are to be protected. There is no such thing as protection of *dharma* other than the people who follow it. The *dharma*, the order, is meant for the people. When it is said that, *dharma* is to be protected, what is meant is that the people are to be protected.

Kṛṣṇa had made it very clear that there were no *kartavya*, to-be-done action, for him or for anyone who has the knowledge of *ātmā*. There is no mandate that says you should continue to do *karma*. Whatever an *ātmavit* does is only for the blessing of the world. This being the contention, Kṛṣṇa told Arjuna that he should determine what is to be done for the good of the people alone. And then he should do it. If Arjuna were to tell the people that there is no action to be done, *kartavyaṁ nāsti*, it would be wrong. And if he set a wrong example by performing no action himself, others would be disturbed. As a word of advice to those who already have knowledge of the self, this theme was repeated by Kṛṣṇa in the next verse.

Verse 26

***An ātmavit does not disturb people
who lack discrimination***

न बुद्धिभेदं जनयेदज्ञानां कर्मसङ्गिनाम् ।
जोषयेत्सर्वकर्माणि विद्वान्युक्तः समाचरन् ॥ २६ ॥

*na buddhibhedaṁ janayed ajñānāṁ karmasaṅginām
joṣayet sarvakarmāṇi vidvān yuktaḥ samācaran (26)*

karma-saṅginām – of the people who are committed to the results of action; *ajñānām* – of the people who are ignorant; *buddhi-bhedam* – disturbance of one's understanding; *vidvān* – one who knows (the *ātman*); *na janayet* – should not create; *yuktaḥ* – the wise person steadfast in the knowledge; *sarva-karmāṇi* – all actions; *samācaran* – performing them well; *joṣayet* – should encourage (the ignorant people)

> The one who knows (the *ātman*) should not create any disturbance in the understanding of the ignorant who are attached to the results of action. The wise person, steadfast in the knowledge, himself performing all the actions well, should encourage (the ignorant) into performing (all actions).

In this verse, Kṛṣṇa is saying, 'May this *ātmavit*, the one who knows the *ātmā*, not produce any disturbance in the attitude of those who are ignorant, those who are committed to the results of action, *karma-phala*.' *Karma-saṅgīs* are those who have *saṅga*, attachment, meaning, here, an attachment to the results of *karma*. Lacking discrimination, these people are not *karma-yogī*s and Kṛṣṇa was telling Arjuna not to disturb them— *na buddhi-bhedaṁ janayet*.

Those who know a little Vedanta often say to others, 'What is this *karma* that you are doing? These rituals and prayers are not going to help you. Why do you go on chanting, '*Hare Rāma, Hare Kṛṣṇa*' all the time? You are wasting your time.' Such statements do nothing but create unnecessary problems. Therefore, Kṛṣṇa said, 'Do not disturb their understanding.'

These people need only be encouraged to do *karma* according to *dharma*, nothing more. *Dharma* and *adharma* can be discussed with them in terms of their various pursuits. But they should not be disturbed by being told not to do any *karma*, since they are not ready for what that really means. Had Kṛṣṇa and Arjuna lived their lives doing nothing, and had all the enlightened people around them also done nothing, people would certainly have concluded that the right thing to do was nothing.

People who are thought to be enlightened, are considered to be the elite in a given society and whatever they do tends to become law for the others. Therefore, such people are leaders, *śreṣṭha*s. And these leaders, including the *ātmavit*, should not disturb the minds of those who follow them.

Just as you cannot alter the direction of a river unless you do it very gradually, so too, the direction that a person's life is taking can only be altered gradually. A sensitive person, one who really cares for another person, brings about a change in that person by going with the flow, altering the direction of his or her life, little by little, in a helpful way.

The word *vidvān* in the second line of this verse refers to a wise person who is asked not to disturb the understanding of an *ajñānī*, one who is ignorant. *Yuktaḥ* is another word for *vidvān*, meaning, one who is *jñānena yuktaḥ*, endowed with knowledge. Even though such a person does not have anything to accomplish and does not lose anything either, he or she sets an example for others to follow.

For example, a *vidvān* does not pass a temple, but enters, offers prayers, and may even compose a verse in praise of the Lord. A *vidvān* does not need to go into the temple because the person is a temple unto himself or herself. In this way, a *vidvān* performs all the *karmas* that are to be done. Śaṅkara consecrated many temples and composed verses in praise of the Lord. If the *vidvān* happens to be a *gṛhastha*, the *karmas* mandated for this particular *āśrama* are followed by him or her. And if the person happens to be a *sannyāsī*, a *sannyāsī*'s life is followed. Here, Kṛṣṇa was talking about *gṛhastha*s.

A *gṛhastha* is a householder; he or she is not a renunciate. For such a person, there are different levels of *karma* – obligations to the society, to one's parents, to one's own immediate family members, to the *devatās*, and so on. In this verse, Kṛṣṇa instructed the wise who is a *gṛhastha*, to set an example for others because it was the best way to teach them.

There are two types of teaching. Teaching can be done by setting an example as is done with reference to *karma* and *dharma*. Of course, the one who is teaching also says that certain things are to be done and not to be done. For the most part, however, *karma* and *dharma* are best taught by example. Only then will the words of the one who is teaching carry any weight. The words of a person who has lived a good life always carry more weight than those of one who has not.

In the case of *ātma-jñāna*, the teaching is not by example; it is to be taught by using words. This, then, is the other type of teaching. You cannot follow an *ātma-jñānī*. You cannot say that because he or she does this or that, I will do the same and become enlightened. It does not work this way because we are dealing with knowledge. Therefore, unlike a life of *dharma*, *ātma-jñāna* cannot be taught by example. It must be taught by words, *śabda*, whether few or many, words being the *pramāṇa* here.

In teaching any subject matter, if the person knows what he or she is talking about, the words carry weight; they sound true. As the words are spoken, you see their meaning. Naturally, the words of a person who knows what he or she is talking about are different from those of everyone else. Still, teaching by using words is not teaching by setting an example.

What example are you setting when you tell someone that he or she is Brahman? Do you close your eyes? Do you walk around or remain seated? There is no example involved in telling a person that he or she is Brahman. When Kṛṣṇa compared a wise person to an ignorant person by saying what was night for one was day for the other, he was speaking from a position of desperation in terms of setting an example. To say that when the ignorant are sleeping, the wise person is awake and when they are awake, the wise person is sleeping, simply means that they never meet. We see something similar in today's families where the father works so hard that he leaves the house too early in the morning to see his children and comes home so late to find them again sleeping.

Just as the father and children never meet, the wise person and the other-wise also never meet. What is night for one is day for the other, and what is day for one is night for the other. Example setting is only with reference to *dharma-śāstra*, not with reference to *jñāna*. This point needs to be recognised because there are those who advocate teaching *ātma-jñāna* by example. The only way a wise person can set an example here is by doing *karma* properly. When he does the *karma* well, a wise person makes others do their various *karma*s because the people will follow him or her.

Verse 27

How a person gets attached to karma

प्रकृतेः क्रियमाणानि गुणैः कर्माणि सर्वशः ।
अहङ्कारविमूढात्मा कर्ताहमिति मन्यते ॥ २७ ॥

prakṛteḥ kriyamāṇāni guṇaiḥ karmāṇi sarvaśaḥ
ahaṅkāravimūḍhātmā kartāham iti manyate (27)

prakṛteḥ guṇaiḥ – by the *guṇa*s of *prakṛti*; *sarvaśaḥ* – in various ways; *karmāṇi* – actions; *kriyamāṇāni* – are performed; *ahaṅkāra-vimūḍhātmā* – one who is deluded by the I-notion; *aham kartā* – I am the doer; *iti* – thus; *manyate* – thinks

Actions are performed in various ways impelled by
the *guṇas*[10] of *prakṛti*, the body, mind, and senses.
Deluded by the I-notion, one thinks, 'I am the doer.'

Prakṛti means cause, that out of which all things come,
the potential cause of anything. There are two aspects to an
individual – *puruṣa*, meaning *ātmā*, the self, *caitanya*, consciousness,
and *prakṛti*, also called *avidyā* or *māyā*. Your body, mind,
and senses are modifications, *vikāras*, creations, born of *prakṛti*,
which depends entirely on the *puruṣa*, the *vastu*, the thing to
be understood.

Prakṛti being the cause, anything born of it is called *prakṛti-*
vikāra or *prakṛti-guṇa*, meaning modification. The word *guṇa*
has to be seen in its proper context in order to understand its
meaning because it has many meanings. It can be any simple
attribute, *viśeṣaṇa*, like the yellow colour in a yellow flower.
Any adjective is a *guṇa*.

Guṇa is also a technical term for *sattva*, *rajas*, and *tamas*,
which indicate certain conditions of the mind as well as the
constituents of *māyā* or *avidyā*.

A virtue is also called *guṇa*. For example, a person of ethics,
one who has a good heart and stately qualities, is called *guṇavān*.
Another meaning of *guṇa* is 'knot.' And, in Sanskrit grammar,
guṇa is one of the many technical names given by Pāṇini. It
indicates the vowel '*a*' and the diphthongs, '*e*' and '*o*'.

---

[10] The word '*guṇa*' has many meanings. In this verse, *prakṛteḥ guṇaiḥ* means,
by the modifications of *prakṛti*, meaning, by the mind, senses and the
physical body.

Guṇa is also a particular modification, *vikāra*. In this verse, we have '*prakṛteḥ guṇaiḥ*–by the modification of *prakṛti*, meaning by the mind, senses, and physical body. All three are called *prakṛti-guṇa*s. In the technical language of Sanskrit this body mind sense complex is called *kārya-karaṇa-saṅghāta*. We have already seen that the physical body is *kārya* and the mind, senses, and *prāṇa* are *karaṇa*. The assemblage, *saṅghāta*, of the physical body, mind, and senses is called *guṇa* here being the modification of *guṇa*s of the *prakṛti*. All actions are performed by these *prakṛti-guṇa*s, the physical limbs, mind, and senses, alone.

Actions are performed in various ways, based on various sources of knowledge, for the purpose of achieving various ends. Thus, there are actions enjoined by the Veda, *vaidika-karma*, and all other activities, *laukika-karma*. All types of activity are covered here, whether they are pursuits meant for gaining knowledge or for gaining various other results, here or in the hereafter.

A *vimuḍhātmā* thinks, 'I am the doer'

The person who thinks he or she is doer of these various actions is referred to in this verse as *ahaṅkāra-vimuḍhātmā*[11] meaning one who is deluded by the notions he or she has about the I, the *ātmā*.

---

[11] Śaṅkara resolves this compund as follows:
अहङ्कार-विमूढात्मा – कार्यकरणसङ्घाते आत्मप्रत्ययः अहङ्कारः । तेन विविधं, नानाविधं मूढः आत्मा अन्तःकरणं यस्य सः । The I-notion placed in the *kārya-karaṇa saṅghāta* is called *ahaṅkāra*. The one whose *ātmā, antaḥ-karaṇa* is deluded in various ways because of this false 'I-notion' is called *ahaṅkāra-vimūḍhātmā*.

The I-notion or I-sense has all the attributes. When you say, 'I am so and so,' the *kārya*, the physical body, and *karaṇa*, the mind and senses, are an integral part of your *ahaṅkāra* alone, the person has become deluded *vimūḍha* in many ways. In fact, the delusion is multifaceted – one delusion with varieties of nuances, one big knot with innumerable knots within knots. These knots are the varieties of problems and notions that a person has.

Ahaṅkāra implies many notions, beginning with 'I am a mortal.' The I-notion is connected to hundreds of notions about oneself. For example, religious notions brands one as religious. Then the person says he or she belongs to this or that religion, and so on. This is just one of the innumerable problems brought about by notions. All such notions are about this 'I' and are expressed by this 'I.' The *ahaṅkāra* itself includes all these notions.

The starting point for *ahaṅkāra* is the *kārya-karaṇa-saṅghāta*, the body-mind-sense complex centred on which is the conclusion, 'I am as good as this body, mind and senses.' And over a period of years, we keep gathering a variety of notions about this 'I.' No baby thinks, 'I am white or black, Caucasian or Negroid.' Only as the child grows up, does he or she slowly begin to pick up such notions. One's whole life is spent gathering more and more notions about oneself and this is what is meant when it is said, his mind is deluded, *vimūḍha*.

The *vimūḍhātmā*, the one whose mind is deluded in a hundred different ways by the *ahaṅkāra*, thinks that he or she is a doer, *ahaṁ kartā*, even though it is the physical body, mind, and senses that perform the actions. The person is the one who is aware of all the actions – in other words, the one who lights them up. He or she knows what does what; but, at the same time, is still able to think, 'I am the doer.' This, therefore, is no ordinary *avidyā*; it is not ignorance of an object or of a discipline of knowledge. It is self-delusion. Because the self is not clear, the obvious is not at all obvious. On the other hand, one who knows the *ātmā*, the *ātmavit* or the *jñānī*, does not take oneself to be the *kartā*, as we shall see in the next verse.

To tell someone who looks upon himself or herself as the *kartā*, that he or she is not the *kartā* will only confuse the person. Nothing is ever said in the *śāstra* to suggest that one should not do *karma*. The *śāstra* says you are not the doer and that this knowledge is *mokṣa*. You can live a life of renunciation or you can live a life of *karma-yoga*. In either case, knowledge is *mokṣa*. This is what is said.

To tell a person, who thinks he or she is a *kartā*, not to do *karma* is meaningless. Even if someone does no *karma*, it does not mean that one is not doing *karma*. As long as the person is a *kartā*, one's every move is a *karma* – standing is a *karma*, listening to someone is a *karma*. Everything becomes *karma* because the person thinks he or she is the *kartā*. As long as this notion is there, one will always be doing one thing or the other thinking that one is the doer. If at all you are to teach such a person, you will have to try to make the person understand that he or she is *akartā*. This understanding is purely *jñāna* and has nothing to do with doing or not doing *karma*.

Verse 28

The wise are not attached to karma

तत्त्वविन्तु महाबाहो गुणकर्मविभागयोः ।
गुणा गुणेषु वर्तन्त इति मत्वा न सज्जते ॥ २८ ॥

tattvavit tu mahābāho guṇakarmavibhāgayoḥ
guṇā guṇeṣu vartanta iti matvā na sajjate (28)

tu – whereas; *mahābāho* – O the mighty armed (Arjuna)!; *guṇa-karma-vibhāgayoḥ* – of the distinction between the body-mind-sense complex and action; *tattvavit* – knower of the truth; *guṇāḥ* – senses, mind, and organs of action; *guṇeṣu* – in *guṇa*s; *vartante* – express themselves; *iti matvā* – knowing this; *na sajjate* – is not bound

Whereas, Arjuna, the mighty armed! the knower of
the truth of *guṇa*s and actions is not bound, knowing
that the *guṇa*s express themselves in *guṇa*s (body-
mind-sense complex).

In this verse, Kṛṣṇa contrasted the *jñānī* with the *ajñānī*
mentioned in the previous verse. The ignorant person takes
the body mind sense complex, *kārya-karaṇa-saṅghāta* as oneself
and oneself to be the *kārya-karaṇa-saṅghāta*, thereby making no
distinction between the two. This lack of discrimination is
where individuality comes from, that which makes one seem
unique and distinct.

The *jñānī*, on the other hand, while taking the body mind
sense complex as himself or herself no doubt, does not take
the self to be the body, mind, and senses. If the *jñānī* were not

identified with the body mind sense complex, in this way, talking, walking, seeing, hearing, and thinking would not be possible. Since the *jñānī* thinks, does actions, and so on, he or she also naturally has an *ahaṅkāra*. Here the *kārya-karaṇa-saṅghāta-ātmā* is being called the *ahaṅkāra*.

The nature of delusion

Thus, both the *jñānī* and the *ajñānī* have this *ahaṅkāra*, the difference between the two being that the *jñānī* does not take the self to be *kārya-karaṇa-saṅghāta* whereas the *ajñānī* does, which is why there is *saṁsāra* for him or her. *Saṁsāra* is in the self, for the self.

Because the *ātmā* is taken to be the *kārya-karaṇa-saṅghāta-ātmā*, there are individuals, each of whom is unique and distinct from every other individual. Thus, there is an 'as though' division, an 'as though' duality, *dvaita*. The *śruti* does not say there is *dvaita*; it says only that there is 'as though' duality – *dvaitam iva bhavati*. Wherever there is this 'as though' duality, there is death, *mṛtyu*; there is time, there is *saṁsāra*.

The *jñānī* is referred to as *tattvavit* in this verse. The suffix 'tva' is added to a noun to convey its abstract sense, its essence. For example, the truth or essence of a pot, *ghaṭasya tattvam*, becomes *ghaṭatva*, potness. In English, the suffix 'ness' is used in the same way.

'That' is a pronoun and as such can stand for anything. Thus, *tattva* refers to that which is the truth or essence of everything, *tasya-bhāvaḥ*. The one who knows the truth about oneself, the world, and God is called *tattvavit* and the one who does not know this truth is called *atattvavit*. In this verse, *tattvavit* refers to one who knows the truth of the *guṇas*, the modification that is the body-mind-sense complex, as well as of the *karmas*, meaning that the person can distinguish between the two. The distinction, *vibhāga* here is that the body mind sense complex is an instrument, a *karaṇa*; it is not the *ātmā*.

I, the *ātmā* is not the *karaṇa*, the sense organs or the mind, or the *kārya*, the physical body. While the mind and senses perform their actions, they are only *karaṇas*, instruments. *Ātmā* is not an instrument. It is the self, the content of the subject, the doer. Therefore, a distinction is to be made between the essence of the subject and the instrument.

The subject cannot be taken as an instrument because the instrument, being wielded by the subject, is necessarily in the hands of the subject. You are handling the body, you are handling the mind and senses. The subject cannot be taken as the very thing that it handles, just as you cannot take the spoon or fork that you eat with as yourself. That you are holding the fork in your hand does not mean that the fork is you. It is simply an instrument that you wield. Similarly, you wield your mind and senses; you operate them. You wield your physical body; you operate it. Therefore, they are merely instruments and the doership imputed to *ātmā* is simply a thought belonging to the mind.

The one who knows the *karaṇa* as the *karaṇa* and the *ātmā* as the *ātmā* is one who knows the truth of both. The one who knows the truth of *ātmā* also knows the truth of *anātmā* and is therefore a *tattvavit*. This, then, is what is meant by *guṇa-vibhāga*.

Ātmā is not the *kartā*. *Ātmā* does not perform any action; only the *guṇas* perform action. Action does not come from the *ātmā*. It emanates from the *guṇas*, from the *kārya-karaṇa*, from the physical body, mind and senses, alone.

Any fancy or desire is a modification of the mind. But you may not go along with the desire or fancy. Many desires rise and fall simply because we do not bother about them. This happens because of a particular function of the mind that enables you to decide whether to go along with the desire or not. In such a decision, there are various considerations, pragmatic and ethical considerations, among others. 'Is this necessary for me?'– is a pragmatic consideration undertaken by the *ātmā* in the form of *buddhi*.

With the organs of action or the sense organs you perform *karma*. Whatever you do – eat, walk, or engage yourself in any kind of pursuit – some sense organ is involved. The truth of this *karma*, however, is that *ātmā* is not directly involved in the activity. *Ātmā* is not a desire or a decision. Nor does it desire or make decisions. Desires and decisions are always in the form of *vṛtti*s, modifications of the mind. These *vṛtti*s are *ātmā* no doubt, but *ātmā* is none of them. Thus, all *karma* emanates from modifications of the mind, *vṛtti*s, and does not come from the *ātmā*.

Everything is a modification of prakṛti alone

The one who knows the nature of *karma* and the nature of *ātmā*, and therefore the distinction between the two, looks upon *prakṛti* as it really is. *Prakṛti*, also called *māyā*, in its entirety is the cause for everything in that it modifies itself into everything. The body, mind, and senses are *prakṛti* and the sense objects, the world, *jagat*, are also *prakṛti*. All are modifications, *guṇas*, of *prakṛti* alone. And these two *prakṛti*s are in touch with each other. One *prakṛti* is *kārya-karaṇa-prakṛti*, in the form of instruments of perception and action and the other *prakṛti* is in the form of objects, *viṣayātmika-prakṛti*.

This verse explains that the *guṇas* in the form of instruments of perception and action engage themselves in activity in the spheres of their respective objects – *guṇeṣu*. So the eyes engage themselves in the sphere of forms, *rūpa*, the forms being *guṇa*. Sight itself is *guṇa* and the seen object is also *guṇa*. Similarly, hearing is *guṇa* and the objects heard, the sounds, are also *guṇa*. In this way, these *guṇas guṇeṣu*, with reference to objects, *vartante*, engage themselves in activity. This means that I do not perform any action at all. Knowing this, the wise person is not bound, *matvā na sajjate*.

Knowing the truth of *ātmā* and *karma*, the *tattvavit* does not become attached to any *karma*. Such attachment is not possible because the person knows that he or she does nothing. To become attached, there must be a *vṛtti*, which is non-separate from *ātmā*, while *ātmā* is always free from any *vṛtti*. Because there is no connection, no attachment, between the *vṛtti* and *ātmā* there can be no attachment to any *karma* for one who knows that *ātmā* is always free, that is, for the one who knows that *ātmā* is *asaṅgaḥ*.

The problem arises when you say you must become *asaṅga*, detached. You do not become *asaṅga*; that, you are *asaṅga* is a fact to be known. There is no becoming here. You can never become detached. What you want to be detached from is always in your head; therefore, you can never detach from it. Even when you say you are detached from it, you are already attached because you are talking about it. A person who throws away some garbage and says, 'I gave away my garbage,' still has the garbage in his or her head. The garbage was outside and now it is inside! This is exactly how we have collected so much garbage!

As the nature of *ātmā*, detachment is already an accomplished fact. Knowing this, one is not bound – *iti matvā na sajjate*. The person looks upon himself or herself as a non-doer, *akartā aham asmi*, actionlessness itself. Previously, Kṛṣṇa said that by not performing an action, a person does not gain *naiṣkarmya*, the state of actionlessness. Knowing the self to be free from any type of action, doership is not there. When there is no doership, there is no *karma*. In this sense, knowing there is no doership, a person is free from all *karma*. This, then, is the difference between the *tattvavit* and the *atattvavit*.

How to help others in terms of this knowledge?

When this is so, what should you do? Suppose you know you are *akartā* and the other person, whose welfare you are interested in, takes himself or herself to be *kartā*. Should you tell the person not to do *karma*? Definitely not. If at all he or she is available for this knowledge, all you can say is, *ātmā* is *akartā*. This alone is the truth and anything else is a distortion of it. To tell someone not to do *karma* is the same as saying that performing *karma* is bondage. If the person still looks upon oneself as *kartā*, being deluded in this way, one will only become lazy, nothing more!

Therefore, all you can do is tell the person to do *karma*, but to do it according to *dharma*. You can say only this much. This is what the scriptures also enjoin. Not performing any action will eventually result in a person doing something that is not to be done. What is not proper for you is not proper for the other person also. There are universal implications inherent in all action. If you compromise with this universal fact, for example, by robbing someone even though you yourself do not want to be robbed, you may think you can get away with it, but you cannot. This, the scriptures tell you. Otherwise, you would not need a scripture; common sense would be enough.

The scripture does not need to tell me that it is wrong to rob. This, I knew even as a child. When my elder brother took the chocolate out of my hand, I complained to the heavens! I cried and created havoc in the house because I knew very well that he robbed what I held as mine. He took it away. Everyone is very clear on this point and does not need a scripture for it. Nor do we need someone to come and preach us about things we already know. What the scriptures and preachers are saying, however, lest we do not know it, is that we should not think we can get away with improper actions.

This, then, is an extra revelation, extra information provided by the scripture. It says that the reason you do not get away with improper actions is because there is a law that is impossible to get around. The moment you commit a wrong action, a debit is registered against your name. The whole law is based on credit and debit, both of which are automatically recorded to your account. Also, there is no way of manipulating this law. It is already programmed to record whatever action you perform. Everything has been taken care of. This law is not a computer that you, the wizard, the *kartā*, can manipulate. You can, however, erase it by means of a different operation. This is additional information that a scripture may talk about. Because the information is revelation, something that we have no other way of knowing, the scripture is given the status of revealed knowledge.

A person who performs action because he or she looks upon himself or herself as the *kartā* should not be told to refrain from action because *karma* is bondage. It is bondage, no doubt, but telling the person so is not going to make him or her free. If, however, you really care for the person, and he or she cares for your words, then you can share what you know. Otherwise, your talk will just go over the person's head. It is like someone who is interested in this knowledge trying to explain to his or her parents what he or she is studying. Because the parents do not understand, they will only ask themselves what they did wrong for their child to have been steered in such a useless direction. 'We must have been a little too severe and that is why our child listens to this Swami,' they may say. To attempt an explanation is only to make them feel guilty because it is impossible to convince them of the true worth of this knowledge.

You may care for the welfare of those who do not understand, but they too have to care for your words. Otherwise, they will only sympathise with you, feeling that you are completely deluded! And if they do care for your words, you can tell them the truth, that *ātmā* is *akartā*. In the modern literature on Vedanta, you may read that you must become *asaṅga*. This is why some people spend an entire lifetime trying to become *asaṅga*. It is also sometimes said that you should experience the *asaṅga ātmā*. There is an experiencer, an object of experience, and *ātmā* is to be experienced by another *ātmā* who is an experiencer. All that you experience in this way is *anātmā*, not *ātmā*.

Because *ātmā* as *asaṅga* is a fact to be recognised, Kṛṣṇa further cautioned the wise not to confuse those who still think of themselves as doers.

Verses 29&30

People are bound in terms of *guṇa* and *karma*

प्रकृतेर्गुणसम्मूढाः सज्जन्ते गुणकर्मसु ।
तानकृत्स्नविदो मन्दान्कृत्स्नविन्न विचालयेत् ॥ २९ ॥

prakṛterguṇasammūḍhāḥ sajjante guṇakarmasu
tān akṛtsnavido mandān kṛtsnavinna vicālayet (29)

prakṛteḥ guṇa-sammūḍhāḥ – those who are deluded by the modifications of the *prakṛti*; *guṇa-karmasu* – in terms of the body-mind-sense complex (*guṇas*) and actions; *sajjante* – become bound; *tān* – those people; *akṛtsnavidaḥ* – those who do not know; *mandān* – those who are not discriminative; *kṛtsnavit* – one who knows; *na vicālayet* – should not disturb

Those who are deluded by the modifications of the *prakṛti* become bound in terms of the body-mind-sense complex (*guṇa*s) and actions. One who knows (the self) should not disturb those who do not know (the self), who are not discriminative.

Here, *prakṛteḥ guṇa-sammūḍhāḥ* refers to those who are deluded with reference to *prakṛti-guṇa*, which are the modifications of the *prakṛti*. They take the self to be the body-mind-sense complex. This expression can also mean that people become deluded because of the mind and senses, their ignorance with reference to these being the origin of their problems. Looking upon themselves as doers, such people become bound, attached, *sajjante*, with reference to the body, mind, and senses (*guṇa*), and with reference to action (*karma*).

To take the body, mind, and senses as oneself means, 'I am only as good as the body, mind, and senses,' with all their limitations; to think this way is bondage. The people discussed in this verse have become bound with reference to *prakṛti-guṇas*, such as the body-mind-sense complex, *kārya-karaṇa-saṅghāta*, and also to their *karma*s. The bondage manifests in terms of actions such as, 'This is my *karma* and I perform it for the sake of this result.'

Because people experience success and failure, they are bound by the results of their action. And if they have *śraddhā*, *puṇya* and *pāpa* are also involved. Then success and failure, *puṇya* and *pāpa* become the ruling factors in their lives. Thus, such people have both *dṛṣṭa* and *adṛṣṭa* conflict, attached as they are to the seen and unseen results of their actions.

The verse also tells us a little more about those who are bound in terms of *guṇa* and *karma*. They are described as *mandas*, those who have no *viveka*. *Mandatva* means 'dullness,' the sense you have when you have indigestion, for instance, and do not feel like eating or doing anything. You develop a complete dispassion even towards foods that you like and it lasts for as long as the discomfort lasts, at least. And if this *mandatva* happens in our thinking, we have a definition for the person, *manda*, discussed in this verse. Nothing ignites in the brain of such a person. There is no fire, whatsoever! Although situations unfold around the person, there is no assimilation, no response.

The word '*mandatva*' is used here only as a definition for the condition of the mind. It is not meant as a criticism either of oneself or of another. The word simply indicates a person who does not discriminate between *ātmā* and *anātmā*. Two other words are used in the verse to make the same distinction between one who has the knowledge and one who does not.

Kṛtsnavit is a wise person, one who has complete, *kṛtsna*, knowledge with reference to *ātmā* and *anātmā*, whereas *akṛtsnavit* refers to everyone else. Because the *akṛtsnavit* does not know that he or she is not the doer, the person has problems. The *akṛtsnavit* may understand that *anātmā* – the body, mind, and senses – performs action, but may think of *ātmā* as something other than himself or herself, something that is not known. Therefore, one has some knowledge but does not know totally, which is the meaning of *akṛtsnavit*.

For a person who knows nothing, there is no problem. Ignorance is bliss, as they say, provided, of course, the ignorance is total. For example, there is no problem in sleep because you do not think of yourself as a *kartā*, *bhoktā*, or anything else. Only when there is some knowledge is there a problem. Those who are dull, *manda-prajñas*, who have no discrimination, *viveka*, with reference to *ātmā* and *anātmā* are referred to here as *akṛtsnavits*. These are the people that a wise person should not disturb, *tān na vicālayet*, by telling them that *karma* will not produce *mokṣa*. They should not be told, 'Karma' is all bondage. Why do you do *karma*? Why do you pray? Why do you go to church or to the temple? Why do you do *japa* and meditation? This is all nonsense. Only *jñāna* will give you *mokṣa*.' Such comments should not be made because they do not help anybody.

A person should not be told not to work or that working for money is useless. Let the person work; otherwise, one will become lazy. Such people will end up at your door, telling you that you said not to make money and now they need some! People need food and place to live. Whom else will they come to but the person who told them not to make money. Therefore, do not tell them not to make money. Tell them to do so, following *dharma*. You can even give them some ideas on how to go about it. There is nothing wrong with making money; it is a resource, Lakṣmī, and as such should not be abused.

If, on the other hand, you are talking to a person who has seen that money is not an end in itself and he or she has some *viveka*, then you can talk about *karma-yoga* or *sannyāsa*. It all depends on the person to whom you are talking. Kṛṣṇa's point here was that the person should not be disturbed unnecessarily. Even a person who is a *mumukṣu*, who has *viveka*, should not be indiscriminately told to take *sannyāsa*. For someone who still has *rāgas-dveṣas*, *sannyāsa* will not work; it will only be abused. Such a person should be told to perform action as a *karma-yogī*, as Kṛṣṇa told Arjuna in the next verse.

मयि सर्वाणि कर्माणि संन्यस्याध्यात्मचेतसा ।
निराशीर्निर्ममो भूत्वा युध्यस्व विगतज्वरः ॥ ३० ॥

mayi sarvāṇi karmāṇi sannyasyādhyātmacetasā
nirāśīrnirmamo bhūtvā yudhyasva vigatajvaraḥ (30)

sarvāṇi – all; *karmāṇi* – actions; *mayi* – unto me; *sannyasya* – renouncing; *adhyātma-cetasā* – with a mind that is discriminating; *nirāśīḥ* – devoid of expectations with reference to the future; *nirmamaḥ* – devoid of any sense of 'mine-ness'; *bhūtvā* – being; *vigata-jvaraḥ* – without any anger or frustration; *yudhyasva* – fight!

Renouncing all actions unto me, with a mind that is discriminating, devoid of expectations with reference to the future and any sense of 'mine-ness,' without any anger or frustration whatsoever, fight (act).

The word 'fight!' in this verse can refer to anything, beginning with one's daily battle of getting out of bed in the morning. Throughout the day also there are a number of situations to be faced. For Arjuna, what had to be faced was an actual battle. The battle was a *kartavyaṁ karma*, a 'to be done' action for him. Given all that Arjuna and Kṛṣṇa had said before, Kṛṣṇa's mandate, 'Get up and fight!' was to be expected. It was neither a command nor advice; it was teaching. Having presented his arguments, Kṛṣṇa simply said, 'Do it!' Thus, there was a definite 'therefore' implied here, indicating teaching rather than a command or advice. The rest of the verse deals with how Arjuna was to fight. First, 'giving up all activities, fight! *sarvāṇi karmāṇi sannyasya yudhyasva.*'

The real meaning of renunciation

There are two types of *sarva-karma-sannyāsa*, as we have seen. How can you fight if you have renounced all activities? It won't work. If, on the other hand, the mandate is, 'Renouncing all actions, go to a teacher and listen to the *śāstra – sarvāṇi karmāṇi sannyasya śravaṇaṁ kuryāt, gurumevābhigacchet.*' Giving up all activities, burning all your bridges behind you, and your boats, too, if you have any, go for *mokṣa*. The giving up is meant for learning alone, meaning that you go to a teacher and study until you gain the knowledge that is *mokṣa*. Renunciation is purely for *mokṣa*, not for anything else.

We have seen how *sannyāsa* is a particular lifestyle that enables a person to renounce all activities in order to pursue knowledge. But, here, *sannyāsa* is used in conjunction with the mandate, 'Renouncing all activities, fight! *sarvāṇi karmāṇi sannyasya yudhyasva.*' Fighting being an activity, what does giving up all activity mean? Does it mean that Arjuna is not to do anything other than fight? Performing only one action, give up every other activity – prayer, ritual, eating, sleeping, helping, everything – and fight!

Obviously, because activity in the form of fighting is involved, this *sannyāsa* is other than what we have seen before. Here, it relates to doing what is to be done, which for Arjuna happens to be *yuddha*, fighting. Kṛṣṇa was not suggesting that Arjuna give up all activities and fight. This would not have been possible. What was intended here becomes much clearer when the word, '*mayi* unto me' is taken into account. 'Unto me' means 'unto the Lord,' thereby connecting the giving up, *sannyāsa*, with *karma-yoga*, meaning that all one's activities are offered unto the Lord.

In his commentary of this verse, Śaṅkara compares this offering of one's actions, to how a servant of a king goes about doing various activities without questioning how or why it is to be done, 'I have been placed here to do this particular activity. This is how I have been asked to do it and therefore I do it.'

Similarly, whether you like it, you find yourself in a given situation that calls for a particular action. For Arjuna, it happened to be a battle, a fight. For another person, it may be something else. And, although Arjuna was a *kṣatriya*, doing what was to be done would not always mean fighting. If he had taken the expression '*sarvāṇi karmāṇi sannyasya yudhyasva*' wrongly, he may have thought that he should always fight, which was not what was intended. Doing what is to be done is to be understood within the context of the situation one finds oneself in. Certain situations call for certain actions. Therefore, *yudhyasva*, can be taken to mean *kuruṣva*, do what is to be done and do it with an awareness of Īśvara.

Awareness of Īśvara is pointed out in the verse by the word, *adhyātma-cetasā*; *cetasā* meaning 'with the mind.' The mind should have *viveka*. *Adhyātma* means with reference to oneself. *Adhyātmacetas* enables you to know what is and what is not the right thing to do. This capacity is also called *viveka-buddhi*.

A *viveka-buddhi* says, 'I am a doer, of course, but I do this for the sake of Īśvara as a *bhṛtya*, the one who serves – *ahaṁ karta, īśvarasya bhṛtyavat karomi.*' The person who performs action in this way is a *mumukṣu*, a seeker. Because the person thinks of himself or herself as a *kartā*, he or she is a *karma-yogī*. There is an evolution that can take place here. One who is not a *karma-yogī* and who is totally deluded, *vimūḍhātmā*, is also a *kartā*, but still does *karma* for the results alone. His thought is, 'For my sake, I am doing this.' For a *vimūḍhātmā*, expediency and convenience take precedence over a more appropriate means when choosing a course of action. Even though he or she may have one eye on *dharma*, the other eye can be somewhat blind if the person thinks there is any justification for going against *dharma*.

Everything belongs to Īśvara alone

The *karma-yogī* on the other hand, performs action quite differently–for the sake of Īśvara. Therefore, an awareness is necessary, which is *viveka* here – *adhyātma-cetasā* – with a mind that is awakened to Īśvara. 'Do all the activities that you are going to do, surrendering them unto me,' Kṛṣṇa said here. Why? Because you are placed in situations that you did not create. Nor does anything really belong to you; everything belongs to Īśvara alone. Thus, you are placed in certain situations and the order of *dharma* governing such situations is the Lord. The order determines what is expected of you in each situation and as a *karma-yogī* you do it with an awareness of this fact.

Further, Kṛṣṇa said, *nirāśīḥ nirmamaḥ bhūtvā yudhyasva.* *Nirāśīḥ* is one from whom all notions about the future, *āśā*, have gone. Future plans, goals, grandiose schemes, and priorities can stifle and inhibit one's present course of action with reference to what is to be done now. A person who thinks only of the future will compromise what is to be done in the present, thereby becoming a schemer. Such a person is not a *karma-yogī*; he or she is an *avivekī*, one who performs *karma* for the results alone. What is to be done is not done if it is inhibited by your own *āśā*. Thus, *nirāśī* is one who is not inhibited by futuristic ambitions, nor devoid of ambitions.

Nirmama means one from whom the *mamatva*, the mine ness, is gone. Such a person no longer thinks in terms of, 'this is mine, this is not mine,' which also inhibits what is to be done. 'This is not my job. I am not getting anything out of this. Why should I do this when it is his job? He is supposed to do it.' This mine-ness or *mamatva* is the greatest villain in the maturing process of a person because, to be mature, one has to see only what is to be done. Therefore, *mamatva* should not interfere with one's doing what is to be done.

We can see by these two words *nirāśī* and *nirmama*, that *karma-yoga* is not an ordinary thing; it requires a lot of maturity and an awareness of the laws that are Īśvara. *Karma-yoga* does not mean that you should not receive wages for the work you do, although there may be situations where it would be more appropriate not to. What makes you a *karma-yogī* is simply the awareness of Īśvara, as we have seen before and will see again.

Another word given in this verse describing how one is to perform action is *vigatajvaraḥ*, meaning to be free from all anger and frustration. Suppose a man wants to do what is to be done in a given situation that Īśvara has placed him or her in, but thinks that Īśvara has placed him in a wrong situation? He acknowledges that Īśvara knows what he is doing, but still thinks of it as a wrong situation and becomes frustrated. This frustration is what is meant by *jvara*, leading to murmuring, complaining. By using the word *vigatajvara*, Kṛṣṇa told Arjuna to fight cheerfully without an iota of complaint, frustration, despair, or anger.

Verse 31

Those who follow the teaching gain mokṣa

ये मे मतमिदं नित्यमनुतिष्ठन्ति मानवाः ।
श्रद्धावन्तोऽनसूयन्तो मुच्यन्ते तेऽपि कर्मभिः ॥ ३१ ॥

ye me matam idaṁ nityam anutiṣṭhanti mānavāḥ
śraddhāvanto'nasūyanto mucyante te'pi karmabhiḥ (31)

śraddhāvantaḥ – people who have faith; *anasūyantaḥ* – those who do not find fault (with the teaching or the teacher); *ye* – those; *mānavāḥ* – people; *me* – my; *idam* – this; *matam* – teaching; *nityam* – constantly; *anutiṣṭhanti* – follow; *te* – they; *api* – too; *karmabhiḥ mucyante* – are freed from the hold of the *karmas* (*karma-phalas*)

Those people who constantly follow this teaching of mine, full of faith, without finding fault with the teaching or the teacher (*anasūyā*), they too are freed from the hold of the *karma-phalas*. (They gain *mokṣa*.)

We have seen the three types of people who perform *karma*. One type were kings like Janaka, who were also *jñānīs*, wise men, all of whom remained active, even though they had the knowledge. They engaged themselves in activities simply because it was in their *prārabdha* to do so. They had to do it and therefore they did it. There was no reason not to. They had nothing to lose and others benefited from their actions.

Those who do nothing but teach, having gained the knowledge, can also be included in this group, teaching being an activity. *Sarva-karma-sannyāsa* is the renunciation of all activities in terms of knowledge alone. It is not to be taken literally, as we have seen. In terms of knowledge, you are not the doer. Knowing this frees you completely from all action, whether you perform activities. You may be a *sannyāsī* or you may be very active in the world. In this way, then, there are two types of enlightened people, *sannyāsīs* and non *sannyāsīs*, with reference to lifestyle. But in terms of knowledge, there is *sarva-karma-sannyāsa* for both.

Although Janaka was a king, engaged in a lot of activity, he was considered to be enlightened. Here, Kṛṣṇa told Arjuna that even if he was enlightened, he could continue to do *karma* for the benefit of the world, as Janaka did, for the sake of establishing *dharma* so that the people would be protected. Kṛṣṇa knew very well what his own mission was, saying: 'Look at me. I too perform actions, not because I have something to accomplish, but because if I do nothing, others will follow my example, which would not be good for them.' All this Kṛṣṇa pointed out.

The second type of people who perform *karma* are *avivekīs*, those who have no discrimination and therefore no desire for *mokṣa*. They are only interested in fulfilling their likes and dislikes, for which they engage in activities. More often than not, such people cut corners and sometimes take the wrong path in order to accomplish their ends. These people can only be asked to come to *dharma*. Let them pursue whatever they want to pursue according to *dharma*. That itself is a blessing.

One's choice is surrendered to what is proper

Finally, for those who are *mumukṣu*, who have *rāga-dveṣas*, Kṛṣṇa pointed out *karma-yoga*. Such people can either take to *sannyāsa* or *karma-yoga*, either of which involves giving up, *tyāga*. For a *sannyāsī, tyāga*, means *karma-tyāga* as well as all other *tyāgas*, covering any pursuit or attachment. The person has to grow out of each and every one of them, renouncing them all, before becoming a *sannyāsī*.

Or one can be a *karma-yogī*. Such a person does what is to be done simply because it is to be done. The *karma-yogī*'s commitment to *mokṣa*, being what it is, his or her choice of action has nothing to do with what he or she likes to do.

If, on the other hand, the emphasis is on doing what is convenient and what one likes to do, even a child will eventually question why he or she cannot do certain things. He or she will say, 'Who are you to stop me? That is how you brought me up. Why, now that I am sixteen, are you trying to stop me from doing what I want to do? It doesn't make sense. You have always asked me what I want and this is what I want!'

The psyche tends to react in this way when this particular approach is taken.

Such an approach is not always right, nor does the world necessarily operate in such a way. So, what is proper becomes important. To do what is proper may involve sacrifice in terms of your own pleasures, your own likes and dislikes. Unless you can give them up, it is impossible to always do what is to be done, *kartavya*. Therefore, propriety, not convenience, should be the ruling factor, all of which is implied in *karma-yoga*.

A *karma-yogī* is a *bhakta*, a devotee. Without devotion, without the awareness of Īśvara, there is no *karma-yoga*. Having said all this before, Kṛṣṇa again picked up this thread. Performing all activities for the Lord's sake is one great *yajña*, one great offering. What you have to do in the situation you find yourself in, is done as something that is dictated by Īśvara, meaning *karma*. *Karma* is the law and the law is Īśvara. The choice of doing this or that is given to you and that choice is surrendered to what is obvious. Each situation is nothing but *karma* unfolding itself and inherent in it is an obvious course of action, an expected action. This is what you do because this is how you have placed yourself based on your own past actions. And, whatever are the results of the actions you perform, you simply receive them as *prasāda*.

The verb in this verse is *anutiṣṭhanti*, meaning 'follow,' 'practice,' or 'live according to.' *Mānavāḥ* means those who come under the mandate of Manu, the ordainer of the law that is Īśvara – in other words, all human beings. And how long do they live this way? *Nityam*, always. This is not just a morning or evening practice; nor is it a Monday, Friday, or Sunday practice. It is a constant practice. And what is it that is practised? What do the people follow? They follow what was said by Kṛṣṇa, his vision, *me matam*, this particular *sādhana*, *karma-yoga*. And they follow it properly with *śraddhā–śraddhāvantaḥ anasūyantaḥ*—and with no intolerance towards the Lord, his vision, or the *karma-yoga* that he has advised as a means for gaining liberation, *mokṣa*.

Śraddhā in the śruti as a pramāṇa is necessary

The *śraddhā* mentioned in this verse is looking upon the words of the *śāstra*, the Veda, as unfolded by a teacher, as true. Whether one understands these words to be true or not, one at least accepts them in good faith. This *śraddhā* extends to the words of the *Gītā* as well, since the *Gītā* does not say anything other than what is said by the Veda. The English translation for *śraddhā* is faith. *Śraddhā* is operative when, even though these scriptures may seem to be contradictory according to your perception, you accept them and enquire into their message. *Śraddhā* grants you the disposition, the attitude, necessary for further pursuit.

When you look at the *śāstra* in the form of sentences, you derive a certain meaning from it, based on what you already know. Only on the basis of what you already know can you absorb or understand any sentence, in fact. In other words, you do not understand more than what you already know. What you will understand of the *śāstra* is determined by where you are coming from and where you are right now. Based on your past experiences and present understanding, there is a predisposition to what a sentence can reveal to you. Therefore, when you look at a sentence that has a new message to give, what can it give you? Can the intentions behind the sentence be understood?

The intention of a sentence is important in communication. When someone forms a sentence, the person has an intended meaning to convey and that meaning is what you should receive. Sometimes, however, the words spoken do not convey the intended meaning of the speaker. And even when the intended meaning is clearly conveyed, it is anyone's guess whether the listener or the reader will pick it up. This is especially true if the message is unlike anything that the listener already knows, whereas if the message is similar to what he or she knows, it is much easier for the person to pick it up. Using the knowledge one already has, the person can go further in one's understanding of what is being conveyed. But if the message is entirely dissimilar, meaning that it is against everything the person has so far concluded about himself or herself and the world, it is not even mind boggling; it simply sounds silly.

How can everything be one when all I see are differences? To say that these differences are false, that everything is *mithyā*, when so much of what is experienced is tangible – the walls, physical bodies, objects, even the microbes that bother me so much – makes no sense whatsoever because everything seems to be so real. This is because the word *mithyā* is not properly understood. Nor do the various translations help. One will translate *mithyā* as 'false,' another as 'illusion,' and still another as 'delusion.' To say that the world is any of these does not agree with my experience.

To say the world is an illusion is itself an illusion. The very concept is an illusion. If you consider the world an illusion, where does that leave you? Are you not in the world? And since you are, does it not mean that both you and your statement are an illusion? If the one who talks is an illusion and that which is talked about is illusion, then talking also is illusion. This being the case, everything becomes *satya* because the one who talks and what is talked about belong to the same category! If everything is illusion, where is *satya*? Thus, you can call everything *satya* or you can call it illusion. In Buddhism, everything is *mithyā* and, therefore, *mithyā* is *satya*. To say everything is *mithyā* means that everything becomes *satya*.

Therefore, words like illusion, delusion, and so on, simply do not convey what is intended unless there is an understanding of what *satya* is and what *mithyā* is. To appreciate their meanings, you must know Vedanta, which means you must know what the statement, *tat tvam asi* means. And, unless you know *tat tvam asi*, you will not understand *tat tvam asi*! Thus, we have an interesting paradox here. If you already know, *tat tvam asi*, you need not study *tat tvam asi*. And if you do not know 'tat tvam asi,' how are you going to understand, *tat tvam asi*? It is for this reason that one needs a lot of *śraddhā* and a teacher who is well-established in the knowledge. It is not a simple matter. To study Vedanta requires *śraddhā*; otherwise, it will have no meaning whatsoever.

Vedanta can never be the subject matter of academic pursuit because it is based purely upon *śraddhā*. The *śraddhā* is in the *śāstra* as a *pramāṇa*, for which supporting logic is given. Only when Vedanta is looked upon as a *pramāṇa*, a means of knowledge, does it have a value; otherwise, it has none.

When I say Vedanta is a *pramāṇa*, you have no way of proving that it is not a *pramāṇa* because one *pramāṇa* cannot be dismissed by another *pramāṇa*. This is because, for a *pramāṇa* to be dismissed by another *pramāṇa* it should be within the scope of the other *pramāṇa*. But, what a particular *pramāṇa* makes you know is not available for verification or dismissal by another *pramāṇa*. For example, when I see an object as yellow and it is really blue, only the eyes can disqualify what I saw as wrong. I may still see the object in the same way, but the eyes alone have to say, not the ears, that it is not yellow, it is blue. Due to some problem in the eyes, I may not be able to see it as blue. No other *pramāṇa* has a scope here.

Once a *pramāṇa* is accepted as an independent *pramāṇa*, then it has to prove itself as a *pramāṇa*, as a means of knowledge. For it to do so, you have to give the *pramāṇa* a chance. If you do not give the *pramāṇa* a chance, you should not talk against it. You cannot establish that a means of knowledge is not a *pramāṇa* just by talking about it. This is an unreasonable position to take and a person who knows it as a *pramāṇa* will have no interest in refuting such a stance. You have not allowed the *pramāṇa* to prove itself to you. A reasonable stance can only be taken after you have analysed the *pramāṇa* and worked with it. But you can only do this if you accept it as a *pramāṇa* in the first place – and to do this requires *śraddhā*. Therefore, when you work with it with *śraddhā*, it works. Only then can it prove itself.

The *pramāṇa* says you are not a *jīva*, an individual, that individuality is just a notion. It says you are *param-brahma*, a statement that is not something to be simply swallowed. It is to be understood. Because the *pramāṇa* is saying something desirable, what basis do you have for any objection? None. Since the *pramāṇa* says you are Brahman, then until you see that you are Brahman, you should work with it. If you see that you are Brahman, there is no problem. And if you do not, on what basis can you say you are not Brahman? You can only say, 'Vedanta says I am Brahman. But I don't think I am and, besides, other people tell me I am an idiot. This seems to be more reasonable to me because it seems to be truer.'

When what is said by the *pramāṇa* is desirable, 'You are the whole. You are Brahman,' then you have to go for it. No one needs to tell you that you are not Brahman. This you knew long ago. That you are not Brahman is not something that you have to be taught by a scripture, a religion, prophets, or messiahs. The *śruti* is not telling you something you already know; it is telling you something you do not know. It says you are Brahman, which is something desirable. To hear that you are the whole is definitely not undesirable because the whole is exactly what you want to be.

Behind all your pursuits is the conclusion that you are small and it is from this conclusion that you seek to be free. The *śruti* tells you that you are already free from being small.

Therefore, you have no basis for saying that what the *śruti* says is wrong.

You cannot prove that you are not Brahman. If you could, then Brahman would be within the scope of perception and inference, which it is not. Perception and inference are the means of knowledge available to you, the subject, *ātmā*, whose essence is Brahman. *Ātmā* is Brahman. Because *ātmā* is not an object to be known by perception or inference, you cannot prove that the self is not Brahman. This is why *śraddhā* in the *śruti* as a *pramāṇa* is necessary. And, because you have to understand what the statement, *tat tvam asi* is, to be able to know it, you must go to someone who knows – a teacher.

You may say that if a teacher can come to know, then you also should be able to figure it out. But the teacher came to know because he or she had a *guru* and that *guru* came to know because he or she also had a *guru*. Like this, it goes on right back to the first teacher. Lord Kṛṣṇa said, 'By me alone it was taught at the beginning.' And it works – if you have *śraddhā* in the *śruti* as a *pramāṇa*.

Śraddhā is an attitude that enables you to say, 'The words are true; my understanding alone is not proper.' And if *śraddhā* is not there, you will give it up, saying, 'I have studied so many *Upaniṣads* and have concluded that Vedanta is just another trip. The *Upaniṣads* say that you are Brahman and other scriptures say that you are not. Which should I accept? They are all speculations. The very *Upaniṣads* themselves are contradictory.' In this way, you can dismiss it all because of a lack of *śraddhā*.

Without *śraddhā* confusion is inevitable

While writing an introduction to the translation of Śaṅkara's *brahma-sūtra-bhāṣya*, the author who had translated it as part of the Max Mueller Series wrote that Śaṅkara did not know the difference between Brahman and Īśvara. He based his conclusion on a few passages, saying that where the word Brahman appears in the text, Śaṅkara used the word Parameśvara and where the text says Parameśvara, he used the word Brahman. Translations by such people are very dangerous in that they totally miss the point. Whether the word is Parameśvara, *paramātmā* or Brahman, it is all the same. The word *jīva* can also be included, since *jīva* and Brahman are also one and the same.

Śaṅkara used the word Īśvara in the sense of Brahman as the cause of the creation, *jagat-kāraṇaṁ brahma*. Sometimes he used *paraṁ-brahma* and sometimes he used Parameśvara. The meaning is the same, as he explained very clearly. He used Brahman in the way he did because that is how the *śāstra* used it. The word Brahman is like that. Parameśvara is Brahman; Brahman is Parameśvara because he is the cause of the whole *jagat – jagat kāraṇatvāt brahmaiva parameśvaraḥ.*

When you accept the *pramāṇa* with *śraddhā* you do not dismiss what it says; rather, you doubt your understanding of what it says.

Because Arjuna had this attitude, he did not tell Kṛṣṇa that his words were contradictory; he merely said that they seemed to be contradictory. This is what is meant by *śraddhā* and you need it all the way. Because *mokṣa* is in the form of knowledge, you require *śuddha-antaḥ-karaṇa*, a proper mind. And for that, you require *karma-yoga*, which is based upon *śraddhā* in the sense that you want to know that you are Brahman. Because this knowledge is contained in the *śāstra*, you have *śraddhā* in the *śāstra* as a means of knowledge, a *pramāṇa*. The people mentioned in the verse under study have this *śraddhā*, which is why they are called *śraddhāvantaḥ*.

Those who have *śraddhā* are also described here as *anasūyantaḥ*. To understand the meaning of this word, there are two Sanskrit words we need to look at – *asūyā* and *mātsarya*. *Mātsarya* can be translated into English as jealousy. Suppose someone has gained something, some success, skill, wealth, knowledge, or some possession or other. Seeing the achievement of this person, another person may become unhappy. This unhappiness is jealousy. In Sanskrit it is paraphrased as, *parotkṛṣṭaṁ dṛṣṭvā jāyamānaḥ santāpaḥ mātsaryaḥ*.

The words, '*jāyamānaḥ santāpaḥ*' describe this jealousy, *santāpa* meaning sorrow, sadness, some affliction or uneasiness in the mind, and *jāyamāna*, meaning 'being born.' This uneasiness or discomfort that occurs in the mind is called jealousy. It can be seen even in the way the jealous person looks at the other person. This is *mātsarya*, jealousy.

Then there is *asūyā*, which means intolerance, another form of jealousy. *Asūyā* is when a person tries to find a defect in a person who has some virtues, *guṇeṣu doṣa-darśanam*. When a man praises the virtues of another man, you may say that he is praising him because he does not know him and you do. In fact, you have a long list of things to prove that the person is not at all virtuous.

Asūyā is the characteristic of always trying to find some skeletons in a person's closet – some lack, some blemish, in the person. You try to find some defect among the person's virtues or in the very virtues themselves. Jealousy is unhappiness, in different degrees, over the success or happiness of others. But *asūyā*, also an expression of jealousy, goes one step further and finds fault with the people themselves.

People who have *śraddhā* get liberated

Kṛṣṇa is talking here about people who have *śraddhā* in his vision, which is the *śruti*'s vision. Such people do not try to see defects in it so that they need not follow it. Those who attempt to find defects in the *śruti* always try to justify that what it is saying is not true. But this justification is always backed by a prior conclusion. Any justification is preceded by a conclusion. You conclude and then justify.

Even though the *śruti* can give the person *mokṣa*, still he or she finds some blemish in it. Such people will say, '*karma-yoga*? I have seen a lot of *karma-yogīs*. They suffer as much as I do! What have they accomplished? Nothing. They are still the same.' How does the person know they are the same? They alone know what they were before and what they are now; no one else knows. To say they are the same is nothing but the person's perception and that is not exactly a reliable criterion to follow here.

Those who have *śraddhā* in the vision of the *śruti* are different. They accept that *karma-yoga* will give them the *antaḥ-karaṇa* necessary for gaining the knowledge. Such people do not have any *asūyā*, meaning that they accept what is said by Kṛṣṇa gladly, and are therefore, *anasūyantaḥ*.

The verse says that they also get liberated, released by the *karmas – te api karmabhiḥ mucyante*. By *karma-yoga*, when these people gain *antaḥ-karaṇa-śuddhi*, they are able to assimilate the knowledge that 'I am *jagat-kāraṇaṁ brahma*.' And because of this knowledge they are free of all the *karma-phalas* standing in their account, that is, all the *sañcita-karmas*. This is what is meant by – *te api karmabhiḥ mucyante*. Because Arjuna wanted to be a *sannyāsī*, Kṛṣṇa tells him, '*sannyāsīs*' are liberated and *karma-yogīs* are also liberated.

There is no question of *karma-yogīs* being second rate here. The only difference between the two is that *sannyāsīs* pursue knowledge directly, to the exclusion of everything else, and *karma-yogīs* prepare themselves for pursuing knowledge. There may be a time lag for a *karma-yogī*, with reference to gaining the knowledge, but this will also happen for a *sannyāsī* whose *antaḥ-karaṇa-śuddhi* is not complete.

The point here is that knowledge has to be gained. *Karma-yogīs* are also *mumukṣus*. They also gain liberation. Liberation is not gained by *sannyāsīs* alone. Without giving up *karma*, *karma-yogīs*, as well as *sannyāsīs*, are liberated from all *karmas*. Thus, the word *api*, when taken to mean 'also,' can create confusion, whereas when it is taken to mean 'as well' there is no confusion at all.

Verse 32

*People who are critical of the
śruti's vision are totally deluded*

ये त्वेतदभ्यसूयन्तो नानुतिष्ठन्ति मे मतम् ।
सर्वज्ञानविमूढांस्तान्विद्धि नष्टानचेतसः ॥ ३२ ॥

*ye tvetad abhyasūyanto nānutiṣṭhanti me matam
sarvajñānavimūḍhāṁstān viddhi naṣṭān acetasaḥ (32)*

tu – whereas; *ye* – those who; *abhyasūyantaḥ* – being critical
without reason; *etat* – this; *me* – my; *matam* – vision; *na
anutiṣṭhanti* – do not follow; *sarva-jñāna-vimūḍhān* – deluded in
all realms of knowledge; *acetasaḥ* – devoid of discrimination;
tān – them; *naṣṭān* – as lost; *viddhi* – know

> Whereas those who, being critical of this (teaching)
> without reason, do not follow my vision, who are
> deluded in all realms of knowledge, and devoid of
> discrimination, know them as lost.

In the previous verse, Kṛṣṇa spoke of those who followed
his vision, his *mata*, meaning the vision of Īśvara, *īśvarasya
matam*. Such people follow with *śraddhā*, without having any
asūyā, without trying to find fault with the vision. In other
words, they are *karma-yogīs*. They too, *te api*, gain liberation
just as *sannyāsīs* do.

For Kṛṣṇa to have said that two types of people gain
liberation, *mokṣa*, is in keeping with what he said in the beginning
about there being only two lifestyles, *niṣṭhas* for *mokṣa* – either

sannyāsa or *karma-yoga*. There is no third *niṣṭha* at all. Whether one is a renunciate or a *karma-yogī*, liberation can be gained.

Throughout the *Gītā*, there is often a '*tu*, whereas,' indicating that a contrast, which may seem to be a criticism, is being made to bring out the point Kṛṣṇa was making. Suppose, for example, Kṛṣṇa had said, 'This particular thing will release you and is therefore good for you.' He would then also say, 'And if you do not follow this, you will have this particular problem.' In other words, if you have knowledge, you are free and if you do not, you have *saṁsāra*.

Here, the particle '*tu*' is to denote such a contrast. This particle also indicates an answer to a question, even though the question may not actually be stated. The question may simply be implied and the answer to it is introduced by '*tu*'. '*Tu*' is also used for emphasis. In this verse, however, '*tu*' contrasts people who do not follow the Lord's vision with those who do.

Jñāna-yoga or *sannyāsa*, of course, is too far removed for those who do not follow Kṛṣṇa's vision, whereas *karma-yoga*, on the other hand, is possible for such people. But, even this they do not follow – *na anutiṣṭhanti*. Instead, they perform *karmas* solely to fulfil their own *rāga-dveṣas*, without considering whether this approach can give them what they really want in life.

Human life implies the use of reason, *viveka*; it is not just a matter of doing whatever one wants. People tend to think that they have to fulfil whatever desire pops up in their heads. This behaviour is natural for an animal, but not for a human being.

If a dog feels like barking, it is natural for it to bark. The dog need not think about whether it should bark or not, nor does it have the discriminating *buddhi* to do so. Whereas, if you feel like shouting, you can always refrain from doing so because you have a free will with a discriminating *buddhi*.

Human life implies discrimination at all levels

In order to live the life of a human being, a person has to make use of this *buddhi, viveka*. Kṛṣṇa was talking here about those who do not make use of their *viveka* – in other words, those who do not follow his *mata* because they have *asūyā*; they are *abhyasūyantaḥ*. To justify how they are living, they find some blemish or other with reference to Kṛṣṇa's vision. They criticise it, disregard it, and put forth endless arguments to justify what they are doing. Being critical, finding blemishes in this *mata*, they do not follow it.

With reference to these people, Kṛṣṇa says, 'Please know them, *tān viddhi*.' Understand those who do not follow this vision to be *sarva-jñāna-vimūḍhāḥ* – *sarveṣu-jñāneṣu vimūḍhāḥ*, deluded in terms of all forms of knowledge.

Such people are deluded about their familial and social obligations, which come under *karma-yoga*. They are deluded with respect to national obligations also. They do not even remember or think about the many forces, *devatās*, that are constantly at work to keep them going and towards whom there are certain obligations. All these obligations are disregarded by those who do not follow Kṛṣṇa's vision. Instead, they think that the family, the society, and the nation are obliged to them! They think that the society should protect them and help them gain whatever it is that they want and, if the society fails to do this, then the national government should do it.

People who think this way are self centred, interested only in their own welfare, which means fulfilling their *rāgas* and *dveṣas*, unmindful of the welfare and interests of others. Thus, with reference to *dharma* and *adharma*, right and wrong, they are deluded, *vimūḍhas*. They are also *vimūḍhas* with reference to *ātmā* and *anātmā*, what is real and not real, what is true and not true. With reference to all human pursuits *dharma*, *artha*, *kāma*, and *mokṣa*, they are *vimūḍhas*. Even with reference to eating, they are deluded – they do not know what to eat, what not to eat, how much to eat, and so on. Without becoming a faddist, a person should know the basics of what is important in life. But, for these people, delusion is rampant; it exists everywhere. This is the meaning of *sarva* in the expression, *sarva-jñāna-vimūḍhāḥ*. At all levels of understanding, there is delusion. Thus, we are to know that the people being discussed here are totally deluded.

At all levels of understanding there is *viveka* involved. This *viveka* has to be applied with reference to performing actions and responding to situations. When people do not have *viveka*, we should understand that they are deluded. Their delusion is not in terms of having a low IQ. If such were the case, we would not be talking about them at all. Their only problem is that they lack discrimination in the sense that they have the capacity to discriminate, but they do not make use of it. Therefore, they are *avivekīs*. Kṛṣṇa referred to them as *acetasaḥ*. And because they lack discrimination, they are deluded in every way.

Such people are to be understood as lost. So he says, *tān naṣṭān viddhi* – know them to be lost. *Naṣṭa* is one who is lost to everything; one who does not get what is to be gained in this world. Even though the people being discussed here may have money and power, from the standpoint of *viveka*, from the standpoint of what they really want, they are definitely *naṣṭas*. If, in the process of gaining money and power, a number of conflicts are also gained, one has to question whether the money and power are worth having.

A *vivekī* is one who always thinks about whether what he or she wants is good for him or her. One may want money for one's own happiness and peace, but if, in the process, one also buys a lot of conflicts, sorrow, and sleepless nights, then the money is worthless to him or her. It may be useful to someone else, but not to him or her. If conflict accompanies any gain, the bargain is a bad one. How bad it is has to be seen and your ability to do so is always in proportion to the discriminative power you have.

A mature person, one who has *viveka*, is one who sees the immensity of the loss involved when something is gained. When whatever you want to gain involves a great loss in terms of your happiness, your peace of mind, *śānti*, you should be able to see the laws at work and refrain from the pursuit. This is what is meant by *viveka* and maturity. When you take all the pros and cons into account, you may find that what seemed like a good bargain is not really a bargain after all.

Thus, the *vivekī* is one who is not *naṣṭa*, lost. Those who are *naṣṭa* are lost in the sense that they do not get anything here in this world, much less in the hereafter. They are not dead; they are lost and this we are to know. In the second chapter, we have seen how this same idea was expressed. There too the word *praṇaśyati*, he is destroyed, was used.[12]

There it was said that, for the one who dwells upon a given object, *dhyāyataḥ puṁsām*, there develops an affection, some love, for the object. And what a person loves, he or she wants to have; thus, with reference to the object, a desire is born – *kāmaḥ upajāyate*. If the desire is fulfilled, there is no problem. Only if it is not fulfilled is there a problem.

Not fulfilling a desire is more common than fulfilling it. Therefore, the unfulfilled desire leads to *krodha*, anger. And once anger comes, you are lost. Among other things, anger brings about an inner torpor and prevents you from understanding the true situation. Whatever you had learned in the past from similar situations is not available to you when you are angry. You may have burned your fingers before, but the wisdom gathered in the past is not at your service once *krodha* has overtaken you. In the midst of anger, the memory, *smṛti*, does not work and your discriminative power, *viveka-śakti* is gone. The knowledge one has with reference to what is to be done, what is not to be done, the *kārya-akārya-viveka*, your enquiry, etc., are all lost. That is, *buddhi-nāśa* takes place.

---

[12] Refer to the verses 62 and 63 of chapter 2 (Volume 2 - page 355)

When the *buddhi, cetas,* is gone, the person is destroyed, lost – *praṇaśyati.* Why? Because it is the *buddhi* that makes the person a human being. If the *buddhi* is gone, there is a problem. While we are to understand that such a person is lost, the loss is not an irretrievable one. At any time, the person can become a *vivekī;* therefore, he or she is only lost for the time being. This also we must know. Because of some grace, these people may again question what they are doing and thereby alter their course. Any person given to crime can become a saint. The possibility for change is always there because the person has a *buddhi.* But, for the time being, the people Kṛṣṇa was talking about in this verse are lost.

Śaṅkara introduces a question here in his commentary. Given that Kṛṣṇa had made his vision, his *mata,* so very clear, why do these people not follow it? What Kṛṣṇa had said is reasonable and well-explained. When the *niṣṭhā,* the *karma-niṣṭhā,* he talks about, has been so carefully reasoned out, why do the people not follow it? Why do they follow something else?

The reason given is that each one acts according to his or her nature, *svabhāva.* Because animals are programmed to behave in a certain manner, nothing can be done about it. Thus, when a donkey brays or a tiger kills, it is because it is their nature, their *svabhāva,* to do so. A human being also has a *svabhāva.* Some past, perhaps even a remote past, is there for the person and that becomes his or her *svabhāva.* The next two verses are particularly beautiful in this respect.

Verse 33

*Whatever one does is in keeping with
one's svabhāva alone*

सदृशं चेष्टते स्वस्याः प्रकृतेर्ज्ञानवानपि ।
प्रकृतिं यान्ति भूतानि निग्रहः किं करिष्यति ॥ ३३ ॥

*sadṛśaṁ ceṣṭate svasyāḥ prakṛterjñānavānapi
prakṛtim yānti bhūtāni nigrahaḥ kiṁ kariṣyati (33)*

jñānavān – a wise person; *api* – even; *svasyāḥ* – one's own;
prakṛteḥ – of nature; *sadṛśam* – in keeping with; *ceṣṭate* – acts;
bhūtāni – beings; *prakṛtim* – (one's own) nature; *yānti* – follow;
nigrahaḥ – control; *kim* – what; *kariṣyati* – will do

Even a wise person acts in keeping with his or her own
nature. Because all beings follow their own nature, of
what use is control?

Prakṛti is used to mean 'nature' here because cause is
involved in the sense that one's actions are determined by one's
nature. This applies to everyone, Kṛṣṇa says, even to a person
who has knowledge, *jñānavān api*. The only difference is that
the nature, the *prakṛti*, of a wise person is good and, therefore,
his or her actions will be good. This is the idea being conveyed
here. And, if even a *jñānī*, a person of knowledge, performs
actions according to his or her own *svabhāva*, nature, what
control is possible?

Action in keeping with one's own *svabhāva* applies to all
living beings, including trees. If a tree is a sandalwood tree, the
whole tree will have a particular aroma, not just its flowers alone.

Every tree, flower, plant, insect, bird, animal, and human being, including the *jñānī*, behaves and acts according to *prakṛti– prakṛtiṁ yānti bhūtāni.*

Prakṛti being what it is, neither the doer of the action nor anyone else can control it. Kṛṣṇa himself cannot control it, as Śaṅkara points out in his commentary. This is because the person has been given free will, which gives him or her the capacity to say no to anything. Therefore, what is there that can control it – *nigrahaḥ kiṁ kariṣyati?* Unless one listens to Kṛṣṇa's vision and decides to behave differently, how is one going to stop a particular behaviour or action? And if the person chooses not to listen, there is no 'don't' that can control what such a person does.

Because everyone acts in keeping with his or her *svabhāva,* no control is possible, be it Kṛṣṇa's or the person's own control. Even if the *guru* says to stop a particular behaviour, how is the person going to stop? All that will happen is that he or she will continue the behaviour stealthily. The *Gītā* also is incapable of controlling the person since it is his or her *svabhāva* to act in such a way.

However, if everyone behaves according to his or her own nature, are we not going to have a problem? Where is free will in all this? If everyone were in the hands of *prakṛti* doing whatever is to be done according to his or her nature, no one would have any say over his or her action. Of what use is free will then?

If free will is not a factor, there is no such thing as right and wrong. For right and wrong to be, free will must have a sphere and, if all action is in keeping with *prakṛti*, there is no such sphere. So there seems, then, to be no scope for *dharma-śāstra* in all of this. If free will is not involved, what is the use of such statements as, 'Go to a *guru* and listen,' 'Do this or that; otherwise you will get into trouble,' 'Do this and you will get this,' and so on? All such advice, along with the entire *dharma-śāstra* and *vedānta-śāstra*, would have no usefulness.

Since you have free will, these books do have a usefulness. Therefore, the guru can say, 'Do this and don't do that.' The Veda says not to eat meat, drink alcohol, or hurt another person. These are all mandates of the *śāstra*. But they are not simply arbitrary mandates. Why certain things should be done and other things should not be done is explained in a most reasonable way and the necessary rationales are presented. But to whom are these reasonable mandates given? If everyone is behaving according to one's own nature, why is there a *dharma-śāstra* at all?

The animals do not have a *dharma-śāstra* because they behave according to their nature. Animals also do not have any will. Even if you nicely ask a tiger not to kill anyone, it may pounce on you because it thinks you are going to attack it. Nor can you ask a cat not to mew. It will simply keep on mewing. This is why such creatures do not have books on ethics and scriptures. Nor do they join any congregation, let alone work for *mokṣa*.

The mandates are addressed only to human beings because they have free will. But, here, Kṛṣṇa was saying that each one behaves according to his or her *prakṛti* and nothing can stop it.

This came like a big bombshell for Arjuna because he had always thought that he should do something. Now Kṛṣṇa was saying, 'No, no. You just go by your *prakṛti* because nothing can stop it anyway.' What does this all mean? Here there is something that we need to understand and Kṛṣṇa explains in the next verse.

Verse 34

Likes and dislikes are there towards every object

इन्द्रियस्येन्द्रियस्यार्थे रागद्वेषौ व्यवस्थितौ ।
तयोर्न वशमागच्छेत्तौ ह्यस्य परिपन्थिनौ ॥ ३४ ॥

indriyasyendriyasyārthe rāgadveṣau vyavasthitau
tayorna vaśam āgacchettau hyasya paripanthinau (34)

indriyasya indriyasya arthe – with reference to the object of every sense organ; *rāga-dveṣau* – attachment and aversion; *vyavasthitau* – are there; *tayoḥ* – of these two; *vaśam* – spell; *na āgacchet* – may one not come under; *hi* – because; *tau* – these two; *asya* – one's; *paripanthinau* – enemies

There are longing and aversion (potential) in every sense object. May one not come under the spell of these two because they are one's enemies.

Repetition of the word *indriyasya* here is an example of a language style used in Sanskrit, called *vīpsā*. First, let us take the expression *indriyasya arthe* – with reference to an object, *arthe* of a given sense organ *indriyasya*; in other words, a sense object. By repeating the word *indriyasya*, in the phrase, *indriyasya indriyasya arthe*, the meaning conveyed is, with reference to every sense object. The repetition conveys the meaning of 'every.'

The verse tells us that, with reference to every sense object, there are two factors present – *rāga* and *dveṣa*, likes and dislikes. This verse is the key to everything that has been said thus far and contains the entire psychology of the *Gītā*. The senses themselves do not have an aversion or an attachment to the sense objects. They are merely reporters. What is said here is that with reference to every sense object, there can be *rāga* or *dveṣa* on the part of a human being – *indriyasya indriyasya arthe rāga-dveṣau vyavasthitau.* This is a statement of fact.

May you not come under the spell of likes and dislikes

With reference to any sense object – sound, *śabda*; touch, *sparśa*; form or colour, *rūpa*; taste, *rasa*; or smell, *gandha* – there are likes and dislikes. Everyone has his or her own likes and dislikes, even the *devas*. Angels also have their own likes and dislikes. And why are these likes and dislikes present? Because of *prakṛti*, one's own nature. In this, you have no say at all.

This is why when you tell someone, 'I love you,' and the person asks, 'Why?' you can only invent an answer! You do not really know why you love a person. Although one can say it is without reason, there is definitely a reason. So, if you look into your psyche and ask yourself what is it that makes you like a particular person, you will find a reason. This is why everyone has a person to like. In fact, he or she has been looking for that person. So many others came before, but not this one. Then, suddenly the person appeared and there was an electrifying experience.

All that can be said is that you love someone because of your *svabhāva*, which can be called your subconscious. There is something, causing you to love the person. The subconscious is the *prakṛti*, which may be the result of one's own past. If a man has to live his life with a certain woman or if a woman has to live her life with this man, however miserable the person may be, there will be a liking for the person and the Lord alone knows why!

Being married to and living with another person is no joke. It is something that is definitely going to change the person's life. Both pain and pleasure will be there, depending upon who the person is. And why did you choose this person from among all the other people in the world? You cannot say that the Pizza Hut where you first met was responsible! You have seen many people in the Pizza Hut and nothing happened. If you had not met there, you would have met somewhere else. So it is not a particular place that is responsible. This particular meeting took place because of something within yourself. That which connects two people in this way is called *karma*.

Śaṅkara says that *karma*, *prārabdha-karma*, plays a role – *saṁskāra*s of *dharma* and *adharma*, *puṇya* and *pāpa* being there in everyone. This is why one person likes another person. In this life too, from childhood onwards, one picks up a lot of likes and dislikes unknown to oneself. These are all buried in the person's subconscious and this 'sub,' like a submarine, will also surface. And it always surfaces at the right time.

In the previous verse, Kṛṣṇa said that everyone acts in accordance with his or her own nature. One expresses one's nature in terms of *rāgas* and *dveṣas*, over which no control is possible. In the present verse, in the second line, free will is brought in, 'Do not come under the spell of these two likes and dislikes, *tayoḥ vaśam na āgacchet.*'

Kṛṣṇa did not say, 'do not have likes and dislikes.' Such a statement would have been meaningless. He was simply saying, 'May you not come under their spell.'

You cannot avoid having certain thoughts

The mind behaves according to its own logic. It is meaningless to tell someone not to entertain a particular thought. The more the person tries not to have this thought,the more he or she will have it. In fact, it may even become an obsession, a fixation. If you try to avoid anything, in the name of avoiding it, it is necessarily right there in your mind. For example, if I tell a man that when he chants a particular *mantra*, he should not think of a monkey, what will happen? Because he wants to follow my advice, before chanting the *mantra* he will remember my advice, 'Don't think of a monkey.' In order to avoid thinking of a monkey, he must think of the very thing that he is to avoid – monkey! And, after some time, he will not just see one monkey; he will see all the varieties of monkeys he has seen in his life.

If I ask you to think of a monkey, only one monkey will come to mind. One that has previously created an impact on your mind. One person may think of a rhesus monkey or an Indian monkey. Another may think of a chimpanzee or of King Kong. In any event, only one monkey will come to mind.

However, if you want to avoid the thought of this particular monkey, you would find any number of monkeys coming, one by one, starting with your own monkey, followed by a rhesus monkey, then a chimpanzee, a gorilla, King Kong, rat monkeys, and a variety of African monkeys! They will all come, one by one, all because you want to avoid thinking about a monkey.

To tell someone not to think of a particular object is meaningless. This is where free will comes in. The statement, 'Do not come under their spell, *tayoḥ vaśam na āgacchet*, implies your will. Problems always arise when we try to avoid the thoughts themselves. Some people spend their lifetime trying to avoid certain thoughts because they are told that some thoughts are good and others are bad. In the process, they remain stuck with the very thoughts they are trying to avoid! In fact, these thoughts have nothing to do with you; they have only to do with *prakṛti*.

Therefore, what can you do about thoughts? If a commoner happens to see a princess and develops a *rāga*, a desire, for her, what is he to do? Because of his status, he cannot even enter the palace and yet he has a great love for the princess. He can love her alright, but he can hardly proceed on that love.

What control do you have over liking a person? None. Nor should you have any control. In fact, you should leave it alone because if you try to control it, you will be in trouble. You will be meddling with your mind and when you rub against your mind, you rub against nature. And in this process you get rubbed too.

Some of our modern spiritual literature is replete with statements declaring that you should avoid having certain thoughts. There are so many do's and don'ts that a seeker becomes nothing but a pack of nerves! Prior to becoming a seeker, the person was much more acceptable to himself or herself, but after reading so many books, the person finds so much garbage in his or her mind. Because *mokṣa* is beyond all concepts of good and bad and beyond concepts themselves, cultivating and avoiding good and bad thoughts becomes meaningless. All thought is *prakṛti*.

Use your free will to do what is right and avoid what is wrong

And how is your will involved here? Will is not to determine what you should and should not think, but how far you should go with the thoughts that arise. Your activities are not caused by the likes and dislikes appearing in your mind but by your identification with them. Because you are identified with your *rāga-dveṣas*, you go along with them –'you' being the will.

The commoner who discovered a love for the princess just leaves his *rāga* alone if he is an intelligent man, that is, if he is a *vivekī*, one who has discrimination. If he is not a *vivekī*, he will go along with his *rāga* and get beaten up in the process.

So, allow the *rāga-dveṣas* to be what they are. The mind is a beautiful instrument as long as you let it think and do not meddle with it. Otherwise, you will be in for problems. It takes very little time to become insane.

What is being said here is, while you can go by your likes and dislikes, you should make use of your free will to do what is right and avoid doing what is wrong. This is *karma-yoga*. Do not come under the spell of your *rāga-dveṣas*. Because, if you do, they become enemies for you. The *rāga-dveṣas* themselves do not form the enemies; it is your coming under their spell that turns them into your foes. When you are under the spell of your *rāga-dveṣas*, you do not do what is to be done and you do what is not to be done. In this way, *rāga-dveṣas* become obstacles for you. This means that likes and dislikes are those into whose hands you deliver yourself. It is these *rāga-dveṣas* that become your obstacles. Such likes and dislikes become binding and, therefore, enemies. Because they rob away your reason, they are likened to thieves and become your enemies— *tau hi asya paripanthinau*. Therefore, without worrying about what happens in the mind, simply go by what is to be done and not to be done.

Verse 35

Following one's svadharma, svakarma
is the basis of karma-yoga

श्रेयान्स्वधर्मो विगुणः परधर्मात्स्वनुष्ठितात् ।
स्वधर्मे निधनं श्रेयः परधर्मो भयावहः ॥ ३५ ॥

śreyān svadharmo viguṇaḥ paradharmāt svanuṣṭhitāt
svadharme nidhanaṁ śreyaḥ paradharmo bhayāvahaḥ (35)

su-anuṣṭhitāt paradharmāt – as compared to the well performed *dharma* of another; *viguṇaḥ* – imperfect; *svadharmaḥ* – one's own *dharma; śreyān* – better; *svadharme* – in one's own *dharma*; *nidhanam* – death; *śreyaḥ* – is better; *paradharmaḥ* – the *dharma* of another; *bhayāvahaḥ* – is fraught with fear

> Better is one's own imperfectly performed *dharma* than the well performed *dharma* of another. Death in one's own *dharma* is better. The *dharma* of another is fraught with fear.

We have seen that with reference to sense objects – forms, sounds, smells, tastes, etc., certain objects are looked upon as desirable while others are not. These likes and dislikes arise in your mind in the form of various types of wants, for which you are not responsible. It is here that the *śāstra* comes in.

Wherever there is doer-ship and enjoyer-ship centred on free will, wherever free will has access, the *śāstra* has its sphere of influence. The *śāstra* deals with *dharma* and *adharma*, right and wrong, *satya* and *mithyā*, the real and the unreal. All these are dependent on *viveka*, *vicāra*, discriminative enquiry, for the person who is free. Therefore, the *śāstra* is not deemed to be useless simply because the previous verse declared that each person behaves according to his or her own nature, which cannot be controlled.

This *prakṛti*, one's nature, is only with reference to the appearance of *rāga-dveṣas* in the form of various thoughts arising in your mind. It is true that your *svabhāva*, your nature, is responsible for the appearance of these *rāga-dveṣas*, but whether you go along with them depends entirely upon you. There are always certain governing factors for any course of action. What is proper, what is useful to you, what is feasible, all determine which *rāga*, which like, you choose to follow or fulfil. Certain norms of pragmatism and ethics, *dharma* and *adharma*, also have to be taken into account.

An ethical person need not necessarily be a karma-yogī

If there is an awareness of Īśvara in your choice of action, it is *karma-yoga*. Until then, it is simply the choice of a mature person. A mature person is one who has ethics, for which one need not have religion. Bertrand Russell, for example, wrote a book called, 'Why I am not a Christian.' He never claimed to have any religious leanings and even wrote, in so many words, that he had nothing to do with such matters. At the same time, this man was a clean person and the first to raise his voice against the proliferation of nuclear weapons. He was a man of great ethics without having any religion.

Any thinking person understands ethics. Everyone knows what others should and should not do to him or her; everyone also knows that others expect the same in return. Thus, ethics are born of common sense, not of religion, and can be understood more clearly and assimilated if the person has a certain degree of maturity. One's own experiences in life and understanding are enough to understand what is proper and improper. Thus, no one needs religious scriptures or mandates in order to be an ethical person.

However, the religious scriptures of the world add something to ethical values. They say that if you perform an improper action, you cannot get away with it; you will have to pay for it later. This is where the concepts of *puṇya* and *pāpa*, merit and demerit, come in. According to the *karma* performed, there is a certain result that comes to you. It is like a ticket you get from a parking violation, which is not going to be as severe as a ticket from a speeding offence. Similarly, according to the *karma* performed, there is a result called *adṛṣṭa-phala–puṇya* and *pāpa*. That there is such a result as *adṛṣṭa-phala* is additional information gleaned from the scriptures. But for merely understanding what is ethical and unethical, religion is not required.

A person can be ethical without being a *karma-yogī*. One becomes a *karma-yogī* only when there is an appreciation on the part of the person that Īśvara is the giver of the results of action, *karma-phala-dātā*. A *karma-yogī* is a *bhakta*, a devotee, one who does not look upon one's possessions as one's own. For such a person, a physical body is given, a mind is given, the world is given, opportunities are given, resources are given, skills are given, time is given, place is given. Everything is given.

Only when one appreciates the given, and also the giver behind the given, is there *karma-yoga*. Ethically, therefore, one can be clean, but this in itself is not *karma-yoga*– all of which has been pointed out.

Spontaneous action

If what is to be done by you at this time and place and what you want to do, happen to concur, then your action is spontaneous and no thinking is required. Also, when what is not to be done is something that you do not want to do, avoidance or withdrawal from such an action is spontaneous. Even if someone asks you to do it, your 'no' is spontaneous because you do not have any such inclination and, also, the action is not to be done.

Thus, with reference to certain *rāgas* and *dveṣas* there is spontaneity because you are in harmony with *dharma*. You do not rub up against anything. The laws are not being rubbed against; in fact, you are in harmony with the whole set up. But if your *rāga-dveṣas* do not conform to right and wrong, *dharma* and *adharma*, there is a rub. This is why Lord Kṛṣṇa also said here, 'Death in your own *dharma* is better; the *dharma* of another is fraught with fear – *svadharme nidhanam śreyaḥ paradharmo bhayāvahaḥ*.'

The choice you have is only with reference to what you are going to do, you have no choice whatsoever about what happens in your head. Thoughts just happen and you have no control over them. But whether you go along with them or not, is definitely subject to choice. *Svadharma* means what is to be done by oneself, one's own *dharma, dharma* meaning *karma* here.

In a society where the duties are very well spelled out, each person knows exactly what is expected of him or her. In the Vedic culture, for example, each of the four groups of people, *varṇas*, had certain duties, which were very clearly defined. For a person of a given *varṇa* who is a student, there are certain duties. Then, as a householder or married person, he or she has a different set of duties. So, too, for a *vānaprastha*, one who is preparing for a life of renunciation.

Although such clearly defined systems no longer operate in the world, one thing is clear – in any given situation, there is a certain response required on your part in terms of action and this becomes your duty. Duty is not something that you have to be told about by someone, really speaking. It becomes evident as you look at the situation that you are in and understand it as it is. In this way, what is to be done becomes obvious to you.

If you do not understand the situation you find yourself in, you can always seek the help of someone in order to understand what your duty is in terms of what should and should not be done. Someone who is more informed, who has more experience, or who is more capable, and placed in such a way that he is able to spell out your duties, can do this for you.

The concept of *svadharma* needs to be seen also in the spirit of this verse. In terms of one's own *karma*, *svadharma*, what is to be done is to be done even if one is destroyed in the process. Doing one's own *karma* is far better than doing the *karma* of another person, meaning that it is useless to want to do what someone else is doing. Do only what you have to do.

Suppose the goalkeeper in a soccer game decides to run like the other players do, because the ball never seems to come to him anyway, it would be a disaster. In other words, if he decides to do the job of the other players, even though it is his job to stand between the posts, it would not work. What is being said here is that if standing between the posts is your job, you had better do it. If the ball does not come to you, it means the other team is not scoring goals and, if it comes too often, you can enjoy the action. It is not as though you are always going to be just standing there. Sometimes, there will be some action to perform. Just because the other players run, does not mean that you should also run.

Similarly, the job of a bolt in a piece of machinery is to sit tight. But, suppose the bolt is teased by the piston that says, 'Why aren't you doing any action? I am the only one doing anything here. All you are doing is sitting there tightly. Why don't you do something?' Hearing this once or twice, the bolt may simply say, 'This fellow is just blabbering. My job is to sit tight. That's how my maker, the manufacturer has made me. Therefore, let me ignore what the piston is saying.' But, eventually, the bolt may think, 'Why should I not also move? I think the piston is actually making some sense. After all, I do sit tightly all the time while he keeps going. Should I not also do something? Then he may become my friend. I am also a part of the machinery. Why shouldn't I do anything?'

Having decided thus, the bolt has to struggle to move because it has been sitting so tightly for a long time. It tries to move one way and cannot. Then it tries to move the other way and begins to shift. Happily, it says, 'I am also doing now. I am also doing now. I am also doing now. I am also doing now...' Whereupon the bolt falls to the ground! Before any time at all, the piston also falls out and the entire mechanism comes to a standstill – all because of one bolt wanting to do someone else's job!

Can any job be said to be really better than another? Which is better for the bolt – sitting tightly or moving? Jobs differ.

One fellow's job is to sit tightly. Another's job is to move. One is not to do the job of the other person in the overall scheme of things. Because someone is working hard on a construction site does not mean that someone else has to do the same. Working hard is not the issue. What is to be understood is that there are different types of work. Sitting tight is also difficult work because, even though there is a tendency to move, you should not move if, for example, you are an orderly in an intensive care unit.

Similarly, each one has his or her own duty to perform in a given situation and that duty is only to be done by the person whose duty it is. It is better to die guarding your post than to do something else just because it is more convenient, more remunerative, more likeable, and so on. This does not work at all.

You see this problem everywhere in today's society. If you have monetary satisfaction, you may not have job satisfaction and, if you have job satisfaction, you may not have monetary satisfaction. You may love your job, but you cannot own even a small house. Paying rent is also a problem so that you find yourself still living in a one room apartment. If you have job satisfaction, but such satisfaction does not produce the money you need, what kind of job satisfaction is this?

A man who is in this situation usually becomes more practical when he marries. He gives up the job he loves and takes another. In terms of money, it is a better job, but now he is sitting in front of a computer all day long, the additional money providing him with no job satisfaction whatsoever.

Svadharma and satisfaction

When we see someone else doing something that seems to be making the person happy, we want to do it, too. But *svadharma* does not work that way. In any given situation, in any given position, whatever is to be done by you, whatever that is appropriate for you, that alone is your *karma*, your *dharma*. This does not mean that you should not switch jobs. Both, money and job satisfaction, are important, but a number of other factors must be taken into account.

If you are an artist, try to make money with your art. Produce something that will make money, something that is good. In this way, you will have job satisfaction and money also. This is the intelligent way to live; otherwise, you will have neither money nor satisfaction.

What kind of job is it, after all, that does not produce money? How can there be any real satisfaction in such a job? Your art will definitely be affected because being without the essentials of life that money provides, you will often be disgruntled. Your paintings will be angry paintings. The colours themselves will reflect your inner life. Of course, there are people who will like such paintings because they, too, are angry. So, you may even sell some of them!

In the verse under discussion, Kṛṣṇa also said that the duty of another is definitely fraught with fear, *bhayāvahaḥ*, when you take it as your own. This being the case, it is better to do one's own duty, to do whatever is proper and appropriate, even if it amounts to death, than to do someone else's duty. In this way, you will have the satisfaction of knowing that, at least until your death, you did what you had to do.

Also, if you neglect your own duty and do something else, you will be dying everyday of your lifetime. You will have nothing but conflict, regret, guilt of omissions and commissions. What was to be done was omitted, what was not to be done was committed – all of which is a living death. While you are living, you go on dying!

Exercise your choice

Even though you have *rāga-dveṣas* that have no connection with your *dharma*, you still have a choice. You can choose not to go along with your *rāga-dveṣas*. You need not have anything to do with them. The only connection there need be, is that they happen in your mind; you need only recognise them, nothing more. You can even be so amused by them that you will not need to read another thriller. Reading your own mind will be enough! Your mind can provide you with pages and pages of entertainment by your simply witnessing what is going on. But in terms of choice in action, you go with what you want in accordance with the norms of *dharma*.

One's *svadharma* may not be as productive, as convenient, or as pleasant as one might want. Duties are certainly not always pleasant; they can be unpleasant also. Nor may they be remunerative or convenient. But, you have to do only that which is your *svadharma*. Even though it may be *viguṇa*, devoid of any enticing, pleasing, fascinating, or satisfactory features, your own duty is definitely better for you to perform than the *dharma* of others. Because the *dharma* of others is not your *dharma*, it is not to be done by you.

So, each person has certain things to do and these are what he or she must do. One need not do what others do. The one common factor between your *dharma* and others' *dharma* is that each of you 'do.' The actions to be done differ, situations differ, expectations differ, but each of you do what is to be done by you alone. In this way, you find your *karma* becomes a *yajña*.

If you can appreciate the phenomenal forces in your life as so many *devatās*, as aspects and features of Īśvara, and not just dumb forces, you give them the status of deities or God. For instance, Sūrya, the sun, is not just an implosion that is taking place. It can be explained this way scientifically, but it is actually a blessing. That this implosion takes place there and not here is definitely a blessing! It is also a blessing that the sun rises in the morning. As a part of the whole *jagat*, as the centre of the entire system, the sun is a blessing. It is a blessing in every way.

Just as the sun is a blessing, so too is the air, water, earth, every plant, insect, and so on. The elements are all forces that can be looked upon as *devatās*. By recognising them as such, you need not tell yourself that you should work for the welfare of people. It will be spontaneous because, by recognising these forces that are working for you, you will automatically recognise fellow beings and living creatures. With this sensitivity, you will not need to be told to be kind to people, to be appreciative of their needs, to do unto others what you would have them do unto you. By being able to include the *devatās*, all others are naturally included.

The books that talk about conduct and values, the *dharma-śāstra*, recognise this fact. If, for example, you cut a tree for any purpose, the *dharma-śāstra* says that, you should plant and care for ten more trees. This is to ensure that at least one of the ten will survive. I am told American forestry departments follow this rule now.

The principle of non-injury

The thinking behind this rule is that to cut a tree is to perform an injury, *hiṁsā*. There is nothing wrong with cutting a tree if it is necessary but, at the same time, there should be an awareness of the principle of non-injury, *ahiṁsā*, with reference to trees and all other forms of life. Jainisim is completely based on *ahiṁsā*, as is Buddhism to a lesser extent.

Mahavira, the founder of Jainism, highlighted *ahiṁsā* to such an extent that he instructed his followers to sweep the path in front of them as they walked so as not to trample on any insect that may be there. Also, the sweeping was to be done with feathers so that the insects would be removed from the path as gently as possible. When a person is talking, his or her mouth is to be covered to avoid bugs entering and being killed by the person. This is a kind of discipline and reflects an awareness that killing is wrong.

By creating certain situations, as Mahavira did, there is a symbolic heightening of one's sensitivity. A person, who sweeps the path before walking on it, out of fear of killing an ant, will definitely not be able to kill a fellow human being. This is what is meant by *ahiṁsā*.

Human values are all based on the principle of 'live and let live' and, at the same time, are much more than that. In fact, you live in the awareness of how others make your life possible and, in return, you too make their life possible rather than miserable. Their lives should definitely be as happy as you want yours to be. In this way, each member of the society performs his or her duty and gains *śreyas*.

The Vedic culture is based upon duty alone, according to the person's group and stage of life, *varṇa* and *āśrama*.[13] It was in the spirit of this culture that Kṛṣṇa intends to convey here when he says, 'To die performing one's own *dharma* is better, *svadharme nidhanaṁ śreyaḥ*.' If a man is a *brāhmaṇa*, his job is only to study and teach the Vedas, along with the performing of the rituals, religious duties, and prayers for the welfare of the society. If this is his job, he should do it, without comparing himself to someone else. That someone else also should do his or her duty. Remuneration did not form the basis for choice of duty. Duty was prescribed.

The results of abandoning one's dharma

Because many *brāhmaṇas* have abandoned their *svadharma*, there are very few people who are capable of performing the religious activities that the *brāhmaṇas* are responsible for. And these few tend to be those who cannot be engineers, doctors,

---

[13] Please note that the *varṇa-āśrama* system is not being prescribed to cure the ills of our society. The system itself has brought about many of these ills and no system can work forever. But the Vedic vision of this system has certain logic and spirit which is to be understood. The spirit behind the concept of 'duty' is still valid.

businessmen, soldiers, and so on! This is why the so called religious people of today are not truly religious.

Suppose, however, remuneration and satisfaction, are not the criteria in terms of what I do. Because I was born in a particular family and because my aim is *mokṣa*, I know exactly what is to be done by me. My life becomes a preparation for *mokṣa* in that it enables my mind to become mature, to gain *antaḥ-karaṇa-śuddhi*. Preparing the mind in this way is not an ordinary task. One's entire lifetime may be necessary to make the *antaḥ-karaṇa* mature, along with the numerous lifetimes that may have preceded this one. A person can reach his or her eighties and still have the old phobias and childhood problems that he or she had before. It seems as though one lifetime is not enough. And because each lifetime starts with the same innocence, we have the same problems for which there seems to be no solution.

If inner maturity is such an important factor and *mokṣa* is to be gained, what money do you need to have beyond what you need to live a simple life? Of course, you must be able to buy your food and other basic necessities. Therefore, the need for money depends entirely upon your aim. Because its vision is *mokṣa*, the Vedic society is based upon duties so that the mind may be purified and be able to grasp the vision.

If the aim is *mokṣa*, there is no competition. Which job you have is not an issue. And because you bring a certain attitude to it, you love doing the job that is yours to do. You know that what you require is maturity of mind and that by performing what is to be done by you, you will gain it.

Changing jobs is only necessary when the aim is money. Nowadays, there are even consulting agencies to advise you about which courses you should take, which field is currently open, where the easy jobs are, the better jobs, the more remunerative jobs. These agencies are staffed by people who earn money by giving such advice to others. The whole approach to learning and doing now has its basis in what will bring more money. For example, if a glut occurs in the field of Chemical Engineering, everyone becomes disinterested in that field and turns towards electronics. And when there is a glut there, those who were interested in electronics go into Chemical Engineering. Like this, everything keeps changing and people keep switching.

Duties and rights are one and the same

When power and money are the criteria, your whole attitude changes, whereas if *antaḥ-karaṇa-śuddhi* is the main aim, what job you do means nothing and how well you do it means a lot. Therefore, in the Vedic society, there are only duties; there are no rights whatsoever. In fact, they are one and the same. We see this also in the American constitution, or in the constitution of any country for that matter, where a person is granted certain rights, even the right to carry a gun. But, along with that right are certain responsibilities. You must have a license and you cannot shoot simply because you happen to have a gun.

Any right naturally implies a certain responsibility. You can emphasise the rights and spell out the responsibilities, the duties, which is what modern constitutions do. They specify the rights of citizens and then mention the duties associated with those rights. Or, you can emphasise the duties and not mention rights at all. When you emphasise rights, you have to mention the duties and enforce them also. But, when you emphasise the duties, you need not even mention the rights.

Why is this? If you analyse duties, you find that all duties are interpersonal and interrelated – duties towards the *devatās* or gods, towards the forefathers, towards parents, towards other members of one's family, towards fellow beings and all living creatures. In this way, you have widening circles of duty.

In India, even today, the emphasis on duty is reflected in a person's speech. If you ask a man if he can come to see you, he will not say he has to go to work. He will say he has duty. And if he takes up a new job, he will say he has joined duty, he has reported to duty, he is just coming from duty, this is his duty. This concept of duty is called *dharma, svadharma,* one's own duty.

Being a husband, for example, is a role that comes with certain duties. There is no such person called 'husband;' it is merely a role. Related to someone, a man is a husband to that person. And every role has a script, which is one's *svadharma.* As a husband, then, a man performs his duties according to the script, *svadharma.* In this way, his wife receives certain rights. Similarly, in her role as wife, she also performs her duties and, as her husband, he receives his rights. How can either person's rights be denied when each one performs his or her *svadharma*?

Similarly, as a citizen we perform our duties. The state also performs its duties, which become my rights as a citizen.

The citizen's duties become the state's rights. Therefore, all that we have are duties. Rights come to us as a natural consequence. But we do not go after them; we do not command or demand our rights. We try only to perform our duties.

Only when we do what is to be done by us is *antaḥ-karaṇa-śuddhi* possible. When our likes and dislikes are one thing and our duty is quite another, we put aside our *rāga-dveṣas* and go by duty. In the process, everyone gets his or her right and there is no fight. To demand one's right always means fights. One person says, 'This is my right,' and the other person says the same. Neither person will fight, saying, 'This is my duty!'

There is no demand in duty

Duty is either done or not done. In the concept of duty, there is no demand whatsoever, whereas when one's rights are emphasised, there is always an element of demand. And wherever there is demand, there are denials and counter demands, the natural results of demanding. This is because no one has the right to demand when he or she has not fulfilled the demands of the other person – 'When did you write to me that I should write back to you?' 'When did you take me out that I should take you out?' 'When did you phone me that I should phone you?' 'Why didn't you visit me when I was ill? Why should I visit you now that you are ill?'

Demand means there is always a rub in the form of a counter demand or denial. There is friction. We see this in our own homes and in the society in which we live. Daily life is nothing but demands and more demands. When people are always demanding, the society will naturally be a demanding one. We can see this by reading the newspaper columns – everything is one continuous demand. Even groups are demanding – teachers, nurses, doctors, patients, ethnic groups, males, females, states, and so on. The gods also seem to have become demanding. They seem to say, 'Unless you remember us, no rain for you!' 'If you don't remember us, BANG! an earthquake.'

When you have duties you will find there is amity. And because you can never fulfil your duties completely, there is also humility. But if each person at least tries to fulfil his or her duties, as father and son or husband and wife, for example, they will meet somewhere. In so doing, understanding is possible. Otherwise, there are problems. This is why *dharma* is called *mānava-dharma* or *mānuṣa-dharma*, the *dharma* of a human being.

Can there be any other basis for our interaction with each other that will benefit us all? If people are to live together, at home, in a community, in the society, or globally, this is the only way; there is no other way. Our *śāstra* goes even further and tells us to take into account all the forces. Cosmically speaking also, then, there is only one way – appreciating one's position, one's situation, one's station, seeing what is to be done, and doing it. Following one's own *dharma*, *svadharma-anuṣṭhāna* in this way, and not that of someone else, is the very basis of *karma-yoga*.

Verse 36

Arjuna asks a question

Having said all this, Lord Kṛṣṇa might have become quiet,
whereupon Arjuna asked a question:

अर्जुन उवाच ।

अथ केन प्रयुक्तोऽयं पापं चरति पूरुषः ।

अनिच्छन्नपि वार्ष्णेय बलादिव नियोजितः ॥ ३६ ॥

arjuna uvāca
atha kena prayukto'yaṁ pāpaṁ carati pūruṣaḥ
anicchannapi vārṣṇeya balādiva niyojitaḥ (36)

arjunaḥ – Arjuna; *uvāca* – said;
vārṣṇeya – O descendent of the *vṛṣṇis*, (Kṛṣṇa)!; *atha* – now;
anicchan api – even though not desiring; *ayam* – this; *pūruṣaḥ* –
person; *kena* – by what; *prayuktaḥ* – impelled; *balāt iva* – as
though by force; *niyojitaḥ* – pushed; *pāpam* – sin; *carati* –
commits

Arjuna said:

Vārṣṇeya (Kṛṣṇa)! Impelled by what, does a person
commit sin, as though pushed by some force even
though not desiring to?

Previously it was pointed out that there are likes and
dislikes with reference to every sense object and all you have
to do is not fall under their spell–*tayoḥ vaśam na āgacchet*. It
was also said that even though one's *svadharma* –what one
must do – is not very pleasant, it is better to follow that, than
to follow something else that is more pleasing and convenient.

Hearing all of this in terms of *karma-yoga*, Arjuna asked what it is that impels a person to perform an action that he or she knows is not proper. Some kind of pleasure may be there, but still the person knows that the action is not becoming and will produce sin, *duḥkha*. If the person did not know, of course, it would be different and understandable.

Why does a person do a *karma* that he or she knows to be an improper action – *kena prayuktaḥ pāpam carati pūruṣaḥ?*[14] Impelled by whom or what does he or she do this action? Posing this question, Arjuna addressed Kṛṣṇa here as Vārṣṇeya, one who is born in the family of *vṛṣṇis*.[15]

Arjuna described such a person as one who is as though, *iva*, impelled or pushed into performing improper actions by some force, *balāt niyojitaḥ*, *niyojita* implying a devilish force. Further, the person is pushed into it, even though he or she does not want to do it. The person knows it is not right, *anicchan*, meaning that he or she does not have any real intellectual value for performing such action. But still, it is done. Why? Impelled by whom, *kena prayuktaḥ*? This was Arjuna's question.

---

[14] *Puruṣaḥ eva pūruṣaḥ* – the word *pūruṣa* is the same as *puruṣa*, meaning a person.

[15] *Vṛṣṇi* – one of the name of ancestors of Kṛṣṇa by whose name the entire clan is known. Because he belongs to the clan of *vṛṣṇis*, he is known as a Vārṣṇeya. However this word can be interpreted differently. *Brahmānandaṁ varṣatiiti vṛṣṇiḥ samyag-bhodaḥ; tena avagamyateiti Vārṣṇeyaḥ*–that which showers on one the fullness of Brahman is called *vṛṣṇi*, the clear knowledge of Brahman, *brahma-vidyā*; the one who is known by this knowledge is Vārṣṇeya.

Duryodhana was once asked, 'Why do you do all this *pāpa-karma*? You come from a good family and have been brought up so well. You are a prince. What impels you to do such things?' In a verse attributed to him, Duryodhana responded, 'I know what is right, *jānāmi dharmam* and I also know what is not right, *jānāmi adharmam*. My problem is not that I have any innocence or confusion with reference to what is right and wrong. The problem is, that I know *dharma*, but I do not pursue it, *jānāmi dharmaṁ na ca me pravṛttiḥ*. And I know *adharma*, but I cannot refrain from it, *jānāmi adharmaṁ na ca me nivṛttiḥ*.

Duryodhana then went on to say, 'in whichever way I am impelled by the one sitting in my heart, in that way I do, *kenāpi devena hṛdi sthitena yathā niyukto 'smi' tathā karomi*'[16] It may have been a person or a force, but Duryodhana did not know who or what it was. Thus, Duryodhana and Arjuna had the same question, 'Who or what is it that is sitting in the mind forcing the person to do what he or she knows to be wrong, even when the person does not want to do it?'

Verse 37

Kṛṣṇa answers

श्रीभगवानुवाच ।
काम एष क्रोध एष रजोगुणसमुद्भवः ।
महाशनो महापाप्मा विद्ध्येनमिह वैरिणम् ॥ ३७ ॥

---

[16] जानामि धर्मं न च मे प्रवृत्तिर्जानाम्यधर्मं न च मे निवृत्तिः ।
केनापि देवेन हृदिस्थितेन यथा नियुक्तोऽस्मि तथा करोमि ॥ (महाभारत)
*jānāmi dharmaṁ na ca me pravṛttirjānāmyadharmaṁ na ca me nivṛttiḥ
kenāpi devena hṛdi sthitena yathā niyukto 'smi' tathā karomi (Mahābhārata)*

śrībhagavān uvāca
kāma eṣa krodha eṣa rajoguṇasamudbhavaḥ
mahāśano mahāpāpmā viddhyenam iha vairiṇam (37)

śrībhagavān – Lord Kṛṣṇa; *uvāca* – said;

eṣah – this; *kāmaḥ* – desire; *eṣaḥ* – this; *krodhaḥ* – anger; *rajo-guṇa-samubhavaḥ* – born of the *guṇa, rajas*; *mahāśanaḥ* – a glutton; *mahāpāpmā* – a great sinner; *iha* – here in this world; *enam* – this; *vairiṇam* – the enemy

Śrī Bhagavān said:

This desire, this anger, born of the *guṇa rajas*, is a glutton and a great sinner. Know that to be the enemy here in this world.

In his commentary to this verse, Śaṅkara discusses the six fold *bhaga*, qualities, possessed by the one who is called Bhagavān – total overlordship, *aiśvarya*; the strength to create, *vīrya*; all fame, *yaśas*; all wealth, resources, *śrī*; all-knowledge, omniscience, *jñāna*; and total dispassion, freedom from any sense of want, *vairāgya*. This *vairāgya* is not a *sādhana*, a means for gaining the knowledge; it is absolute *vairāgya* that comes with complete fullness. Therefore, Bhagavān is the one in whom these six fold qualities always remain in their entirety.

Everyone has these qualities in a small measure. All have limited *jñāna* and *vairāgya*. Certainly, with reference to garbage, almost everyone has *vairāgya*, although what is garbage for one may not be for another. In Bhagavān, however, each of the six qualities is without any hindrance or obstruction whatsoever.

Śaṅkara goes on to say that Bhagavān is one who knows about the creation and the dissolution, *utpattiṁ pralayaṁcaiva.* He also has complete knowledge of the good and bad ends of all beings. He also has complete knowledge about the time, type, and place of birth and death of all beings, *bhūtānām āgatiṁ gatim.* Whatever be their lot – pleasure, pain, *sukha, duḥkha* – he knows that too. He also knows knowledge and ignorance of the *bhūtas, vettividyām avidyāṁ ca.* Here the word *avidyā* also means *karma.* 'This is the one who is to be called Bhagavān, *sa vācyo bhagavān iti,*'[17] quotes Śaṅkara.

Improper actions come from desire alone

In this verse, Bhagavān told Arjuna that what impels a person to do an action of *pāpa* is but a thought. A thought itself is not a person; it depends upon a person. Therefore, it is not a real substantive. But, because the *ātmā* is with the thought, a thought assumes a certain force. This thought, Kṛṣṇa said, is *kāma,* desire.

The expression, 'this desire, *eṣaḥ kāmaḥ,*' indicates that it is something known to everyone. Thus, Kṛṣṇa was telling Arjuna, 'You can know this desire by looking into yourself.' When you ask why a person performs an improper action, do you really think there is some devil or something in there? You are the only devil. There is no other devil, no separate

---

[17] उत्पत्तिं प्रलयं चैव भूतानामागतिं गतिम् ।
वेत्ति विद्यामविद्यां च स वाच्यो भगवानिति ॥ (विष्णु-पुराण - ६.५ .७८)

upattiṁ pralayaṁ caiva bhūtānāmāgatiṁ gatim
vetti vidyāmavidyāṁ ca sa vācyo bhagavāniti (6.5.78)

This is another way of describing Bhagavān. We saw the first definition in Volume 1- page 42- footnote 5.

satanic force, sitting there interfering with Bhagavān's work. There is no second force more powerful than Bhagavān. You are both the devil and the angel here. It is your own desire alone and this desire is something that is very well-known to you.'

To say that a person performs improper actions, even though the desire to do so is not there, simply means that the will does not seem to have the force necessary to stop the want, *kāma*. The want becomes so powerful and your identification with the want becomes so complete that whatever wisdom may be there, telling you that what you want is not good for you, is silenced.

In this way, *kāma* can be very powerful. Desire is born out of *rajoguṇa* alone, *rajoguṇa-samudhbhavaḥ*, whereas wisdom is born out of *sattva*. When *rajas* is predominant, there is desire. Because *rajas* is a force, *kāma* is also forceful.

Kāma is said to be your enemy, *vairī*, an enemy being one who does what is not good for you. *Kāma* is inimical to you when it makes you go after things that you do not really want or need, things that you can afford to be without. In this way, it is your enemy.

Kāma also has another form – *krodha*, anger. *Krodha* is simply another stage of *kāma*. If *kāma* is destroyed in any way, if it is obstructed and not allowed to fulfil itself, then it will turn into anger. Arjuna was only too well aware of how this can happen. Born of Indra's grace, Arjuna was considered to be Indra's son. Indra thought he would reward Arjuna, who had been doing *tapas* in the forest for a long time, by sending the beautiful

Urvaśī to him. Urvaśī was a celestial damsel, the most beautiful *apsarā* in heaven, and therefore the dream of all men, including the men in heaven.

When Arjuna told Urvaśī that he did not want to have anything to do with her, that he was already married and that he considered her as a mother, Urvaśī became very angry and put a curse on him that he would lose his masculinity and become a eunuch. Lord Indra intervened on behalf of Arjuna and made Urvaśī modify the curse such that Arjuna would become a eunuch only for the period of one year and that he could choose the time when the curse would take effect. Later this curse turned out to be a blessing for Arjuna, since it made him eligible to teach dance and music to the ladies in the palace during the year he was to remain incognito. At the beginning of the thirteenth year of exile, Arjuna opted for the curse to take effect and became Bṛhannalā and spent that year teaching dance and music.

Arjuna had therefore experienced how desire can turn into anger. When Urvaśī's desire for Arjuna was not fulfilled, it became anger. A person whose love has been rejected can even become violent towards the object of his or her love. Rejected love means that *kāma*, want, is there. It is not like the love that one has for the stars, the moon, the sky, and so on. There one's mind has no demands as to how they should be or should not be. The mind totally accepts these as they are and enjoys them as they are. Therefore this kind of love does not cause any problem. It is not the case with a *kāma* that is demanding, and therefore binding. This binding *kāma* can be called by many names.

In the beginning, it is called 'want,' then 'passion,' and then 'anger'– all these are born out of *rajoguṇa*.

Kāma as *krodha*, anger, was referred to here as *mahāpāpmā*, a great sinner, because it is the cause of those actions that a person regrets for his or her entire lifetime. Such actions have to be paid for and *kāma* alone is the cause. *Ātmā* has nothing to do with them, nor do the body, mind, and senses. And although your ignorance has something to do with performing improper actions, ignorance itself has nothing to do with it. Who does it? Desire alone, *kāmaḥ eva*, does it.

There is also a *mantra* to this effect, chanted by adults and children alike. The *mantra* is, 'Desire did it, anger did it. Oh! Lord, my salutations – *kamo' kārṣit manyurakārṣit namo namaḥ!'* This *mantra* is repeated 1008 times on a certain day of the year. It is not just a prayer; it carries a message too. It implies that 'I did not do it.' If knowledge is there, there is no problem, which is why Kṛṣṇa said, 'Understand, *viddhi*, that this *kāma* alone is your enemy.'

As your enemy, *kāma* forces you to perform actions that you know are improper and that you do not really want to do. Just as Duryodhana said, 'There is someone sitting in my heart impelling me to do wrong actions, but I don't know who the person is,' Arjuna also did not know. Here, Bhagavān made it very clear that this person is none other than *kāma*.

Desire is insatiable

There is one more word given in the verse to describe *kāma* – *mahāśanaḥ*, one who is a great glutton. *Kāma* never says, 'Enough!'

Of course, its fulfilment may be enough for some time, but eventually the *kāma* will start up again, just like a glutton, who barely takes time to swallow the food being eaten before wanting more. This is the nature of want; any want is always replaced by further wants. There is no end to the gluttony of *kāma*, Kṛṣṇa said here.

To suppose that by continuing to fulfil one's wants there will be a day when none remains is not a reasonable assumption. Like fire, *kāma* always wants more; it will never say, 'Enough!' Therefore, there is no possibility of *kāma* coming to an end. It just goes on breeding. This is why we always have wants.

Verse 38

Kṛṣṇa tells how kāma operates

धूमेनाव्रियते वह्निर्यथादर्शो मलेन च ।
यथोल्बेनावृतो गर्भस्तथा तेनेदमावृतम् ॥ ३८ ॥

dhūmenāvriyate vahniryathādarśo malena ca
yatholbenāvṛto garbhastathā tenedam āvṛtam (38)

yathā – just as; *vahniḥ* – the fire; *dhūmena* – by clouds of smoke; *āvriyate* – is covered; *ādarśaḥ* – mirror; *malena* – by dust; *ca* – and; *yathā* – just as; *garbhaḥ* – foetus; *ulbena* – by the womb; *āvṛtaḥ* – covered; *tathā* – so too; *tena* – by that (binding desire); *idam* – this (knowledge); *āvṛtam* – is covered

Just as the fire is covered by clouds of smoke, just as a mirror is covered by dust, and just as a foetus is covered by the womb, so too, knowledge is covered by (binding) desire.

Even though fire is self revealing, *prakāśātmaka* being effulgent and requiring no light to be seen, still the smoke coming from the fire can cover the fire itself. In the same way, one's discrimination, *viveka*, knowledge of what is to be done and what is not to be done – is covered by *kāma*, which is born of the mind alone.

There are two types of *vivekas* – *dharma-adharma-viveka*, meaning *kārya-akārya-viveka*, what is to be done and what is not to be done, and *ātma-anātma-viveka*, the ability to discriminate between the real and the unreal. This two-fold is required to conduct your life. If you have *kārya-akārya-viveka*, then *ātma-anātma-viveka* will follow naturally. These two *viveka*s constitute knowledge, *jñāna*.

The mind, *buddhi*, that has this knowledge, *viveka-jñāna*, is covered by *kāma*, just as fire can be covered by its own smoke. Like fire, your *jñāna* is also self-revealing; therefore, it should be able to serve you. But, because it is covered, it cannot. When the *kāma* comes, it takes you over so completely that your murmuring wisdom is nowhere to be found!

Kṛṣṇa provided two other examples here – a mirror covered by a coat of dust and a foetus covered by the womb. The mirror and foetus are not seen, simply because they are covered. You can see the mirror but, at the same time, it is not clear at all. Similarly, you know an unborn child is there, but you cannot see it because it has yet to see the light of day. So, too, in the first example, you know fire is there because you see the smoke, you cannot see the fire because it is covered.

Simple viveka will dismiss many desires

There is a specific reason why Kṛṣṇa used three different examples to make his point here. Everyone has certain *kāmas* that rob his or her wisdom away, but only for the time being. With a little *viveka*, a little discretion, you can dismiss them. There are always so many fancies going on in your head, but they need not hold you for any length of time. It is like walking through a department store. You may see many things that you would like to buy, but you just walk away without buying any of them, which is just as well because, if you fulfilled every fancy, your home would become the department store! Such fancies take hold of you temporarily, but then, by some enquiry, *vicāra* – by considering your purse, by seeing whether you need the objects or not, whether you really want them or not–you are able to dismiss these fancies.

So, with reference to certain wants, all you require is a short *vicāra*. Other wants, of course, may require a longer *vicāra*. Mere *vicāra* may also not be enough; some force of will may be necessary to dismiss the desire. Still, you will come out the victor because you have the necessary will. You may have to say 'No!' aloud, most emphatically, if you really want to do a particular thing. For example, when someone asks you to go somewhere and you want to go but you know you should do something else instead, you may reply with a loud 'No!' In such cases, half the 'no' is for the other person and the other half is for yourself! This is why it comes out twice as loud. What this 'No!' is all about is so well-known in India that, if you say it when you are eating, you will be given one more helping of food!

Saying 'No!' requires will on your part. *Vicāra* itself is not enough. This way of dismissing a desire is likened here to the mirror that is covered with dust. To merely blow on it is not enough. Not only will the mirror remain dusty, it will become hazy as well. You have to take a wet cloth and wipe the mirror clean, which requires both will and effort. Similarly, not giving into your desires requires *vicāra* and will. Talking with someone who understands such matters, which requires effort, or some other action, may also be necessary.

The example of the unborn child in the womb is much stronger in that the time factor, *kāla*, must also sometimes be taken into account with reference to not giving into one's desires. It takes nine months for a child to be born. Similarly, it may take time to understand your desires and to gain certain mastery over them. When time is required and you try to circumvent it, the whole effort will be aborted. Therefore, you need to bide your time. The covering illustrated in this verse is binding desire and its modifications.

Verse 39

Discriminative knowledge – viveka – is covered
by the insatiable kāma

आवृतं ज्ञानमेतेन ज्ञानिनो नित्यवैरिणा ।
कामरूपेण कौन्तेय दुष्पूरेणानलेन च ॥ ३९ ॥

āvṛtaṁ jñānam etena jñānino nityavairiṇā
kāmarūpeṇa kaunteya duṣpūreṇānalena ca (39)

kaunteya – O Arjuna!; *jñāninaḥ* – of the wise; *nityavairiṇā* – by the constant enemy; *kāmarūpeṇa* – whose form is desire; *ca* –

and; *duṣpūreṇa* – insatiable; *etena analena* – by this fire; *jñānam* – knowledge; *āvṛtam* – is covered

Knowledge is covered by this insatiable fire of desire,
the constant enemy of the wise, Kaunteya (Arjuna)!

The word 'this, *idam*,' used in the preceding verse, refers to knowledge, *jñāna*. Here, this knowledge is said to be covered by the enemy in the form of *kāma* – *kāmarūpeṇa*, just as the fire, mirror, and foetus are covered by the smoke, dust, and womb, respectively.

And by what kind of *kāma*s is the knowledge covered? By the *kāma*s that are difficult to fulfil, *duṣpūreṇa*, and impossible to satiate, *analena*. *Anala* means fire. Fire is never satiated – the more fuel you offer it, the more it wants. All its tongues are out, demanding more. Therefore, fire is called *anala*. Like fire, desire also has no satiability. So it is referred to here as *anala*.

There is no such thing as fulfilling all your desires so that after retirement there will be none remaining. There is no such thing as a last desire, the last dregs of all one's desires. At no time can you say that you have only five remaining desires and that if you just fulfil these five, everything will be perfect because you will be *pūrṇa*, limitless.

All desires flow from our sense of limitation

Desires themselves are born out of *apūrṇatva*, one's sense of being limited. Every desire is an expression of this sense of limitation. This sense is like a perpetual spring from which all desires flow. New desires will keep flowing to the surface. Even if you have no particular desire at a given point in time, the *buddhi* will say, 'You are not even capable of desiring.' In the face of this new condemnation, you will again feel limited and desire to be free of the limitation.

The adjective, *nityavairiṇā*, meaning 'by the permanent enemy,' indicates that *kāma* is permanent. Śaṅkara provides an excellent commentary on the word *nityavairī*. Knowledge can be covered by desire, even for one who is mature and knows what is to be done and not to be done. This desire is difficult to fulfil and is both insatiable and inimical to those who are discriminative. And why is this enemy described as permanent? Śaṅkara goes on to say that even before the desire comes, the person is a *kārya-akārya-vivekī*, knows what is to be done and not to be done. But this knowing what is proper and improper does not mean that the person will act accordingly. Even the discriminative person, knowing a particular desire is not good for him or her may still try to fulfil it because the desire can be more powerful than the wisdom of discrimination. Because the person knows, both before and after, that a given desire is not for one's well-being, desire is referred to as a permanent enemy, *nityavairī*, of the discriminating people.

One who is not discriminating knows only later that the binding desire is useless, whereas at the time of desiring, the person thinks that to act on this particular desire will be wonderful; it seems to be the right thing to do. For example, a person who wants to make a killing on the stock market may say, 'I have a new scheme and I am going to make it work. In one month's time, you will see how great my plan is.' But, after the time has passed, all there is to see is that the person is broke!

'I should have thought it over,' the person will say. 'I never thought of the possibilities of loss.' Only later is there the discovery that the desire was costly, *anartha*, and, also, that it was the cause of the person's subsequent problems. 'If I had not been greedy, I would not have become involved in this mess!'

Śaṅkara says that *kāma* is *nityavairī* for the discriminative because it is a consistent enemy. Before and after acting, they know that the desire will not benefit them in anyway. Whereas, for the non-discriminating, *kāma* appears to be an enemy only after they have acted – the action not producing the benefits they had expected. Arjuna wanted to know who or what impelled people to perform improper actions. And, because Arjuna also wanted to know how to be free of that which impelled improper action, Kṛṣṇa told him how to deal with this *kāma*.

Verse 40

***Kāma* deludes the person by covering his or her wisdom**

इन्द्रियाणि मनो बुद्धिरस्याधिष्ठानमुच्यते ।
एतैर्विमोहयत्येष ज्ञानमावृत्य देहिनम् ॥ ४० ॥

indriyāṇi mano buddhirasyādhiṣṭhānam ucyate
etairvimohayatyeṣa jñānam āvṛtya dehinam   (40)

indriyāṇi – senses; *manaḥ* – mind; *buddhiḥ* – intellect; *asya* – its; *adhiṣṭhānam* – location; *ucyate* – is said; *eṣaḥ* – this; *etaiḥ* – with these; *jñānam* – wisdom; *āvṛtya* – covering; *dehinam* – person; *vimohayati* – deludes

Its location is said to be the senses, mind, and intellect. With these, it (*kāma*) deludes the person by covering his (or her) wisdom.

Kṛṣṇa had told Arjuna that *kāma* alone impels a person to perform actions he or she knows to be improper. A desire can be so powerful that the means employed to fulfil it is not even questioned by the person. Whenever a particular end is very important to you, you can always compromise the means because every desire is for an end only, not for the means.

Actions can become improper with reference to the means used for gaining a desired end. The end is very rarely wrong, whereas the means are often compromised because the end is so very important to the person. In some cases, both the means and the ends are wrong.

The villain in all of this is not a force outside yourself. Nor is it yourself. It is *kāma*, desire. The self itself is harmless. In fact, it is clean, *śuddha*. Nor can the body do anything right or wrong. It is only a place, a location. So too, the mind and senses are not harmful. *Kāma* alone is what creates the havoc. But *kāma* is only inimical when it is binding in nature. Thus, with reference to various ends, *kāma* is located in various places in terms of physical actions, perceptions, and experiences. Knowing where desire is located makes it possible to do something about it.

This is similar to how the police deal with thieves and other criminals. Investigation agencies keep records on habitual thieves based on certain repetitive patterns of behaviour. Some thieves enter only through windows and others open doors in a certain way. Some thieves pick up only certain things and leave everything else untouched. Each thief knows the places in which he or she can operate safely, meaning with less chance of being caught. People given to crime tend to be habitual offenders in two ways – in the types of offences they commit and how they commit them. All that is required to catch them is to discover their patterns, how they operate, where they spend their time, and so on.

Ātmā is free of desire

Similarly, when the place that one's enemy, desire, operates from, is known, *kāma* is easy to manage and take care of. Where, then, is this *kāma* located? It is not in the *sat-cit-ānanda-ātmā* although, *sat-cit-ānanda-ātmā* is in the *kāma*. Without the *ātmā*, there is no want, no desire, no condition of the mind whatsoever. Whatever the condition, pain or pleasure, *ātmā* is there. But *kāma* is not in the *ātmā*.

If you look into the self there is no want therein. It is always clean, untouched by anything. But, without bringing about any material change in the object, *ātmā* joins everything. If *ātmā* itself has attributes, *guṇas*, its joining with a thought would result in a mixture, a compound. A desire would therefore not be a discrete desire; it would be 'coloured' by *ātmā* which is not the case. *Ātmā* itself, not having any attributes, lends its existence, *sat*, and consciousness, *cit*, to anything obtaining in the mind. Therefore, *ātmā* is said to be free from want, *kāma*.

The body, mind, and senses also do not have wants as such, but the wants involve all these locations. Almost all the *kāmas*, the wants, are with reference to sense objects. And without the senses, these objects are not known and therefore do not become objects of desire. Naturally, then, the senses become the basis, *adhiṣṭhāna*, for the desires to arise in the mind. Therefore, the senses are said to be the *adhiṣṭhāna* of *kāma*. Through the senses, desires can also be fulfilled.

Without the mind, *manas*, there is no want; thus mind is also the location, *adhiṣṭhāna*, for, *kāma*. The *manas* is the one that creates the fancies that are the beginning of *kāma*. Because the decision with reference to the fulfilment of a want takes place in the *buddhi*, the intellect, the *buddhi* too is said to be the *adhiṣṭhāna* for desire. Thus, with reference to *kāma*, the *manas*, the *buddhi*, and the senses are places of operation, as it were.

When one's *kāma* is very powerful, it robs away the person's very wisdom, *jñāna*; it deludes the person. In terms of earlier acquired wisdom, the person is as though blindfolded by his or her desire and is taken for a ride. This ride can be a very long one also because, when you wake up, you find yourself elsewhere with all the damage already done. This is *kāma*.

The removal of delusion

What can you do about this delusion of desire? With regard to your mind, *buddhi*, and senses, the places where, *kāma* operates, be careful. Exercise your capacity to curtail or stop the senses whenever you want something that does not benefit you. Any sense pursuit can be stopped just short of overt expression, as in eating, for example. One can always say, 'Enough!' even when, from inside, the desire keeps saying, 'Come on, have a little more!' To stop a sense pursuit at the level of the senses is called *dama*.

We have seen that one has no control over the wants that arise in one's head because of one's nature. You cannot say, 'I want to avoid this want,' because you cannot avoid it. Your desires do not need to be controlled, in fact. Your *prakṛti*, your nature, is your entire past, the remote past and the immediate past–all of which can give rise to a certain type of thinking and certain wants. Your likes and dislikes just happen; you cannot do anything about them. What you can do, however, is to keep a certain distance between yourself and your likes and dislikes. In other words, you need not deliver yourself to them. This is what is called *śama*.

So, there are two disciplines, *dama* and *śama*, with reference to *kāma*. Although you need not worry about what you think, what you desire, it is also not to your advantage to do whatever you want, based on your desires alone. Therefore, do not fall prey to your simple fancies and wants. Always look into yourself and see what is proper. Is it feasible, necessary, and useful to fulfil a particular desire? Is it proper? There may not be anything wrong with the desire; it may be quite legitimate but not at all necessary. Or it may be feasible to fulfil the desire, you may be able to buy something that you want, but you do not need it. Then why buy it? It may be useful, but is it necessary to have this particular object? Instead of simply buying it, consider first how useful it is in terms of your priorities.

Having weighed all the factors, you can then go with the desire or not go with it. This deliberation is *śama*. And if, having gone along with the desire, you find that you want more and more, you then say, 'No, thus far and no further.' This is where you require *dama*, which can be practised daily whenever you feel like having another helping of food. Only when you practice *śama* and *dama* can you manage your wants. Otherwise, they will manage you and make a mess of your life. Therefore, taking the various factors into account, go with your desires, but do not let them make your decisions for you. To manage your desires in this way, you need to be very alert, as Kṛṣṇa points out in the next verse.

Verse 41

The practice of dama leads to śama

तस्मात्त्वमिन्द्रियाण्यादौ नियम्य भरतर्षभ ।
पाप्मानं प्रजहि ह्येनं ज्ञानविज्ञाननाशनम् ॥ ४१ ॥

*tasmāt tvam indriyāṇyādau niyamya bharatarṣabha
pāpmānaṁ prajahi hyenaṁ jñānavijñānanāśanam (41)*

bharatarṣabha – O the foremost in the clan of Bharata (Arjuna)!; *tasmāt* – therefore; *tvam* – you; *ādau* – at the outset; *indriyāṇi* – sense organs; *niyamya* – controlling; *hi* – indeed; *enam* – this; *jñāna-vijñāna-nāśanam* – the destroyer of knowledge and wisdom; *pāpmānam* – sinner; *prajahi* – destroy

Therefore, Arjuna, the foremost in the clan of Bharata! controlling the senses at the outset, destroy indeed this sinner, the destroyer of knowledge and wisdom.

In this verse, Kṛṣṇa told Arjuna to destroy his *kāma*, which had turned into *krodha* and had robbed him of his wisdom, which in turn would make him a sinner, a *pāpmā*. The *kāma* was to be destroyed in terms of giving it up, as Śaṅkara makes it very clear in his commentary. Giving up the want, not going with it, is the practice of *śama*. If you do not go with the wants as they arise, they will not continue to come up indefinitely. If someone keeps calling you and each time the person says 'Hello' you put down the phone, how long will he or she keep calling? Here, too, if you do not go with the wants, they will go because there is no one to support them.

In this way, whatever *kāma* that is there becomes meaningless. As long as I have a distance between myself and my *rāgas* and *dveṣas*, I can decide to go with them or not to go with them. Let them be there. They need not affect me at all. This is the beauty of what is being said here. We are not trying to eliminate the wants. We only want to maintain enough distance or space, to use the American expression, so that we can decide either to go with the want or not to go with it. This is real space, freedom, and is also the practice of *śama*.

Why is *kāma* called a *pāpmā*, a sinner, here? Because it robs you of your knowledge and wisdom; it is *jñāna-vijñāna-nāśana*. We refer to the people who rob us of our money as criminals, but such petty thieves cannot rob us of our knowledge, the greatest wealth we have gathered. Money can always be gathered again. But, because knowledge is not as easily gathered, it is considered to be our greatest treasure. Knowledge is something that is gathered, garnered, gleaned, over a long period of time from varieties of experiences. To take away such a treasure, therefore, is a great sin. Thus, *kāma* is called a *pāpmā*.

A person who robs you of your money is not a *pāpī*. This term is reserved for that which robs you of your real treasure, your knowledge and discriminative power – *kāma*. Knowledge, *jñāna*, can also be taken here to mean the wisdom that leads to *vijñāna*, the knowledge of realities. The one who is a destroyer of this *jñāna* and *vijñāna* is definitely a *pāpī* – sinner like, a criminal, in other words. Kṛṣṇa told Arjuna to give up *kāma* first by practising *dama* and then by practising *śama*. This is why people practice silence, *mauna*, for a length of time—for an hour, two hours, in the morning, and so on. People make these small vows all the time. The *sādhus* also practice certain disciplines, such as not talking or not eating on certain days. These practices of *dama* lead to *śama*, the capacity to sort out your wants and not go with what you want.

Verse 42

Discover the distance between yourself and your desires

इन्द्रियाणि पराण्याहुरिन्द्रियेभ्यः परं मनः ।
मनसस्तु परा बुद्धियों बुद्धेः परतस्तु सः ॥ ४२ ॥

indriyāṇi parāṇyāhurindriyebhyaḥ paraṁ manaḥ
manasastu parā buddhiryo buddheḥ paratastu saḥ (42)

indriyāṇi – senses; *parāṇi* – superior; *āhuḥ* – they say; *indriyebhyaḥ* – to the sense organs; *param* – superior; *manaḥ* – mind; *manasaḥ tu* – to the mind; *buddhiḥ* – intellect; *parā* –

superior; *buddheḥ parataḥ yaḥ* – whereas the one who is superior to the intellect; *saḥ* – is he (the *ātman*)

> They say that the sense organs are superior (to the body); the mind is superior to the sense organs; the intellect is superior to the mind. Whereas the one who is superior to the intellect is he (the *ātman*).

When Arjuna asked his question about what or who it was that impelled a person to perform improper actions, Duryodhana was standing right in front of him. Duryodhana knew that what he was doing was wrong. Arjuna knew this. These two men had grown up together, had been raised in the same way, and had the same teachers. Besides, right and wrong do not require to be taught. Duryodhana knew what was right and wrong, yet he did what he did because of *kāma*.

Because of *kāma* alone or because of anger which is *kāma* in another form, a person does things that are not to be done. Anger is not something separate from *kāma*; it is a modification, *pariṇāma*, of your own expectation, your own desire. Where there is no expectation, there is no anger at all. If you expect certain things to happen and they do not happen, *kāma* can turn into anger, if you are not ready to accept what faces you. Because *kāma* transforms itself into anger in this way, Lord Kṛṣṇa said, 'This desire is this anger, *kāma esa krodha esaḥ.*'

Kāma can express as want, passion, and anger, Kṛṣṇa said. And because this *kāma* covers your wisdom, it deludes you. It takes you for a ride. However, when you do not want a particular pursuit, based on desire, to go any further, when you are convinced that it has gone far enough, you should be able to stop it, to pull down the shutters on it. The dictating factor here is your wisdom, your understanding, and not your fancies.

Kṛṣṇa was not asking to suppress or repress your desires. He said that to attempt to control likes and dislikes does not serve any useful purpose because the mind has its own ways. But you need not be swayed by them. In this way, your likes and dislikes will be no problem to you. Since your desires are located in the senses, mind, and intellect, you can have complete mastery over them by discovering a distance between yourself and your likes and dislikes.

You cannot stay in the mind itself and have mastery over it. The more you go inside, the more reasons you find for why you are the way you are. This exploration may provide you some understanding, but it cannot remove the reason, which is the problem psychology is faced with. Some understanding, some validation, and so on, is useful, no doubt. But if you are always stuck with the same problem, what is the use of this kind of understanding? How can you deal with the problem? How can you master such a mind?

To address this concern, Kṛṣṇa said here that you have to go one step further – you must be yourself so that you can manage your mind. In this way, you will be able to take care of all your *rāga-dveṣa*s, your *kāma*s. You can take care of your *rāga-dveṣa*s or *kāma*s only when you are able to step outside of the *kāma*s. If you want to weigh something, for example, you cannot be inside of that which you are weighing. If I recall correctly, Newton was supposed to have said, 'If only I could be somewhere a little away from the earth, then I would be able to weigh the earth.'

Similarly, how can you fix up your mind when you are in the very midst of its mess? If you manage to solve one problem, another one will pop up in its place. If you discover, for example, that all your problems are due to your mother, what do you have then? You have the problem of having had this mother! Then you will ask, 'Why did I have this mother? Why didn't I have a better mother? Why did my mother behave like this?' Nothing comes of this in that you are left with the same problem. In spite of the benefit of some validation, some understanding, the problem itself does not really go away.

This is what keeps people going to therapists. And once they begin to go, the going itself becomes yet another addiction. It becomes something that must be done. Although some help may come from the therapy, another problem has definitely been created. Ultimately in order to deal with a problem, you have to step out of it, which is not to discount the usefulness of therapy as such. All that is being said is that you cannot really deal with psychological problems, within *saṁsāra*, unless you step out of it.

And how do you step out of *saṁsāra*? Arjuna already had one foot out, it seemed. By planning to go to Rishikesh as a *sannyāsī*, he thought that he would be stepping out of *saṁsāra*. But this is stepping in, not out. Stepping out does not imply any external change. All that is implied is a situational change in terms of one's understanding, wherein the distance between one's desires, one's likes and dislikes, is discovered; only then can the mind be mastered.

The order involved in mastering the mind

Whatever we master is always mastered from another standpoint, which implies a particular order. Kṛṣṇa was addressing this order here when he told Arjuna that those who know say that the senses are superior; so say the wise – *indriyāṇi parāṇi āhuḥ paṇḍitāḥ*, The word 'superior,' of course, implies comparison and thus the question, 'Superior to what?' To the physical body is the response.

The senses, *indriyāṇi*, are superior to the physical body, which is a part of an individual, a *jīva*. They are superior because they have the capacity to objectify the body. The eyes and other senses can objectify the body.

Another reason that the senses are said to be superior to the body is because they are subtler in nature. Being subtle, the senses have pervasiveness, *vyāpakatva*. For example, the body remains on the ground, whereas the eyes can go to the stars. To do anything at all, the body has to move, whereas the sense of sight, by simply opening the eyes, has already gone to the stars! Thus, the eyes and other senses are more pervasive than the physical body. The superiority of the senses is further established by the fact that they are inside the physical body in the form of the subtle body, *sūkṣma-śarīra*.

Then the verse goes on to say that the mind is superior to the sense organs, *indriyebhyaḥ param manaḥ*, because the mind can go where the senses cannot. For example, the mind alone can go to heaven. It can also suffer an imagined hell, which is something that the senses cannot do. Also, the mind is the one in whose hands the senses are. Without the mind there is no sense perception at all. Thus, the mind is definitely superior to the senses. It has access to regions where the senses have no scope. The mind's accessibility and the dependence of the sense organs on the mind definitely makes the mind superior, according to those who know.

Again, with reference to the mind, the intellect is said to be superior, *manasastu parā buddhiḥ*, because the *buddhi* is able to dismiss a doubt of the mind with proper understanding. *Buddhi* includes your will also. Doubting and vacillation are the mind. Once there is resolve, which is *buddhi*, there is no more vacillation. You cannot say you have both resolve and vacillation at the same time. Once the resolve is there, the vacillating mind, the doubting mind, goes away. Thus, the *buddhi* is definitely superior to the mind.

Recognising you are limitless takes care of your *kāma*

The mind and *buddhi* are the places wherein *kāma* moves. The *kāmas* are located right here. The difference between the mind and *buddhi* is only with reference to the types of *vṛtti* that take place there. We have seen how the desire, located in the mind, can be so powerful that it can take the *buddhi* along with it. Therefore, in order to really deal with your desires, you have to step outside of them. Then you can see exactly where the *kāma* is hiding. This is why Kṛṣṇa went on to say that the one who is above the *buddhi*, is *ātmā*, yourself – *yaḥ tu buddheḥ parataḥ saḥ paramātmā.*

What Kṛṣṇa meant here is that, in order to take care of the *kāmas* you have to recognise yourself as the *paramātmā*. Even though he said to practice *dama* and *śama*, you have also to see that you are not the *buddhi*, the mind, or the senses. You are the *paramātmā* the limitless. Once you are awake to this fact, the enemy, *kāma*, is no more a problem. This, then, is how you deal with *kāma* drastically and finally.

When you are free from any sense of limitation, there is no enemy and the wants you may have become harmless, mere privileges in fact. Your mind is there and you have the privilege of desiring. Desiring is a privilege only when you do not need to fulfil any desire in order to be secure and happy.

Verse 43

A karma-yogī and a sannyāsī has to deal with kāma only through jñāna

एवं बुद्धेः परं बुद्ध्वा संस्तभ्यात्मानमात्मना ।
जहि शत्रुं महाबाहो कामरूपं दुरासदम् ॥ ४३ ॥

evaṁ buddheḥ paraṁ buddhvā saṁstabhyātmānam
ātmanā
jahi śatruṁ mahābāho kāmarūpaṁ durāsadam (43)

mahābāho – O mighty-armed (Arjuna)!; *evam* – in this way; *buddheḥ* – to the intellect; *param* – superior; *buddhvā* – knowing; *ātmanā* – by the self (*buddhi*); *ātmānam* – the mind; *saṁstabhya* – having made steady; *kāmarūpam* – in the form of (binding) desire; *durāsadam* – difficult to understand; *śatrum* – enemy; *jahi* – destroy

Arjuna, the mighty armed! Knowing that which is superior to the intellect in this way, having made the mind steady with the *buddhi*, destroy the enemy, that is in the form of (binding) desire, that which is so difficult to understand.

In the previous verse, Kṛṣṇa revealed a fact – that which is above the *buddhi*, because of which the *buddhi* is illumined, is the *paramātmā*. And because a mastered mind is required to know this *paramātmā*, Kṛṣṇa concluded the chapter here by summing up what is to be done to destroy *kāma*.

The senses and the mind are in the hands of the *buddhi* alone because the *buddhi* is superior to them. Hence, the *buddhi* is their master. The *buddhi*, meaning one's *viveka*, discrimination, steadies the mind and senses, which is why he said, *ātmānam ātmanā saṁstabhya śatrum jahi.*

Here, Kṛṣṇa told Arjuna that he should destroy the enemy in the form of desire, *kāmarūpa śatrum jahi*, by knowing that which is above the *buddhi, buddheḥ parambuddhvā.* To destroy an enemy outside of oneself is relatively easy, especially for Arjuna who had so many special missiles at his disposal. But, to destroy this inner enemy, *kāma*, requires tact, maturity, dispassion, and understanding. To indicate that Arjuna had these resources, Kṛṣṇa addressed Arjuna as 'mahābāho,' one who is mighty armed.

The enemy, in the form of want, is an only expression of ignorance, ignorance being the mother of *kāma* and its brood – anger, jealousy, fear, and so on. Therefore, to destroy the enemy, one must destroy ignorance, which can only be done through *jñāna*, knowledge. This enemy is said to be *durāsada* here, that which is very difficult to understand. It would seem that desires should be very easy to understand since they just appear. But, this is not the case because every desire has a desire behind it. There is always a reason for liking something. And there is a reason for the reason. Therefore, there is no end to the desires that are there, all of which is to be understood. Only when *kāma* makes you suffer by its presence are you a *saṁsārī*, a sufferer. With knowledge, you can enjoy the presence of a *kāma*. Even if you are surprised by it, you can also be amused. You can either go with it or you need not go with it. When you step outside of your desires in this way, in terms of knowledge, all your desires become privileges for you.

Thus, whether you are a *karma-yogī* or a *sannyāsī*, there is no other way of dealing with *kāma*, except through *jñāna*. What better way for Kṛṣṇa to have made this point than to conclude this chapter, entitled *karma*, with *jñāna*, the only true conqueror of the enemy of desire.

ॐतत्सत् ।

इति श्रीमद्भगवद्गीतासूपनिषत्सु ब्रह्मविद्यायां योगशास्त्रे श्रीकृष्णार्जुन–
संवादे कर्म–योगो नाम तृतीयोऽध्यायः ॥ ३ ॥

oṁ tat sat.

*iti śrīmadbhagavadgītāsūpaniṣatsu brahma-vidyāyāṁ
yoga-śāstre śrīkṛṣṇārjuna-saṁvāde karma-yogo nāma
tṛtīyo'dhyāyaḥ (3)*

Om, Brahman, is the only reality. Thus ends the third chapter called *karma-yoga* – having the topic of *karma* – in the *Bhagavad Gītā* which is in the form of a dialogue between Śrī Kṛṣṇa and Arjuna, which is the essence of the *Upaniṣads*, whose subject matter is both the knowledge of Brahman and *yoga*.

The meaning of Om

All the chapters in the *Gītā* end with the above words, the only variation being the title of the chapter.

In the expression, '*Oṁ tat sat,*' '*Oṁ* is the name of Brahman, a phonetic name for the Lord. Apart from this, linguistically, that is grammatically, this term has a meaning too. It means, that which protects everyone, that which sustains everything – *avati rakṣati iti oṁ.*

Phonetically, 'A' is the first and basic sound that you make when you open your mouth. Thus, 'A' is the first letter of the Sanskrit alphabet. Also, when you close your mouth and make a sound, what comes out is the sound, 'M.' And, in between, there is a rounding off sound, 'U.' 'A' plus 'U' is 'O' which along with 'M' is *Om.*

All forms, objects, have names, and all names are words. Words, even the longest ones like 'supercalafragilisticexpialadoshas' are nothing but sounds. These sounds all come between the 'A' that comes when you open your mouth and make a sound and the sound 'M' that comes with the mouth closed. You cannot make any further sounds after this letter 'M.' Thus, these are the two sounds within which all sounds are produced.

Given that the Lord is the Lord of everything, his name should be '*Om,*' and to account for 'everything,' the 'U' is inserted in between. In this way, *Om* becomes the name of Bhagavān, the Lord. Also, each of these three letters has been loaded by the *śāstra* to stand for the whole. This practice is called *āropa* in Sanskrit. Just as a country's flag represents its constitution, here, the 'A' represents the entire gross world, *sthūla-prapañca,* the 'U' represents the entire subtle world *sūkṣma-prapañca,* meaning the mind or inner world, and the 'M' represents the unmanifest condition, like in sleep when everything resolves and, on waking, again comes out.

In this way, AUM stands for the entire realm of cause and effect, which is nothing but Brahman. That Brahman, *Om,* is *tat sat. Tat,* that Lord alone, is *satyam, sat,* and everything else is *mithyā* depending upon that *tat,* the Lord. Therefore, the expression *oṁ tat sat* is a general conclusion. Having said a lot of things, the conclusion is, *oṁ tat sat,* meaning that after all is said and done, *satya* alone is.

The *Bhagavadgītā,* which has the status of an *Upaniṣad,* contains the subject matter of Brahman. The knowledge of Brahman, *brahma-vidyā,* is simply 'You are that, *tat tvam asi.*' The *Gītā* is also *yoga-śāstra,* dealing with attitudes and values with reference to self management, self-improvement, maturity, and so on, which is *karma-yoga.* Even the rules of *sannyāsa* come under *yoga-śāstra* since they are not *jñāna.*

The nature of the dialogue between Lord Kṛṣṇa and Arjuna

This *yoga-śāstra* and *brahma-vidyā,* form the dialogue that took place between Śrī Kṛṣṇa and Arjuna – *śrī-kṛṣṇa-arjuna-saṁvāda,* the dialogue that imparts knowledge. The word, *vāda* means a discussion. A dialogue that imparts knowledge is different from a dialogue between equals, where there is no imparting of knowledge involved, only exploring of knowledge.

There are also two types of dismissing dialogues wherein the other person is declared to be in the wrong. One type is the dialogue of fanatics, *jalpa*, and the other is *vitaṇḍā*, the dialogue of the intolerant where one person cannot stand another person saying something and getting away with it.

The discussion between Lord Kṛṣṇa and Arjuna was neither a *jalpa* nor a *vitaṇḍā*. Nor was it a discussion in order to discover something. It was a dialogue that imparts knowledge wherein one participant knew and the other wanted to know. Therefore, it was a *guru-śiṣya-saṁvāda*, a dialogue between a teacher and student. This particular meaning is denoted by the prefix 'sam' added to 'vāda.' This chapter under study is entitled *karma*, because it deals with the subject matter, Brahman, in terms of *karma*. Therefore it is said, *karma-yogo-nāma-tṛtīyo'dhyāyaḥ*. As we have seen before, the word *yoga* used in each of the titles of the eighteen chapters of the *Gītā*, means 'subject matter.' Thus the third chapter, entitled, 'Karma' in the *Bhagavadgītā* whose status is that of the *Upaniṣad* which contains the knowledge of Brahman and *yoga-śāstra* in the form of a *saṁvāda* (a dialogue that imparts knowledge) between Lord Kṛṣṇa and Arjuna is concluded.

Summary of chapters 1-3

In the first chapter of the *Gītā*, the teacher, Kṛṣṇa, and the disciple, Arjuna, were introduced and the context leading Arjuna to ask Kṛṣṇa for self-knowledge, was given. Previously, Arjuna had only been interested in regaining the kingdom and settling old accounts with Duryodhana. Arjuna had no desire for this knowledge, and even though he had known Kṛṣṇa for a long time, he did not regard him as a teacher.

Arjuna had lived a life of *dharma* and a life of *dharma* necessarily leads one to ask fundamental questions about life. It had given him the necessary *viveka* to ask Kṛṣṇa, 'O Bhagavan, please teach me what is the ultimate good. I am your disciple.'

The first chapter described the battlefield, Arjuna's despair, and his arguments concerning why he no longer wanted to fight. Early in the second chapter, Kṛṣṇa tried to arouse Arjuna's enthusiasm so that he would do what had to be done. He addressed him as follows:

कुतस्त्वा कश्मलमिदं विषमे समुपस्थितम् ।
अनार्यजुष्टमस्वर्ग्यमकीर्तिकरमर्जुन ॥२-२॥

kutastvā kaśmalam idaṁ viṣame samupasthitam
anāryajuṣṭam asvargyam akīrtikaram arjuna

Arjuna! In such crisis from where has this despair come upon you? It is unbecoming of an upright man and does not add to (your) fame. Nor does it lead you to heaven. (2.2)

क्लैब्यं मा स्म गमः पार्थ नैतत्त्वय्युपपद्यते ।
क्षुद्रं हृदयदौर्बल्यं त्यक्त्वोत्तिष्ठ परन्तप ॥ २-३ ॥

klaibyaṁ mā sma gamaḥ pārtha naitat tvayyupapadyate
kṣudraṁ hṛdayadaurbalyaṁ tyaktvottiṣṭha parantapa

Pārtha (Arjuna)! Do not yield to unmanliness. This does not befit you. The scorcher of enemies! Give up this lowly weakness of heart and get up. (2.3)

Arjuna continued to explain why he could not fight, saying that he would prefer to live the life of a *bhikṣu* who lives on alms. This meant that he was thinking of a life of *sannyāsa*, that he wanted to renounce everything and seek *mokṣa*. He knew that a particular knowledge was necessary for *mokṣa* and that a *guru* was necessary for gaining this knowledge. Thinking that there was no better *guru* than Kṛṣṇa, Arjuna asked him for the knowledge, declaring himself to be Kṛṣṇa's disciple.

In response to Arjuna's request, Kṛṣṇa did not simply say, 'Stop talking and fight!' Had he done so, and had Arjuna followed Kṛṣṇa's advice, the *Mahābhārata* would have no *Gītā*. Instead, it looks as though Kṛṣṇa was waiting for such an occasion as this, to teach Arjuna. Otherwise, he would not have started with, '*aśocyān anvaśocaḥ tvaṁ prajñāvādān ca bhāṣase,* you grieve for those who should not be grieved for, even though you speak words of wisdom.' Nor would he have followed this statement up with, '*nāsato vidyate bhāvaḥ, nābhāvo vidyate sataḥ,* the unreal never is and the real is never absent.' In fact, Kṛṣṇa covered the entire teaching in the second chapter, talking about knowledge and about *karma-yoga* – how one has to live

one's life in a manner that helps one gain certain freedom from
the hold of likes and dislikes.

Then, towards the end of the chapter, Arjuna asked Kṛṣṇa
to describe a person who is established in this knowledge:

स्थितप्रज्ञस्य का भाषा समाधिस्थस्य केशव ।
स्थितधीः किं प्रभाषेत किमासीत व्रजेत किम् ॥ २-५४ ॥

sthitaprajñasya kā bhāṣā samādhisthasya keśava
sthitadhīḥ kiṁ prabhāṣeta kimāsīta vrajeta kim (2.54)

Keśava (Kṛṣṇa)! What is the description of a person of
firm wisdom, one whose mind abides in the self?
How does such a person, whose mind is not shaken
by anything, speak, sit, and walk? (2.54)

In asking Kṛṣṇa to describe a *sthitaprajña*, wise person,
Arjuna indicated that the description should cover how the
person walks, talks, and sits. Kṛṣṇa saw the spirit of Arjuna's
question and defined a *sthitaprajña* in these words:

प्रजहाति यदा कामान्सर्वान्पार्थ मनोगतान् ।
आत्मन्येवात्मना तुष्टः स्थितप्रज्ञस्तदोच्यते ॥ २-५५ ॥

prajahāti yadā kāmān sarvān pārtha manogatān
ātmanyevātmanā tuṣṭaḥ sthitaprajñastadocyate

When a person gives up all the desires as they appear
in the mind, happy in oneself with oneself alone,
Pārtha (Arjuna) that person is said to be one of
ascertained knowledge. (2.55)

दुःखेष्वनुद्विग्नमनाः सुखेषु विगतस्पृहः ।
वीतरागभयक्रोधः स्थितधीर्मुनिरुच्यते ॥ २-५६ ॥

duḥkheṣvanudvignamanāḥ sukheṣu vigataspṛhaḥ
vītarāgabhayakrodhaḥ sthitadhīrmunirucyate

The one who is not affected by adversities, who is
without yearning for pleasures, and is free from
longing, fear and anger, is said to be a wise person
whose knowledge stays (unshaken).(2.56)

यः सर्वत्रानभिस्नेहस्तत्तत्प्राप्य शुभाशुभम् ।
नाभिनन्दति न द्वेष्टि तस्य प्रज्ञा प्रतिष्ठिता ॥ २-५७ ॥

yaḥ sarvatrānabhisnehastattat prāpya śubhāśubham
nābhinandati na dveṣṭi tasya prajñā pratiṣṭhitā

The one who is unattached in all situations, who
neither rejoices on gaining the pleasant nor hates the
unpleasant, his knowledge is well-established. (2.57)

यदा संहरते चायं कूर्मोऽङ्गानीव सर्वशः ।
इन्द्रियाणीन्द्रियार्थेभ्यस्तस्य प्रज्ञा प्रतिष्ठिता ॥ २-५८ ॥

yadā saṁharate cāyaṁ kūrmo'ṅgānīva sarvaśaḥ
indriyāṇīndriyārthebhyastasya prajñā pratiṣṭhitā

When, like the turtle that withdraws its limbs, this
person is able to completely withdraw the sense organs
from their objects, his knowledge is steady. (2-58)

We see here that Kṛṣṇa, appreciating the spirit of Arjuna's
question, converted it into, 'How does a wise person interact

with the world?' A *sthitaprajña*, Kṛṣṇa said, is one whose knowledge is steady, meaning one whose knowledge leaves nothing to be desired. Such a person is happy with oneself and does not require anything other than the self in order to be happy. The person is also not afraid of anything. When unpleasant situations occur, he or she faces them without being adversely affected in any way. Nor is such a person elated when pleasant situations occur.

The spontaneous expressions of the wisdom of a wise person become *sādhanas* values or disciplines for the seeker, which is why Arjuna was interested in the qualities of a wise person. Kṛṣṇa described all these qualities to Arjuna. He also told Arjuna of certain obstacles to gaining this wisdom, such as, how by dwelling upon certain objects, *viṣaya-dhyāna*, we give them subjective attributes in addition to those attributes that the objects already have.

For instance, as long as you look upon money as simply a buying power, there is no problem. However, when you look upon it as a source of security, you are creating a problem for yourself because your conclusion is not totally true. Money itself cannot make you secure. Anything that you hold on to, that is other than yourself only confirms your insecurity. As long as you want crutches, you do not stand on your own legs. A truly secure person requires nothing outside of oneself to make him or her feel secure.

Giving objects the attributes that they do not have, seeing certain qualities in them that are not there, and then dwelling upon them, creates attachment, *saṅga*, towards them. Within the flow of what he was teaching, Kṛṣṇa pointed out all this and what comes of this *saṅga*.

ध्यायतो विषयान्पुंसः सङ्गस्तेषूपजायते ।
सङ्गात्सञ्जायते कामः कामात्क्रोधोऽभिजायते ॥ २-६२ ॥

dhyāyato viṣayān puṁsaḥ saṅgasteṣūpajāyate
saṅgāt sañjāyate kāmaḥ kāmāt krodho'bhijāyate

क्रोधाद्भवति सम्मोहः सम्मोहात्स्मृतिविभ्रमः ।
स्मृतिभ्रंशाद् बुद्धिनाशो बुद्धिनाशात्प्रणश्यति ॥ २-६३ ॥

krodhād bhavati sammohaḥ sammohāt smṛtivibhramaḥ
smṛtibhraṁśād buddhināśo buddhināśāt praṇaśyati

In the person who dwells upon objects, an attachment is born with reference to them. From attachment is born desire and from desire, anger is born. (2.62)

From anger comes delusion and from delusion comes the loss of memory. Because of the loss of memory, the mind becomes incapacitated and when the mind is incapacitated, the person is destroyed. (2.63)

Then, Kṛṣṇa said, 'Arjuna, if you really want to know what a wise person is, you have to be wise yourself.' There is no other way of understanding such a person. Behaviour and so on, are not indications of a person's wisdom:

या निशा सर्वभूतानां तस्यां जागर्ति संयमी ।
यस्यां जाग्रति भूतानि सा निशा पश्यतो मुनेः ॥ २-६९ ॥

yā niśā sarvabhūtānāṁ tasyāṁ jāgarti saṁyamī
yasyāṁ jāgrati bhūtāni sā niśā paśyato muneḥ

In that which is night for all beings, the one who is wise, who has mastery over oneself, is awake. That in which beings are awake, is night for the wise person who sees. (2.69)

The difference between those who are wise and those who are not wise is like night and day. So, what the wise people are awake to, the ignorant people are not awake to. What the ignorant are awake to, the wise are not awake to. In other words, what the ignorant think of as reality, the wise do not see as real at all. Here, night and day are taken as ignorance and knowledge. In fact, there is no other difference save that between knowledge and ignorance. A wise person understands that everything is 'I,' the *ātmā*, whereas other people think, 'Everything is getting me.' Thus, the ignorant thinks that the world is out to get him or her, while the wise person sees that the world is oneself.

Having described a *sthitaprajña* as best as he could, Kṛṣṇa had to say to Arjuna, 'How are you going to understand the wise, Arjuna, unless you are wise? Any kind of description is meaningless. To really know what a wise person is, you have to gain wisdom.'

To explain further, Kṛṣṇa used a more positive example:

आपूर्यमाणमचलप्रतिष्ठं समुद्रमापः प्रविशन्ति यद्वत् ।
तद्वत्कामा यं प्रविशन्ति सर्वे स शान्तिमाप्नोति न कामकामी ॥२-७०॥

āpūryamāṇam acalapratiṣṭhaṁ
samudram āpaḥ praviśanti yadvat
tadvatkāmā yaṁ praviśanti sarve
sa śāntim āpnoti na kāmakāmī

Just as water flows into the ocean that is brimful and still, so too, the wise person into whom all objects enter, gains peace, (remains unchanged) whereas, the desirer of objects does not gain peace. (2.70)

The ocean is in no way affected whether the rains happen or the rivers enter it. There is no increase or decrease, no gain or loss, for the ocean. No change affects its ocean-ness, its fullness, because it does not depend upon anything other than itself. In its own glory, without any external support, the ocean is full and complete.

Similarly, the fullness of one who is wise is centred on oneself. 'I am the whole' is a fact to which the wise people are awake; therefore, they require nothing in order to be full. No addition will bring about any change in the wise, nor will any subtraction take away or make any dent in his or her fullness. This, too, was pointed out.

In contrast to an ocean, however, a pond is something that will dry up without rain. And, if there is too much rain, the pond is nowhere to be seen! The *kāmakāmī*, one who has to fulfil certain desires in order to be happy, is like a pond. When something pleasant happens, the person hits the ceiling with elation, and when something unpleasant happens, he or she hits rock bottom and may even consider committing suicide.

Kṛṣṇa concluded the second chapter by saying:

विहाय कामान्यः सर्वान्पुमांश्चरति निःस्पृहः ।
निर्ममो निरहङ्कारः स शान्तिमधिगच्छति ॥ २-७१ ॥

vihāya kāmān yaḥ sarvān pumāṁścarati niḥspṛhaḥ
nirmamo nirahaṅkāraḥ sa śāntim adhigacchati

Having given up all binding desires, the person who moves around, devoid of longing, without the sense of limited 'I' and 'mine,' gains peace. (2.71)

एषा ब्राह्मी स्थितिः पार्थ नैनां प्राप्य विमुह्यति ।
स्थित्वास्यामन्तकालेऽपि ब्रह्मनिर्वाणमृच्छति ॥ २–७२ ॥

eṣā brāhmī sthitiḥ pārtha naināṁ prāpya vimuhyati
sthitvāsyām antakāle'pi brahmanirvāṇamṛcchati

Pārtha (Arjuna)! This is (what is meant by) one's being in Brahman. Having gained this, one is not deluded. Remaining therein, even at the end of one's life, one gains liberation. (2.72)

Kṛṣṇa said, to be a *sthitaprajña* is the very 'state' of being Brahman. Being in the form of knowledge, this 'state' is not one that you will lose, like the waking state or a drug induced state. It is something as true as you are, which is why once this knowledge is gained, there is no question of losing it, because the gain is in terms of knowledge, not experience. The self is understood to be Brahman, the whole, and that understanding is final. Therefore, there can be no falling back into *saṁsāra*, even if you do not gain this knowledge until you are very old, *antakāle enāṁ prāpya na vimuhyati.*

Even when you are in the last throes of your life, with one foot in the grave, if you come to understand that you are the whole, then you are a free person. And if the very elderly are able to gain this knowledge, then those whose eyes are still able to see, whose ears are still able to hear, and those who are able to sit for a length of time in quiet contemplation can surely come to know.

The third chapter began with Arjuna's next question:

ज्यायसी चेत्कर्मणस्ते मता बुद्धिर्जनार्दन ।
तत्किं कर्मणि घोरे मां नियोजयसि केशव ॥ ३-१ ॥

jyāyasī cetkarmaṇaste matā buddhirjanārdana
tatkiṁ karmaṇi ghore māṁ niyojayasi keśava

Janārdana (Kṛṣṇa)! If in your contention knowledge is better than action, why then do you impel me into this gruesome action, Keśava (Kṛṣṇa)? (3.1)

व्यामिश्रेणेव वाक्येन बुद्धिं मोहयसीव मे ।
तदेकं वद निश्चित्य येन श्रेयोऽहमाप्नुयाम् ॥ ३-२ ॥

vyāmiśreṇeva vākyena buddhiṁ mohayasīva me
tadekaṁ vada niścitya yena śreyo'hamāpnuyām

With words that are seemingly contradictory, you seem to confuse my mind. Deciding for good, which is better, tell me the one thing by which I shall gain liberation. (3.2)

Here, Arjuna presented a problem, 'Kṛṣṇa, if I have understood you correctly, you seem to have your heart in knowledge alone. I asked for *śreyas*, *mokṣa*, from you, and you made it very clear that this can only be gained by knowledge, not by fulfilling desires. You even said that all desires are to be given up. Yet, you say I am to perform action. Therefore, I am confused.'

This is how Arjuna understood what Kṛṣṇa had said. In fact, Kṛṣṇa had not said that all one's desires have to be given up. He said that a wise person gives up desires, meaning that he or she has no desire to become secure and happy. The person may have a desire to do something, but by fulfilling this desire, he or she is not going to become more secure. Such delusion is no longer there for the wise. Although this was what Kṛṣṇa actually said, Arjuna took it as he did because he knew that every *karma*, action, is preceded by desire. Without desire there is no *karma* at all. So, he thought, 'If desire is to be given up, then why should I do *karma*? And how am I to gain knowledge? The only way seems to be to give up *karmas*, along with the desires that initiate them, and seek knowledge.'

Since Kṛṣṇa had asked Arjuna to follow *karma-yoga*, to get up and fight, Arjuna was naturally confused. His thinking was, 'If knowledge will give me *śreyas*, that is what I should go for. And for the sake of knowledge, I need not do all these actions. All that is needed is to renounce everything, go to a teacher, and gain the knowledge. Therefore, *sannyāsa* seems to be the answer to my problem.'

In an attempt to resolve the seeming contradiction, Arjuna asked Kṛṣṇa to tell him, once and for all, the one thing that would give him *śreyas*, to which Kṛṣṇa said:

लोकेऽस्मिन्द्विविधा निष्ठा पुरा प्रोक्ता मयानघ ।
ज्ञानयोगेन साङ्ख्यानां कर्मयोगेन योगिनाम् ॥ ३-३ ॥

loke'smin dvividhā niṣṭhā purā proktā mayānagha
jñānayogena sāṅkhyānāṁ karmayogena yoginām

The sinless one (Arjuna)! The two-fold committed lifestyle in this world, was told by me in the beginning[18]– the pursuit of knowledge for the renunciates and the pursuit of *karma-yoga* for those who pursue activity. (3.3)

From Arjuna's question, Kṛṣṇa could tell that Arjuna had not understood what he had been saying. It is true that *sannyāsa* is a lifestyle; but real *karma-sannyāsa* is giving up all actions by knowledge, *jñānena karma-sannyāsa*, while *karma-yoga* is a means, *upāya*, for gaining this knowledge. To clarify the distinction between *sannyāsa* as a lifestyle and renunciation of action through knowledge, Kṛṣṇa reminded Arjuna that no one can remain without performing any action at all, regardless of whether the person is a *sannyāsī* or not:

न हि कश्चित्क्षणमपि जातु तिष्ठत्यकर्मकृत् ।
कार्यते ह्यवशः कर्म सर्वः प्रकृतिजैर्गुणैः ॥ ३-५ ॥

na hi kaścit kṣaṇamapi jātu tiṣṭhatyakarmakṛt
kāryate hyavaśaḥ karma sarvaḥ prakṛtijairguṇaiḥ

Indeed, no one ever remains for even a second without performing action because everyone is forced to perform action by the (three) *guṇas* (*sattva, rajas* and *tamas*) born of *prakṛti*. (3.5)

A *sannyāsī* is a person who, having taken certain vows, has given up the obligatory duties prescribed in the Veda. Having become a non-competing person in the society, the

---

[18] In the Vedas.

sannyāsī pursues knowledge to the exclusion of all else. Kṛṣṇa acknowledged that such a pursuit is available, that *sannyāsa* is a lifestyle dedicated to this pursuit, but cautioned that it is not an easy one. He also explained that *karma-yoga* is another lifestyle and is a means for real *sannyāsa, sarva-karma-sannyāsa,* which can be achieved by both *sannyāsī* and *karmayogī.*

To live a life of *sannyāsa* requires that you have certain mind, certain contemplativeness, which can be achieved through *karma-yoga.* When you live a life of *karma-yoga,* as a householder, for example, you do not lose anything; in fact, you gain. This is true for any *mumukṣu,* any seeker, who is in a stage of life other than *sannyāsa.* Each one gains the same end because knowledge is something that is to be pursued. Therefore, Arjuna could pursue the knowledge even as a *karma-yogī.* This was what Kṛṣṇa wanted him to understand.

We saw, in the second chapter, that one does not become a *karma-yogī* without the proper attitude with reference to Īśvara being the *karma-phala-dātā,* the giver of the fruits of action, and knowing that I am only the performer of action. When I have this attitude, the results of all actions are taken by me as *prasāda.* Also, every action that I perform is a *yajña,* a sacrifice or offering, to the Lord. This attitude was again highlighted and discussed in the third chapter:

देवान्भावयतानेन ते देवा भावयन्तु वः ।
परस्परं भावयन्तः श्रेयः परमवाप्स्यथ ॥ ३-११ ॥

devān bhāvayatānena te devā bhāvayantu vaḥ
parasparaṁ bhāvayantaḥ śreyaḥ param avāpsyatha

Propitiate the deities with this (*yajña*). May those deities propitiate you. Propitiating one another, you shall gain the highest good (*mokṣa*). (3.11)

इष्टान्भोगान्हि वो देवा दास्यन्ते यज्ञभाविताः ।
तैर्दत्तानप्रदायैभ्यो यो भुङ्क्ते स्तेन एव सः ॥ ३-१२ ॥

iṣṭān bhogān hi vo devā dāsyante yajñabhāvitāḥ
tairdattān apradāyaibhyo yo bhuṅkte stena eva saḥ

The deities, propitiated by *yajña*, will give you desirable objects. One who enjoys objects given by them without offering to them in return is indeed a thief. (3.12)

यज्ञशिष्टाशिनः सन्तो मुच्यन्ते सर्वकिल्बिषैः ।
भुञ्जते ते त्वघं पापा ये पचन्त्यात्मकारणात् ॥ ३-१३ ॥

yajñaśiṣṭāśinaḥ santo mucyante sarvakilbiṣaiḥ
bhuñjate te tvaghaṁ pāpā ye pacantyātmakāraṇāt

Those who eat, having first offered the food to the Lord, are released from impurities, whereas those sinful people who cook only for themselves eat *pāpa* (sin). (3.13)

In this detailed way, Kṛṣṇa explained how the attitude of *karma-yoga* can release you from the hold of your likes and dislikes when the action you perform is done as a worship or a sacrifice.

Then, Kṛṣṇa said:

सदृशं चेष्टते स्वस्याः प्रकृतेर्ज्ञानवानपि ।
प्रकृतिं यान्ति भूतानि निग्रहः किं करिष्यति ॥ ३-३३ ॥

sadṛśaṁ ceṣṭate svasyāḥ prakṛterjñānavānapi
prakṛtiṁ yānti bhūtāni nigrahaḥ kiṁ kariṣyati

Even a wise person acts in keeping with his or her own nature. Because all beings follow their own nature, of what use is control? (3.33)

Each one thinks according to his or her own *prakṛti*. Likes and dislikes are something that you cannot stop; they just happen. All thoughts happen in your mind and you have no say over their occurrence. Collectively, they equal your own *prakṛti*, your own disposition.

Whatever you have done in previous lives (*prārabdha-karma*) and in this life also, all your *dharma-adharma, puṇya-pāpa-saṁskāra*s, set up certain thoughts in your mind and there is no way of stopping this from happening. Even Īśvara cannot stop it. He has set it up like this and he cannot cross his own mandate. Nor can anyone else. Neither Īśvara's control nor anyone else's can change a person's *prakṛti*; the person will remain the same. Even if you were to control your thoughts by negating them, you would have to continue this negation throughout your lifetime.

Given the fact that you cannot control your thoughts, is it not better to ask, why thoughts should be considered a problem in the first place? The person for whom thoughts are a problem has a permanent nightmare because thought is always there. Only a long sleep can help! In fact, thoughts themselves are not the problem.

Another question that arises is, if I cannot control my thoughts, what is the purpose of the *śāstra*? If everyone simply performs action according to his or her *prakṛti*, a person can commit murder and say, 'It is my nature, my disposition, to do such things. I cannot do otherwise.' To take care of any such conclusion, Kṛṣṇa also said that you are the one who goes along with or withdraws from the thought of committing murder, which is where your will comes in. You cannot control your thoughts, but you can choose which thoughts you are going to identify with and which you are not going to identify with. This is the only freedom you have and this freedom is enough.

Thus, Kṛṣṇa said:

इन्द्रियस्येन्द्रियस्यार्थे रागद्वेषौ व्यवस्थितौ ।
तयोर्न वशमागच्छेत्तौ ह्यस्य परिपन्थिनौ ॥ ३-३४ ॥

*indriyasyendriyasyārthe rāgadveṣau vyavasthitau
tayorna vaśam āgacchettau hyasya paripanthinau*

There are longing and aversion (potential) in every sense object. May one not come under the spell of these two because they are one's enemies. (3.34)

श्रेयान्स्वधर्मो विगुणः परधर्मात्स्वनुष्ठितात् ।
स्वधर्मे निधनं श्रेयः परधर्मो भयावहः ॥ ३-३५ ॥

*śreyān svadharmo viguṇaḥ paradharmāt svanuṣṭhitāt
svadharme nidhanaṁ śreyaḥ paradharmo bhayāvahaḥ*

Better is one's own imperfectly performed *dharma* than the well performed *dharma* of another. Death in one's own *dharma* is better. The *dharma* of another is fraught with fear. (3.35)

Here, Kṛṣṇa pointed out that even if your own *dharma*, what is to be done by you, is rather unpleasant, it is better to be with it than to be with someone else's *dharma*, a *dharma* that does not belong to you at all. What is not to be done by you, even though it can be done by another person who is in another stage of life, is not your *dharma*.

For instance, a *sannyāsī* does not perform the daily rituals enjoined in the Veda. Nevertheless, this is no reason for a *gṛhastha*, householder, not to do them. Each person has to perform action according to his or her situation. It is better to die doing one's own action, because to do otherwise is fraught with fear. It does not benefit you, nor does it benefit the society in which you live. Therefore, Kṛṣṇa said, each person has to do his or her own *karma*; in other words, one's own *dharma* has to be followed.

Arjuna then raised a doubt:

अथ केन प्रयुक्तोऽयं पापं चरति पूरुषः ।
अनिच्छन्नपि वार्ष्णेय बलादिव नियोजितः ॥ ३-३६ ॥

atha kena prayukto'yaṁ pāpaṁ carati pūruṣaḥ
anicchannapi vārṣṇeya balādiva niyojitaḥ

Vārṣṇeya (Kṛṣṇa)! Impelled by what, does a person commit sin, as though pushed by some force even though not desiring to? (3.36)

Arjuna wanted to know why a person does things that he or she knows are wrong. Although the person is convinced that certain actions are not proper, still he or she does them. Why is that? Is there a force other than oneself, a devil, or something, a Satan? Is there, as some theologies maintain, a force other than the divine? Is there a demonic force called evil in this world, which is independent of the divine force? Is it that the divine force wants you to do right things and the demonic force comes along and impels you to do the wrong thing? If so, the demonic force certainly seems to be more powerful than the divine force.

In fact Kṛṣṇa said, there is no such force. The only devil is the one within. You are it! This he expressed in the following way:

काम एष क्रोध एष रजोगुणसमुद्भवः ।
महाशनो महापाप्मा विद्ध्येनमिह वैरिणम् ॥ ३-३७ ॥

kāma eṣa krodha eṣa rajoguṇasamudbhavaḥ
mahāśano mahāpāpmā viddhyenam iha vairiṇam

This desire, this anger, born of the *guṇa rajas*, is a glutton and a great sinner. Know that to be the enemy here in this world. (3.37)

'Arjuna, it is nothing but your *kāma* alone,' Kṛṣṇa said. *Kāma* does it, *krodha* does it. Once desire becomes a passion, priorities become confused. The power of *kāma* is such. The desire is so virulent, that you no longer care what means you adopt to fulfil the desire. You cut corners wherever you can, compromising the means, because the end has become so important. Kṛṣṇa explained, 'This is the problem, Arjuna. This enemy in the form of *kāma* covers you just as the fire is covered by smoke, the mirror by a coat of dust, and the foetus by the womb.'

This *kāma* is a permanent enemy for the *vivekī*. He or she must deal with it, first by knowing that it operates with reference to sense pursuits and is located in the mind and *buddhi – indriyāṇi mano buddhiḥ asya adhiṣṭhānam ucyate.*[19]

Having understood this, you then have to step outside the *kāma*, about which Kṛṣṇa said:

इन्द्रियाणि पराण्याहुरिन्द्रियेभ्यः परं मनः ।
मनसस्तु परा बुद्धियों बुद्धेः परतस्तु सः ॥ ३-४२ ॥

indriyāṇi parāṇyāhurindriyebhyaḥ paraṁ manaḥ
manasastu parā buddhiryo buddheḥ paratastu saḥ

They say that the sense organs are superior (to the body); the mind is superior to the sense organs; the intellect is superior to the mind. Whereas the one who is superior to the intellect is he (the *ātman*). (3.42)

Here, Kṛṣṇa explained that the *indriyas*, the senses, are superior to the physical body because of their subtler, more pervasive nature. However, the senses themselves are absolutely harmless because the mind is superior to them even though the mind has doubts and so on. The senses are just reporters and do not harm anyone. They are simply instruments that have been given to you for a purpose and are not meant to take you for a ride. They are in the hands of the mind.

The mind itself is a problem because the *buddhi*, the intellect, does not function when the fancies of the mind

---

[19] *Gītā* 3.40

overpower it. The mind is in the hands of the *buddhi*, the mind and the *buddhi* being nothing but different types of thought belonging to the same *antaḥ-karaṇa* alone. Whichever is more powerful, a thought of the mind or of the *buddhi*, is going to rule the day.

If the mind is more powerful, it will definitely rob your wisdom away, making you do what is not to be done and omit what is to be done. To keep these thoughts in their proper places, you have to step out of the mind and the *buddhi*. Only then will you understand a thought as a thought.

The nature of a human being is determined by one's thoughts and conclusions about oneself. The sense that 'I am imperfect, I am incomplete, I am useless, or I am worthless,' is a conclusion. Such conclusions are the basis for your constant attempt to prove yourself to be somebody, to make yourself into someone who will be acceptable in your own eyes. In this way, life becomes a constant struggle. Kṛṣṇa concluded the third chapter by telling Arjuna that there is only one way to solve this problem; and that is to solve it fundamentally. He said:

एवं बुद्धेः परं बुद्ध्वा संस्तभ्यात्मानमात्मना ।
जहि शत्रुं महाबाहो कामरूपं दुरासदम् ॥ ३-४३ ॥

evaṁ buddheḥ paraṁ buddhvā saṁstabhyātmānam
ātmanā

jahi śatruṁ mahābāho kāmarūpaṁ durāsadam

Arjuna, the mighty armed! Knowing that which is superior to the intellect in this way, having made the mind steady with the *buddhi*, destroy the enemy, that is in the form of (binding) desire, that which is so difficult to understand. (3.43)

One must step out of one's *buddhi* by recognising that which is above the *buddhi*, the *ātmā* that is ever pure, *śuddha*, limitless, *ānanda*, full, *pūrṇa*, the only reality, *satya*. Knowing this *satyaṁ-jñānam-anantaṁ brahma*, this *brahmātmā*, you are free.

Once you have this knowledge, all your desires, thoughts, become privileges only. Your *buddhi*, mind, thoughts–all of them become so many adjuncts, *upādhis* for you. In themselves, these *upādhis* are limited, but the person is free from any sense of limitation. Hence, for such a person, the desires become a privilege.

Kāma, desire, is not something that can be easily understood because it comes in hundred different forms and in situations where you would never expect it. But *kāma* can be given up in the sense that you can step out of it. Then the desires are simply known to you; they cannot harm you. This is the only way to deal with *kāma* because there is no end to the desires that can arise. Thus, step out and be free, because you are already free. You need to only discover this fact.

Alphabetical index of verses

Text	Chapter	Verse	Vol	Page
omityekākṣaraṁ brahma	08	13	6	63
oṁ tatsaditi nirdeśaḥ	17	23	8	278
kaccinnobhayavibhraṣṭaḥ	06	38	5	237
kaccid etacchrutaṁ pārtha	18	72	9	568
kaṭvamlalavaṇātyuṣṇa	17	09	8	243
kathaṁ na jñeyam asmābhiḥ	01	39	1	228
kathaṁ bhīṣmamahaṁ saṅkhye	02	04	2	11
kathaṁ vidyām ahaṁ yogin	10	17	6	379
karmajaṁ buddhiyuktā hi	02	51	2	295
karmaṇaḥ sukṛtasyāhuḥ	14	16	8	33
karmaṇaiva hi saṁsiddhim	03	20	3	118
karmaṇo hyapi boddhavyam	04	17	4	104
karmaṇyakarma yaḥ paśyed	04	18	4	106
karmaṇyevādhikāraste	02	47	2	237
karma brahmodbhavaṁ viddhi	03	15	3	92
karmendriyāṇi saṁyamya	03	06	3	42
karśayantaḥ śarīrastham	17	06	8	235
kaviṁ purāṇam anuśāsitāram	08	09	6	50
kasmācca te na nameran	11	37	7	74
kāṅkṣantaḥ karmaṇāṁ siddhim	04	12	4	71
kāma eṣa krodha eṣaḥ	03	37	3	223

Text	Chapter	Verse	Vol	Page
bījaṁ māṁ sarvabhūtānām	07	10	5	337
buddhiyukto jahātīha	02	50	2	290
buddhirjñānam asammohaḥ	10	04	6	333
buddherbhedaṁ dhṛteścaiva	18	29	9	116
buddhyā viśuddhayā yukto	18	51	9	303
bṛhatsāma tathā sāmnām	10	35	6	419
brahmaṇo hi pratiṣṭhāham	14	27	8	58
brahmaṇyādhāya karmāṇi	05	10	4	329
brahmabhūtaḥ prasannātmā	18	54	9	313
brahmārpaṇaṁ brahma haviḥ	04	24	4	193
brāhmaṇakṣatriyaviśām	18	41	9	146
bhaktyā tvananyayā śakyaḥ	11	54	7	104
bhaktyā mām abhijānāti	18	55	9	316
bhayādraṇāduparatam	02	35	2	191
bhavān bhīṣmaśca karṇaśca	01	08	1	188
bhavāpyayau hi bhūtānām	11	02	7	10
bhīṣmadroṇapramukhataḥ	01	25	1	209
bhūtagrāmaḥ sa evāyam	08	19	6	83
bhūmirāpo'nalo vāyuḥ	07	04	5	308
bhūya eva mahābāho	10	01	6	315

Text	Chapter	Verse	Vol	Page
śreyān svadharmo viguṇaḥ	18	47	9	188
śreyo hi jñānam abhyāsāt	02	12	7	194
śrotrādīnīndriyāṇyanye	04	26	4	212
śrotram cakṣuḥ sparśanaṁ ca	05	09	8	100
śvaśurān suhṛdaścaiva	01	27	1	211
sa evāyaṁ mayā te'dya	04	03	4	7
saktāḥ karmaṇyavidvāṁso	03	25	3	140
sakheti matvā prasabhaṁ	01	41	7	83
sa ghoṣo dhārtarāṣṭrāṇām	01	19	1	203
satataṁ kīrtayanto mām	09	14	6	220
sa tayā śraddhayā yuktaḥ	07	22	5	387
satkāramānapūjārtham	17	18	8	266
sattvaṁ rajastama iti	14	05	8	12
sattvaṁ sukhe sañjayati	14	09	8	23
sattvāt sañjāyate jñānam	14	17	8	34
sattvānurūpā sarvasya	17	03	8	230
sadṛśaṁ ceṣṭate svasyāḥ	03	33	3	193
sadbhāve sādhubhāve	17	26	8	284
samaduḥkhasukhaḥ svasthaḥ	14	24	8	47
samaṁ kāyaśirogrīvam	06	13	5	77
samaṁ paśyanhi sarvatra	13	28	7	475

Books by Swami Dayananda Saraswati

Public Talk Series :

1. Living Intelligently
2. Successful Living
3. Need for Cognitive Change
4. Discovering Love
5. The Value of Values
6. Vedic View and Way of Life

Upaniṣad Series :

7. Muṇḍakopaniṣad
8. Kenopaniṣad

Prakaraṇa Series :

9. Tattvabodhaḥ

Text Translation Series :

10. Śrīmad Bhagavad Gītā
    (Text with roman transliteration and English translation)

11. Śrī Rudram
    (Text in Sanskrit with transliteration, word-to-word and verse meaning along with an elaborate commentary in English)

Stotra Series :

12. Dīpārādhanā
13. Prayer Guide
    (With explanations of several Mantras, Stotras, Kirtans and Religious Festivals)

Moments with Oneself Series :

Bhagavad Gītā

Meditation Series :

Essays :

33. Do all Religions have the same goal?

34. Conversion is Violence

35. Gurupūrṇimā

36. Dānam

37. Japa

38. Can We?

39. Moments with Krishna

40. Teaching Tradition of Advaita Vedanta

41. Compositions of Swami Dayananda Saraswati

Exploring Vedanta Series : (*vākyavicāra*)

42. śraddhā bhakti dhyāna yogād avaihi ātmānaṁ ced vijānīyāt

Books translated in other languages and in English based on Swami Dayananda Saraswati's Original Exposition

Tamil

43. Veeduthorum Gitopadesam (9 Volumes)
    (Bhagavad Gītā Home Study Course)

44. Dānam

Kannada

45. Mane maneyalli Adhyayana (7 Volumes)
    (Bhagavad Gītā Home Study Course)

46. Vedanta Pravesike

Malayalam

47. Muṇḍakopaniṣad

Hindi

48. Ghar baithe Gītā Vivecan (Vol 1)
(Bhagavad Gītā Home Study Course)

49. Antardṛṣṭi (Insights)

50. Vedanta 24X7

51. Kriya aur Pratikriya (Action and Reaction)

English

52. The Jungian Myth and Advaita Vedanta

53. The Vedantic Self and the Jungian Psyche

54. Salutations to Rudra

55. Without a Second

Biography

56. Swami Dayananda Saraswati
Contributions & Writings
(Smt. Sheela Balalji)

312

Also available at :

ARSHA VIDYA RESEARCH
AND PUBLICATION TRUST
32 / 4 Sir Desika Road
Mylapore Chennai 600 004
Telefax :   044 - 2499 7131
Email   : avrandpt@gmail.com
Website : www.avrpt.com

ARSHA VIDYA GURUKULAM
Anaikatti P.O.
Coimbatore 641 108
Ph   : 0422 - 2657001
Fax   : 0422 - 2657002
Email   : office@arshavidya.in
Website : www.arshavidya.in

ARSHA VIDYA GURUKULAM
P.O.Box 1059. Pennsylvania
PA 18353, USA
Ph   : 001-570-992-2339
Email   : avp@epix.net
Website : www.arshavidya.org

SWAMI DAYANANDA ASHRAM
Purani Jhadi, P.B.No. 30
Rishikesh, Uttaranchal 249 201
Telefax : 0135 - 2430769
Email   : ashrambookstore@yahoo.com
Website : www.dayananda.org

Other leading Book Stores:

Chennai:	**044**
Motilal Banarsidass	24982315
Giri Trading	2495 1966
Higginbothams	2851 3519
Pustak Bharati	2461 1345
Theosophical Publishing House	2446 6613 / 2491 1338
The Odessey	43910300
Bengaluru:	**080**
Gangarams	2558 1617 / 2558 1618
Sapna Book House	4011 4455 / 4045 5999
Strand Bookstall	2558 2222, 25580000
Vedanta Book House	2650 7590
Coimbatore:	**0422**
Guru Smruti	948677 3793
Giri Trading	2541523

Trivandrum: **0471**

    Prabhus Bookhouse   2478 397 / 2473 496

Kozhikode: **0495**

    Ganga Bookhouse   6521262

Mumbai: **022**

    Chetana Bookhouse   2285 1243 / 2285 3412

    Strand Bookstall   2266 1994 / 2266 1719/

                                         2261 4613

    Giri Trading   2414 3140